The Conservative Party and the Trade Unions

The relationship between the Conservative Party and the trade unions has been at best uneasy and more often than not hostile. The former's principles emphasising individualism, the free market and management's right to manage have ensured that trade unions have been viewed as an obstacle to those principles.

This book examines the attitudes and policies of the Conservative Party towards the trade unions from the nineteenth century onwards, linking these to wider political and economic circumstances and the personalities involved. Peter Dorey shows that there have always been disagreements within the Conservative Party as to how it should deal with the trade unions. These disagreements have in large part reflected divisions within British Conservatism itself, between the paternalist One Nation strand that has traditionally favoured a conciliatory approach to the unions and the economic liberal/social authoritarian strand, which has always hankered after the virtual suppression of trade unionism.

The Conservative Party and the Trade Unions fills a major gap in existing literature and is the first book to deal exclusively with the relationship between the Conservative Party and trade unions from the nineteenth century to the present day.

Peter Dorey is Lecturer in Politics at the School of European Studies, University of Cardiff.

The Conservative Party and the Trade Unions

Peter Dorey

London and New York

First published 1995
by Routledge
11 New Fetter Lane, London EC4P 4EE

Simultaneously published in the USA and Canada
by Routledge
29 West 35th Street, New York, NY 10001

© 1995 Peter Dorey

Typeset in Times by Florencetype Ltd, Stoodleigh, Devon

Printed and bound in Great Britain by
TJ Press Ltd, Padstow, Cornwall

British Library Cataloguing in Publication Data

A catalogue record for this book is available from the British Library

Library of Congress Cataloging in Publication Data

A catalogue record for this book has been requested

ISBN 0–415–06487–2

To Jane, with love

Contents

1 The Conservative Party and the trade unions

Some of the key events in British trade unionism and industrial relations have occurred during periods of Conservative – or prior to the 1830s, Tory – government: the 1799–1800 Combination Acts, the 1926 General Strike and the subsequent 1927 Trade Disputes Act, the establishment of the neo-corporatist National Economic Development Council in the 1960s, the ill-fated 1971 Industrial Relations Act, the two momentous miners' strikes of the 1970s, and the systematic curbing and marginalisation of the trade unions in the 1980s and 1990s, etc. Yet there remains a notable paucity of literature on the Conservative Party and the trade unions, particularly on any period prior to the Thatcher decade of the 1980s. Such material as exists is invariably either fragmentary (dealing with the Conservatives and the trade unions indirectly as part of a wider or different project) or highly partisan and polemical – the Left invariably seeing Conservative policies towards the trade unions as manifestations of 'ruling class' attempts at suppressing and exploiting the working class, the Right instinctively proclaiming that any measure invoked against trade unions by a Conservative government constitutes a valiant defence of freedom and liberty, and the maintenance of a civilised society. Needless to say, this latter perspective has been proclaimed particularly trenchantly and triumphantly since 1979.

It is the objective of this text to provide a more systematic and dispassionate analysis of the perspectives and policies adopted by the Conservative Party towards the trade unions in Britain, from 1799 to the present day, although the bulk of the study will focus on developments and debates since 1945. Certainly, it was from the latter half of the 1950s onwards that the trade unions became widely seen as a problem (and not just by Conservatives), and it is from this time onwards that Conservatives became increasingly preoccupied with 'the trade union question'.

However, trade unions have always been viewed as problematic by the Conservative Party. At almost any juncture during the nineteenth and twentieth centuries, Conservative MPs could be found expressing concern, or expatiating condemnation, on various aspects of British trade unionism. During the early nineteenth century, there was deep concern that trade unionism undermined the operation of the (market) economy, whilst simultaneously constituting a threat to the political order. Such fears forcefully re-emerged amongst many Conservatives from the latter half of the 1950s onwards, becoming particularly pronounced during the 1960s and 1970s, when the decline of the British economy fuelled Conservative concern about the stability of Britain's economic and political system, and the threat allegedly posed to that system by the trade unions. Even during times of economic growth and prosperity, many Conservatives have continued to view the trade unions with distrust and disdain, precisely because they were deemed to constitute a threat to the continuation of economic success.

In addition to these general, perennial concerns about trade unionism traditionally harboured by the Conservative Party, the twentieth century has witnessed the emergence of more specific concerns and objections, pertaining to particular aspects or activities of Britain's trade unions. The most notable of these have been the political levy, the closed shop, increased strike activity (especially unofficial strikes), picketing, and the enhanced role accorded to the trade unions in policy-making at national level during the 1960s and 1970s.

Yet, as already intimated, it was from the latter half of the 1950s in particular that 'the trade union question' assumed increasing urgency for the Conservative Party. From this time onwards, trade unions became particularly problematic for Conservatives at two discrete levels. First, the relative decline of British industry, and the increasingly crisis-ridden character of the economy, became more pronounced during the 1960s, thereby serving to place trade unions under the spotlight by those seeking an explanation or cause for the country's growing industrial and economic problems. For a number of Conservatives, not only were trade unions largely to blame for these problems, but the emergence of these problems was deemed to vindicate the suspicion, and lack of regard, with which they had always viewed trade unionism.

The second reason why trade unions became particularly problematic for the Conservative Party during the 1960s and 1970s concerns the principles and precepts of Conservatism itself. Certainly, the fundamental faith in the virtues and efficacy of capitalism itself is of crucial importance. For Conservatives, the capitalist system is the means by which individual liberty, economic efficiency, and socio-political freedom are attained and secured. As Russel notes,

> capitalism and Conservatism have always gone hand in hand; ever since it was formed, the Conservative Party has believed in, and supported the capitalist system because of its conviction that it offers something better. . . .The party has always been able to agree on that, and it is still the basic bond which holds it together today.
>
> (Russel 1978: 20)

This faith in capitalism, which is intrinsic and integral to Conservatism, clearly constitutes a major reason why trade unions have always been problematic for the Conservative Party, and became ever more so during the 1960s and 1970s as the socio-economic system which Conservatives seek to uphold has repeatedly careered into crisis. For most Conservatives, the trade unions are responsible, directly or indirectly, for a whole host of problems which have afflicted the British economy since the latter half of the 1950s, particularly infla-tion (fuelled by 'excessive' wage demands), low productivity (by virtue of restrictive practices and overmanning), and lost trade and investment (due to strike activity and high labour costs). Consequently, the Shadow Industry Minister Sir Keith Joseph gave public utterance to the opinion of most, if not all, Conservatives, when he declared that 'solving the union problem is the key to Britain's recovery' (Joseph 1979).

Yet widespread recognition of the 'problems' posed by the trade unions has not provided for widespread agreement in the Conserva-tive Party as to how best to tackle these 'problems'. This lack of unanimity is partly due to the fact that Conservatives either prioritise the individual tenets of Conservatism, placing more importance on one than another, or interpret the same tenet differently. Even the overriding commitment to capitalism does not preclude differences of perspective amongst Conservatives as to the precise form which the capitalist system ought to take. One Nation Conservatives have consistently claimed that a considerable degree of government inter-vention in the economy, and a significant role for the trade unions in economic discussions and decision-making at national level, provide for the most efficient and stable form of capitalism. By contrast, neo-liberals consider such a model to constitute a partial abandon-ment of capitalism, and a move towards socialism. The role which

Conservatives thus ascribe to trade unions will, to a considerable extent, depend on their precise conception of what constitutes capitalism, and how its requirements are best served.

Although support for capitalism represents a fundamental tenet of Conservatism, other principles and characteristics are also crucial. Most Conservatives would doubtless concur that individualism, majoritarian democracy, liberty, order, the rule of law, national unity, denial of 'class' politics, authority, and social harmony are all defining features of Conservatism. Yet it can immediately be comprehended that there exists considerable scope for these principles to occasion tensions within the Conservative Party, for as Eccleshall has remarked, Conservatives have simultaneously or successively embraced a cluster of polarities – free trade vs. imperial protection, laissez-faire vs. state planning, traditionalism vs. modernity, individualism vs. collectivism, liberty vs. authority, aristocracy vs. Tory democracy – in a manner which lends credence to Lord Hailsham's admission that the Conservative Party has not been averse to stealing the policies of its opponents when expedient (Eccleshall 1977).

Trade unions have been deemed to conflict with these Conservative principles in a number of ways. They have been portrayed or perceived as organisations pursuing sectional interests against the national interest, and at the expense of national unity; as embodying the principle of collectivism, frequently at the expense of individualism and liberty; of acting without regard for the rule of law; of instigating industrial anarchy, and thereby undermining order and managerial authority in the workplace; and of seeking to 'run the country', in place of the democratically elected government.

Furthermore, specific trade union practices have caused particular problems for the Conservative Party, not least of these being the 'closed shop'. Virtually all Conservatives opposed the closed shop (it was finally outlawed in 1990), on the grounds that it constituted a denial of individual liberty. Whilst the Conservative Party has constantly expressed support for 100 per cent union membership obtained voluntarily, and through persuasion, it has been unequivocal in its condemnation of compulsory trade union membership schemes. Yet whilst repeatedly castigating the denial of individual liberty which the closed shop was deemed to constitute, the Conservative Party often felt obliged to acknowledge the impracticability of prohibiting it outright. To attempt to do so would be to introduce legislation which was unenforceable, and would thereby serve to undermine another key principle of Conservatism, namely the sanctity of the rule of law.

The problem which the closed shop posed for the Conservative Party was compounded by the fact that some Conservatives actually proffered qualified support for it on the grounds that it provides for order and stability (in industry) – two further tenets of Conservatism – and also makes the task of management easier, because employers only need to communicate with one set of union officials representing the whole workforce, rather than wasting valuable time in endless discussion with a number of unions and/or with non-union employees.

The example of the closed shop thus provides an indication of the way in which the eclecticism of Conservatism has often contributed to the manifestation of disagreement within the Conservative Party over issues pertaining to trade unionism and trade union reform. Policy preferences will invariably be informed by the particular precepts and principles of Conservatism which Conservatives attach the greatest importance to, or place the most emphasis on, and this will vary according to which ideas and individuals are dominant in the party at any particular juncture. The Conservative Party of the 1990s, and its attitude towards the trade unions, is vastly different to that of the 1950s.

Trade unionism has also proved problematic for the Conservative Party with regard to the notions of national unity and national interest. Whilst we noted earlier that Conservatives have ritually condemned the 'selfish' sectional interests and 'class' politics pursued by trade unions, different responses have emanated from within the party, partly because of the different conceptions which exist among Conservatives over the most appropriate means of defending the national interest and maintaining national unity. Conservative neo-liberals have constantly placed great emphasis on the polarity of 'the individual' and 'the nation', thereby denying the legitimacy of 'sectional' or 'class' interests. The nation is deemed to be composed of sovereign individuals interacting as producers and consumers, engaged in voluntary exchanges and transactions. Whilst individuals might combine to form groups of one kind or another, they must accept that the interests of other individuals, and of the nation as a whole, are supreme, and must not be subordinated to, or jeopardised by, the interests of the group itself. Conservative neo-liberalism thus favours a policy of 'legal restraint', whereby the activities and powers of trade unions are strictly limited by law, and the institutions of organised labour are deemed to be but one of the innumerable pressure groups in society. Such a policy, its advocates believe, would ensure that the trade unions had neither the ability to place their own interests above those of the nation, nor the power to coerce other individuals, be they trade union members themselves or managers and employers.

By contrast, the One Nation element in the Conservative Party has long been prepared to acknowledge the importance and legitimacy of organised labour as a major sectional interest, as well as partially recognising the historical – if only symbolic – role of trade unions as 'class' institutions. Such Conservatives have long been of the opinion that the most fruitful means of ensuring the supremacy of the national interest, and of securing national unity, is by incorporating the union leadership into the decision-making processes and institutions of the state. By inviting the trade union leadership to form a partnership with leaders of the business community, and the government itself, One Nation Conservatives hoped that organised labour would become more appreciative of the economic 'facts of life', and thus behave more responsibly; i.e. moderate wage demands, co-operate in schemes to increase efficiency and productivity, etc. It was assumed that if trade unions, or more specifically trade union leaders, were acquainted with information about what the country could and could not afford, then they would voluntarily subordinate their sectional interests to those of the nation. As Harris interprets, if labour, capital, and management were functionally, rather than competitively, related, they would share a common allegiance to 'the nation', and its supreme expression, the neutral state (Harris 1972: 111).

Following on from this, One Nation Conservatives have traditionally harboured a sense of unease about the efficacy of a legislative programme for dealing with the activities and powers of the trade unions. Quite apart from the belief that changes ought to be secured through discussion and persuasion, rather than be imposed from above by statute, the One Nation element in the Conservative Party has been concerned that the kind of legislative onslaught against the unions traditionally yearned for by their neo-liberal colleagues would provoke precisely the class politics and class conflict which neo-liberals purport to eschew. The pursuit of vigorous legislation *vis-à-vis* the trade unions, some Conservatives feared, would force trade unionists to close ranks, and resort to more 'militant' or 'extreme' action in order to defend themselves. This might well serve to weaken social stability, bring the law into disrepute, jeopardise national unity, and, ultimately, grievously affect the authority of the state itself. Such fears were held by some elements of the Conservative Party when it was drafting its Industrial Relations Bill, introduced in

1971, and were felt to be vindicated by the response which the Bill elicited from the trade union movement.

It can thus be seen that whilst Conservatism, and hence the Conservative Party, have historically emphasised the paramount importance of tenets such as national interest/national unity, order, stability, the rule of law, the denial or rejection of class politics, strong and effective government, etc., there have always existed differences of opinion and approach amongst Conservatives as to how best to secure the realisation of such tenets.

In seeking to illustrate these issues, and thereby highlight both the discussions and policies which have emanated from within the Conservative Party *vis-à-vis* the trade unions, this text will adopt an approach which is simultaneously chronological and analytical.

Chapter 2 provides an outline of Conservative Party attitudes and approaches towards the trade unions from 1799 to 1945, illustrating the extent to which the outright hostility towards, and fear of, trade unions harboured by Tories at the very end of the eighteenth century were tempered and tamed during the next century and a half, so that by the end of the Second World War, most Conservatives accepted trade unions as a permanent and vital institution in the world of both industry and politics. Even the relapse into hostility evinced by the General Strike and the consequent 1927 Trade Disputes Act is shown to have been tempered by the widespread advocacy amongst Conservatives of greater industrial partnership, and also by the belief that the defeat suffered by the trade unions during the General Strike would engender a more responsible form of trade unionism in future. We illustrate how the period from 1799 to 1945 was one in which the Conservative Party (in Parliament) came to accept the trade unions, and sought to adopt, for much of the time, a more positive, constructive stance towards them, a stance at least partly necessitated by the extension of the franchise to the working class during the second half of the nineteenth century. At the same time, we note that throughout this period a number of Conservatives remained openly hostile towards trade unionism, and thus critical of the increasingly acquiescent approach adopted by the party's parliamentary leadership; for such critics, acquiescence is really nothing more than appeasement.

Chapter 3 illustrates how, from 1945 to 1964, the Conservative Party strenuously and assiduously sought to cultivate a good relationship with the trade unions, both through the avoidance of legislative reform (as routinely demanded by some backbenchers and constituency activists) and the advocacy of greater co-operation and partnership both between management and trade unions in the workplace, and between trade unions and the Conservative governments of the 1950s and early 1960s. The ultimate institutional manifestation of such partnership was represented by the creation, in 1961, of the National Economic Development Council (NEDC). Yet this itself was partly born of the recognition that Britain was experiencing relative economic decline, for which the trade unions were apportioned much of the blame. Whilst incorporation of the trade unions into the machinery of government and economic policy-making undoubtedly gave institutional expression to the One Nation philosophy of Conservatives such as Harold Macmillan (who was party leader and Prime Minister from 1957 to 1963), the real motive for establishing the NEDC was to encourage greater responsibility on the part of the trade unions, by involving them in discussions and decisions concerning industrial and economic policy, and thereby 'educating' them in the 'facts of life' concerning the increasingly serious problems besetting the British economy. Responsibility was thus to be secured through representation.

Yet this approach failed to achieve its objectives, so that by 1964 Conservative critics of the trade unions and their alleged role in Britain's economic decline were becoming both more numerous and more vocal. Even the paternalists who had hitherto insisted on the need to pursue a constructive, conciliatory approach towards the trade unions were, by this time, becoming somewhat exasperated by the apparent inability or unwillingness of the trade unions to behave as expected or exhorted.

As Chapter 4 details, the period from 1964 to 1970, when the Conservative Party was in opposition, witnessed a fundamental reappraisal of its whole approach to contemporary politics. New – more radical – policies were adopted on a wide range of issues, not least with regard to trade unionism. It was during this period that the Conservative Party adopted a legalistic policy (one which sought to solve the problems posed by trade unions by invoking legislation and statutory stipulation, rather than relying on encouragement or incorporation; if the trade unions would not voluntarily behave in the manner desired by government, then they had to be compelled by law to do so instead). It was this policy which culminated in the ill-fated 1971 Industrial Relations Act, a measure which several Conservative MPs had repeatedly warned was misconceived and liable to compound, rather than conquer, industrial relations problems.

Chapter 5 deals with the period of the Heath government, 1970–4, during which the aforementioned Industrial Relations Act was introduced. It prompted a number of conflicts with the trade unions (as its Conservative critics had prophesied) and was then effectively – and humiliatingly – abandoned. In the wake of the debacle of the Industrial Relations Act, the Heath government performed a major U-turn, discarding the free market policies and legalistic approach towards the trade unions with which it had entered office, and resorting instead to the tried and tested policy of seeking a partnership with the unions in the realms of economic policy and wage determination. However, Heath found himself compelled, in the wake of trade union refusal to accept his proposals for a voluntary pay policy, to impose a temporary statutory prices and incomes freeze, which he intended to be the prelude to a more permanent voluntary incomes policy agreed between government and the trade unions. This outraged his neo-liberal colleagues on the Right of the party, who believed that he was betraying the principles which the Conservative Party had traditionally stood for, and the policies upon which it had fought the 1970 general election. What proved particularly damaging, however, was the miners' strike during the winter of 1973–4 in support of a pay increase which exceeded the limits stipulated by Heath. For Conservative neo-liberals, the strike illustrated simultaneously the need to tackle the trade unions and the futility of pursuing incomes policies.

In Chapter 6, therefore, we explain how the Conservative Party once again found itself formulating a new set of policies whilst in opposition from 1974 to 1979, policies which included a renewed commitment to reform of the trade unions, but which this time showed much greater caution, and represented a rather different – but still legalistic – approach to that enshrined in the Industrial Relations Act. Indeed, this 'cautious legalism' produced clearly discernible divisions within the Conservative Party between those MPs who thought that if and when it returned to power it would have to rely too heavily on legislation and coercion, and thus frighten the electorate or find itself at war with the trade unions, and those Conservatives who believed that the leadership was proving too timid and lacked the determination to 'take on' the trade unions. For others, including much of the leadership, if it was being warned simultaneously about going too far and not going far enough, then it was probably pursuing just the right approach. At the same time, similar divisions were evident concerning the issue of whether or not the Conservative Party ought to commit itself to an incomes policy, although towards the end of its period in opposition, opinion in the party hardened against government determination of wages, and in favour of market forces and a return to free collective bargaining.

Chapter 7 examines the Conservative Party's approach and policies towards the trade unions during the 1980s and the first half of the 1990s under the premiership of Margaret Thatcher and her successor, John Major. The adherence to a policy of 'cautious legalism' is noted, with trade union legislation being carefully introduced on a 'step-by-step' basis. For all their radicalism and dislike of trade unionism, the Thatcher governments were determined not to repeat the errors of the Heath government in introducing too much legislation too soon. There was clear recognition that whilst a gradual, 'step-by-step' approach would not appear particularly radical, the longer-term cumulative effect of reforms introduced in this manner certainly would be radical. Also emphasised is the manner in which the Thatcher and Major governments shrewdly introduced reforms which emphasised the rights of trade union members *vis-à-vis* their union leaders and rule books, rather than overtly attacking the trade unions outright (although, of course, the intention was still that of emasculating the trade unions, and rendering them as ineffective as possible). To this end, breaches of the Thatcher and Major governments' trade union legislation were skilfully placed within the ambit of civil, rather than criminal, law. Not only did this place the emphasis for instigating legal proceedings on aggrieved individuals – which perfectly accorded with the renewed Conservative emphasis on individual responsibility – it also ensured that breaches of trade union law would be punishable in financial terms, through the payment of damages and compensation, rather than through the imprisonment of individual trade union members (thus avoiding the risk of creating martyrs). Yet Chapter 7 makes it quite clear that the Thatcher–Major governments did not rely solely on legislation to weaken the trade unions. Also of signal importance were policies such as the toleration of high unemployment, the downgrading and eventual abolition of the NEDC, the clear willingness to 'stand firm' and not 'surrender' in the face of industrial action, and the consistent avoidance of formal incomes policies. The Conservative governments from 1979 were thus able to ignore not only the inevitable trade union opposition to their policies, but also the criticisms and reservations expressed by the dwindling numbers of One Nation Conservatives.

Finally, Chapter 8 places the key features of the Conservative Party's attitudes and policies towards the trade unions in an overall context, noting how economic circumstances, electoral considerations, ideological trends and tensions within the Conservative Party – indeed, within Conservatism itself – have all shaped the party's approach towards the trade unions. Also emphasised is the social composition of the Conservative Party itself, and the manner in which this has changed since 1945. This itself provides a major clue in explaining the adoption of a much more legalistic approach to trade unionism since the latter half of the 1960s. It is not enough merely to claim that because of Britain's economic decline or crises, the Conservative Party automatically developed a more economically liberal/socially authoritarian ideological approach, and, *inter alia*, became more hostile towards the trade unions. It is also important to consider changes within the party itself, noting in particular the emergence of a new generation of Conservative MPs, whose background, and hence ideological or political outlook, was markedly different to that of their predecessors on the Conservative benches in Parliament. In this context, personalities become as important as circumstances. Mere economic reductionism will not suffice.

2 The Conservative Party and trade unionism, 1799–1945

THE COMBINATION ACTS

It was the Tory (forerunner to Conservative) administration of William Pitt the Younger which passed the Combination Acts of 1799 and 1800, thereby instigating Britain's only period of comprehensive legal prohibition of trade unions. Workers were expressly forbidden to combine for the purpose of exerting pressure, or pursuing industrial action, in order to alter wages, working hours, conditions of work, etc. At the same time, the Acts provided for swift recourse to the law for employers whose workers sought to form a trade union.

However, whilst the introduction of the Combination Acts reflected the increasing influence of economic liberalism at the time, and hence the desire to curb any institutions or organisations which would impede the operation of 'the market', the primary motivation for introducing the Acts was political. The French Revolution of 1789, an increase in strike activity and industrial action in Britain during the 1790s, and an uprising in Ireland in 1798, all served to induce fear among Britain's governing classes about the stability of the state and the existing socio-economic order. According to the Home Secretary at the time, even if nothing injurious to the safety of the government was actually being contemplated, associations so formed contained within themselves the means of being converted, at any time, into a most dangerous instrument liable to disturb the public tranquillity (Pelling 1963: 25).

Yet for a number of reasons, the government was rather reticent about enforcing the Combination Acts. First, many Tories were concerned that if the Combination Acts were applied rigorously to workers' organisations, but not to employer's associations, then the image of the state as an impartial institution, independent from, and standing above, sectional interests in civil society, might well be jeopardised. As the Attorney-General acknowledged, in 1804,

> the impartiality of government would be awkwardly situated if, after undertaking a prosecution at the instance of the Masters, against the conspiracy of the journeymen, they were to be applied to on the part of the journeymen, to prosecute the same Masters, for a conspiracy against their men.
>
> (quoted in ibid.: 27)

Second, there existed considerable concern that the active pursuit of legal repression might actually serve to exacerbate the very politico-industrial unrest it was intended to prevent, possibly resulting in an outright challenge to the authority and legitimacy of the state itself.

Third, the Tories soon recognised that the active involvement or intervention by the state in industrial relations might encourage workers to view it as the channel through which their own demands or grievances could be directed and resolved. For if the state were to assume active responsibility for one aspect of industrial and economic activity, why should it renounce responsibility for others? This was a question which more prescient Tories realised might be inadvertently suggested to the minds of workers if the state was active in enforcing the Combination Acts.

Fourth, there were doubts about the wisdom of pursuing legislative measures which were difficult to enforce. Among the difficulties facing the Tory government at the time of the Combination Acts were Britain's lack of a proper police force, the army's engagement in battle with France, and the absence of a prison system. There was thus a need to avoid bringing the law into disrepute, lest respect for both legal and political authority should be undermined.

The fifth, and final, consideration which lay behind the Tory government's reluctance firmly to enforce the Combination Acts was the dilemma between belief in individual freedom, in a market economy, and the fact that some individuals might wish voluntarily to combine. Was this compatible with individual freedom, or did it serve to contradict it? This posed a dilemma for many Tories, and was eventually to be one of the considerations leading to the repeal of the Combination Acts.

In view of those considerations, the Tory government showed a marked reticence about pursuing legal action against workers who combined in defiance of the Acts, preferring, instead, to leave it to employers to press for prosecution. Yet many employers were themselves uneasy about invoking the Combination Acts against their workers, lest this should exacerbate industrial conflict and suspicion even further. Indeed, the Under-Secretary of State at the Home Department (Office) rhetorically asked: 'how is it possible for any Government to protect men who will not protect themselves?' (quoted in Cole and Wilson 1951: 102).

In the event, therefore, the Combination Acts had only limited success in preventing workers from forming trade unions. Indeed, as William Huskisson, the President of the Board of Trade, argued, the Combination Acts had tended to multiply the number of such organisations, thereby greatly aggravating the evil they had been intended to remove. Right from the beginning, therefore, the Tory Party came to recognise that the introduction of a law, and its subsequent enforceability, were sometimes two different things.

REPEAL OF THE COMBINATION ACTS

In 1824, the Tory Party, then led by Lord Liverpool, repealed the Combination Acts, a move which had been urged from across the political spectrum. Home Secretary Robert Peel articulated a perspective which had increasingly been endorsed by Tories, Whigs, Radical Reformers, and Independents alike when he proclaimed that men who had no property except their manual skill and strength ought to be allowed to confer together, if they thought fit, for the purpose of determining at what price they would sell their property (*House of Commons Debates* (hereafter *HC Debates*), new series, vol.12: c.1305). Paradoxically, therefore, the neo-liberal ideology which had originally underpinned the prohibition of trade unions came to provide justification for legalising them.

Strong opposition to this perspective was expressed by Sir John Newport, however, who complained that unions of workers not only regulated what they would take themselves, but wished to compel others to take precisely the same. This was anything but freedom of trade, or liberty of labour, he complained (*HC Debates*, new series, vol.13: c.371–2).

It was not only neo-liberalism which prompted repeal of the Combination Acts. By 1824, the anxieties provoked by the French Revolution had subsided somewhat, so that combinations of workers were no longer viewed with as much fear and foreboding by the government. There had also developed an awareness that the Combination Acts actually exacerbated tension and distrust between employers and workers. As Huskisson pointed out, the Acts had created relations between employers and employed which were diametrically opposite to those which ought to exist (*HC Debates*, new series, vol.10: c.149).

The Report of the Select Committee on Artisans and Machinery (a body set up to investigate the case for repealing the Combination Acts) was presented to Parliament in May 1824. Amongst its resolutions was an acknowledgement that the laws had not hitherto been effectual in preventing such combinations; indeed, the laws had not only *not* been efficient in preventing either combinations of workers, or combinations of employers, but, on the contrary, had a tendency to produce mutual irritation and distrust, and to give a violent character to the combinations, thereby rendering them highly dangerous to the peace of the community. In view of this, Resolution Seven of the Report recommended that masters and workers be freed from such restrictions as regards the rate of wages and hours of work, and that they be left at perfect liberty to make such agreements as they together considered proper. Resolution Eight, meanwhile, urged the repeal of the statute laws that interfered in these particulars between masters and workers, in conjunction with an alteration of the common law which rendered those attending a peaceable meeting liable to prosecution for conspiracy. In advocating the above, the Report referred to the perfect freedom which ought to be allowed to each party, of employing his labour or capital in the manner he deemed most advantageous (*HC Debates*, new series, vol.11: c.811–13).

Such was the change in the political climate that the Act repealing the Combination Laws was passed with little controversy or debate, and with no division in Parliament. Consequently, combinations were removed from the ambit of the law, including the common law of conspiracy, whilst strikes and lock-outs were specifically permitted. In commenting on the 1824 Act, Macdonald notes how the impetus for abrogation of the penal laws came from those who believed in laissez-faire, and thought that it should also be applicable to combinations, provided that the right to combine was not used to coerce either the community or the individual. The Act, he elaborates, reflected a genuine belief, both in and out of Parliament, that repression in this, as in other directions, was overdone, that the Combination Acts were useless irritants, and that the time was ripe for a relaxation of the law (Macdonald 1960: 15–16).

The repeal of the Combination Acts was immediately followed by a rapid growth in the number of workers' associations, accompanied by widespread industrial unrest and violence. In spite of this, there was widespread acknowledgement that the solution was not to be found in reintroducing the Combination Acts. To attempt to do so, it was feared, would probably make matters even worse. Instead, the remedy was deemed to lie in amending the 1824 Repeal Act, a proposal which again had support from all sides of the House.

In 1825, therefore, a further Act was introduced, which amended the previous years' Repeal Act, thereby placing certain restrictions on the liberties and activities of labour combinations. The Tory Party had thus implemented a policy of legalism, whereby trade unions were legally permitted to exist and operate, but with various statutory restrictions placed upon them. This policy of legalism clearly attempted to accommodate the inherent conflict in liberal theory, between the freedom and sovereignty of individuals in 'the market', and the propensity for those same individuals to use their freedom to form associations to defend, or advance, their interests in 'the market', thereby giving rise to collectivism born of individual freedom. This has been a problem for the Conservative Party ever since, albeit to varying degrees, at different historical junctures.

ONE NATION TORYISM AND ORGANISED LABOUR

With the exception of the Molestation of Workmen Act, passed in 1859 by Lord Derby's Conservative (as the Tories were now known) administration, which clearly affirmed the right to strike whilst also removing liability to legal penalties for peaceful picketing, the next Conservative Party initiative concerning trade unions did not occur until the last quarter of the nineteenth century. However, it is worth noting that the 1859 Act owed much to the tenacity of Benjamin Disraeli, who was Chancellor of the Exchequer at the time, in convincing his ministerial colleagues that a constructive policy towards the trade unions was likely to foster greater moderation by the trade unions. Disraeli is widely seen as the 'founding father' of One Nation Conservatism, a strand in the Conservative Party which envisaged that paternalistic policies towards the labouring masses would be reciprocated by widespread support for the established order, and a further reinforcement of the conservatism which has long seemed deeply ingrained in the British working class.

'One Nation' Toryism was derived from Disraeli's view that Britain was characterised by the existence of two nations, the rich and the poor. Such was the gap between the two that Disraeli became concerned with 'all measures calculated to improve the condition of the people'. This certainly did not imply a belief in egalitarianism;

the traditional Conservative themes of hierarchy and authority retained their immense importance. None the less, Disraeli believed that society was – or ought to be – organic, so that 'its respective classes were joined together by powerful ties of mutual obligation' (Beer 1965: 267). Such a perspective, however, placed particular importance on the duties or responsibilities of the upper class(es) towards the 'lower orders' in society. For Disraeli (and One Nation Tories ever since), the privileges, property, and power which were inevitably the preserve of a small minority were to be accompanied by a sense of duty and obligation towards the rest of society, and a concern for 'the condition of the people'. If the ruling class showed indifference to the problems and conditions of the lower orders, then mutual distrust, suspicion, and hostility might well jeopardise social stability and the body politic. In other words, Disraeli warned, 'the palace is not safe, when the cottage is not happy' (quoted in Monypenny and Buckle 1929: 709). However, the 'moral' responsibilities held by the 'ruling class' *vis-à-vis* the working classes were not without a concomitant degree of self-interest; by supporting social reforms to ameliorate the 'condition of the poor', the privileged elite would serve to secure the stability of the existing social order, and *pari passu*, consolidate their own position.

The adoption of One Nation Toryism as a strategy for the Conservative Party, under Disraeli's leadership, was not, however, solely an affirmation of *noblesse oblige*. On the contrary, Disraeli was acutely aware of the electoral advantages which might accrue to the Conservative Party by the adoption of such an approach. Even before becoming party leader, Disraeli had proclaimed the need for the Conservatives to pursue social reforms in order to succeed politically and electorally. With an expanding working-class electorate (by virtue of the 1867 Reform Act), electoral competition with the Whigs (Liberals) took on a new significance. For Disraeli, therefore, it was essential for the Conservatives not only to support social reforms so as to ameliorate the conditions of the poor, but simultaneously to advocate the creation of One Nation, whilst portraying the Whigs as the party of selfish, sectional self-interest and unbridled individualism, which was, therefore, responsible for the existence of 'Two Nations' in Britain. Certainly, during the run-up to the 1874 election, Conservative candidates in industrial constituencies found themselves pressed by working-class voters to state their intentions concerning the 'trade union question'.

Yet, the extension of the franchise to the more prosperous sections of the male working class, via the 1867 Reform Act, did pose problems for the Conservative Party. Given that the Conservatives perceived and portrayed themselves as a 'national' – as opposed to sectional or class-based – political party, there was considerable ambiguity over the extent to which it should make specific appeals, through its policy pledges, to the working class *per se*. As one commentator has noted: 'The Conservatives, as a whole, had no enthusiasm for appealing to the working men or taking up social questions, and their "national party" strategy precluded any pronounced stress on working-class interests.' Yet it was also recognised by many Conservatives that: 'To gain real strength among the working classes the party needed to adopt a more positive approach to them. It needed to show some sympathy for their social aspirations.' However, 'On the trade union issue, which was perhaps the most important to the working men, attitudes were divided', for whilst some Conservatives were antipathetical towards trade unionism, and thus reluctant to grant even more legal power or protection to the unions, 'there was by this time a body of opinion in the party prepared to offer the unions a degree of legal recognition and protection for their funds' (Smith 1967: 122, 123). To a considerable extent, this more positive approach towards the trade union 'question' was born of electoral considerations, the Conservative Party needing to secure votes from the newly enfranchised working class.

Certainly, during his time as Conservative Prime Minister, from 1874 to 1880, Disraeli 'presided over the most notable instalment of social reform undertaken by any single government of the century ... reconciling it ... to the conditions resulting from the political emergence of the working classes' (ibid.: 2–3), having appointed a Royal Commission to consider improving the state of the law between 'master and servant', an issue which Disraeli himself had looked at, prior to the election. As soon as the Commission had reported, the Conservative Home Secretary, Richard Austen Cross, introduced the Employers and Workmen's Act, which made the two sides of industry formally equal before the law, and also made breach of contract a civil, rather than a criminal, offence.

In introducing the Act, Cross proclaimed that, in so far as was consistent with general public order, there should be the greatest amount of individual freedom of action for workers (*HC Debates*, 3rd series, vol.651: c.678). The Employers and Workmen's Act was accompanied by the introduction of the Conspiracy and Protection of Property Act, which established the right to strike, by stipulating that acts carried out by groups of workers in furtherance of a trade dispute would not be indictable as a conspiracy, so long as the same action by an individual would not be punishable in law.

Having introduced the two Acts, Cross explained that it had been his misfortune for many years to see, and to deplore, the quarrels which periodically arose between masters and workers. If they could be persuaded to realise that their interests were very much the same, he declared, then the government would have done a great deal of good. Disraeli, meanwhile, was informing Queen Victoria that the two Acts constituted the most important labour laws passed during her reign, and that: 'We have settled the long and vexatious contest between Capital and Labour' (quoted in Monypenny and Buckle 1929: 711).

The legislation passed by Disraeli's Conservative government thus formally committed the party to a voluntarist strategy, although most of the Cabinet opposed the Acts. According to one commentator, there was also a distinct lack of enthusiasm from 'Tory lawyers ... [who] had been hostile on points of legal interpretation' (Coleman 1988: 147). Disraeli and Cross managed to overcome this opposition from within the party, thereby ensuring that issues such as wages and working conditions were to be determined by the two sides of industry, through free collective bargaining. The government's role, in true voluntarist fashion, would be to maintain the framework of law within which employers and employees conducted their affairs. Disraeli was of the opinion that 'between men and their employers, the law, to my mind, should not interfere' (*HC Debates*, 3rd series, vol.234: c.15–16).

CONSERVATIVE CONCERN OVER TRADE UNION POWER

Some Conservatives, however, remained unconvinced, believing that the trade unions were being granted too much power and immunity, a perspective voiced by C. N. Newdegate, MP, who spoke ominously of a 'moral terrorism' being exercised by the increasing scope and strength of trade unionism in British industry. He believed that 'trade unionism was becoming a source of great power ... creating a new jurisdiction ... with oppressive effect'. He warned that Parliament might eventually find it necessary to resort to regulating the trade unions again (*HC Debates*, 3rd series, vol.125: c. 684–5).

Certainly, Disraeli's belief that the 'labour question' had been resolved proved rather ambitious or premature. The extension of the franchise, and the growth of trade unionism during the remainder of the nineteenth century, gave the question greater significance. Its sensitivity was further fuelled by the economic problems which beset Britain during this period, and which were deemed by many to be a manifestation of the 'excessive power' and 'irresponsible' behaviour of the trade unions which were accused of undermining profitability and productivity, as well as deterring investment. As has been the case ever since, Conservatives were divided on which strategy to adopt: whether to constrain the trade unions through legislation, even at the risk of engendering further industrial conflict and trade union suspicion of the Conservative Party, or whether to incorporate organised labour more securely into the existing political system by pursuing a more conciliatory and constructive approach, one which actually conceded some of labour's demands, thereby encouraging greater moderation and reciprocal respect on the part of the trade unions.

The choice facing the Conservative Party towards the end of the nineteenth century was starkly spelt out by Lord Randolph Churchill in 1891, two days prior to an announcement by Disraeli's successor, Lord Salisbury, that he was appointing a Royal Commission on Labour. Churchill dwelt at some length upon what he claimed was the great issue of the day, namely what was to be done for the labouring classes. This, he declared, was the great issue of the day because it was the workers who 'had the power'. Without their support, Churchill warned, the Conservative Party could not entertain the great political objectives it had in view. He alluded to the threat of a great war between capital and labour, in which the former was banded together on one side, and confronted labour, which was assembled on the other. In such a war, neither side would yield, Churchill argued, so that the outcome might be even more disastrous to the property of the nation than civil war involving armed force. Randolph Churchill suggested that a Royal Commission on Labour would not only give the greatest possible satisfaction to the labouring classes, because they would feel that the Conservative Party was really, anxiously, considering their position, but it would probably be the means of eliciting the most valuable and useful information, which would be of greatest value to the working classes themselves, when it had been deliberated upon (*The Times*, 23 February 1891).

However, with Disraeli no longer party leader, there was little sign of support for One Nation Toryism amongst Conservatives. Whereas Disraeli, and then Randolph Churchill, sought to create a sense of national unity and social cohesion, by explicitly acknowledging a working class with particular interests, and thereby seeking to incorporate it into the existing socio-political order through certain measures and policies intended to improve its conditions of existence, whilst also granting its organisations various legal rights and 'privileges', Conservatives such as Salisbury doubted the wisdom of such a strategy, fearing that it would serve to undermine the social order. Back in 1860, Salisbury had expressed the view that political reforms such as the extension of power to a numerical majority would not so much abolish any evils in society as replace them by even worse ones, such as that of 'the strong, steady, deadly grip of the trade unions'. If Britain ever fell under their power, he warned, 'we should welcome the military despotism that should relieve us' (Salisbury 1860). Elsewhere, Salisbury expressed concern about the possibility that a strengthened working class might act *en masse* (Salisbury 1866).

Meanwhile, some Conservatives warned that if the other classes in society were given cause to fear the working class, then confidence might be destroyed, with the consequence that the capitalist might withdraw his capital. If this situation arose, it was argued, it would be the income of the working class which would suffer most, for whilst capitalists could seek other spheres for their capital, the working man, as labour was his capital, had no field of action except his own country, in the prosperity and harmony of which he was therefore vitally concerned (National Union of Conservative and Constitutional Associations 1873: 3). Indeed, some Conservatives believed that such a warning was vindicated by the economic difficulties which afflicted Britain at the end of the 1870s, difficulties which were partly blamed on labour 'selfishly' pursuing its own interests, and having been 'pampered' by favourable legislation.

In spite of such concerns, there was no real attempt at reversing the labour (and social) legislation passed by Disraeli's government. To have done so would probably have resulted in the very political unrest and exercise of labour's power which Conservatives such as Salisbury feared in the first place. There was also the obvious electoral consideration. Consequently, the Conservative Party, at the end of the nineteenth century, largely tolerated the voluntarist strategy laid down by Disraeli. To have enhanced the position of labour any further might have alienated the Conservatives' rapidly growing middle-class support, whilst to have attempted a reversal of labour's improved position would have meant incurring the wrath of the, by now, fully enfranchised male working class.

However, the general acceptance of a voluntarist industrial relations strategy was accompanied by an initial ambivalence about the extent to which the state should intervene in disputes where collective bargaining had ceased to operate, or where stalemate ensued. The problem arose, to a significant extent, because of the size and scale of British industry which had developed by the end of the nineteenth century; what had previously been disputes between workers and employees, which affected only their own plant or factory, soon had repercussions beyond the immediate source of the dispute, due to the increasingly national, and interconnected, character of British industry, and also because of rapidly growing foreign competition. In this context, there were calls from some Conservatives, such as Sir John Gorst, for a system of compulsory arbitration to be imposed, in instances where 'internecine quarrels' in the country's 'highly organised industries' entailed 'the whole community in suffering' (*HC Debates*, 4th series, vol.31: c.395).

LEARNING TO ACCEPT THE ROLE
OF TRADE UNIONISM

However, when the Royal Commission on Labour published its report, it endorsed the view that compulsion or legislation by the government, in order to solve or prevent disputes between employers and employees, was both undesirable and largely impracticable. In any case, the report exhibited considerable optimism about the future of industrial relations, for it suggested that the course of events was tending towards a more settled and pacific period in which there would be, if not a greater identification of similar interests, then at least a clearer perception of the principles which must regulate the division of the proceeds of each industry, consistently with its permanence and prosperity, between those who supply labour, and those who supply managing ability and capital. Most of the conflicts in industry were deemed by the report to be the result of uncertain rights and misunderstandings, along with the pursuit of separate interests by employers and workers, without due regard to their common interest. The report of the Royal Commission came to the conclusion that the increased strength of organisations in industry might tend towards the maintenance of harmonious relations between employer and employee (Command 7421).

The Conservative Cabinet was thus persuaded that compulsory arbitration ought to be avoided, not least because of its unacceptability to both capital and labour. It was also feared that compulsion might lead to conflict between organised labour and the state.

Consequently, the 1896 Conciliation (Trade Disputes) Act introduced by the Salisbury government avoided any form of compulsion, instead empowering the Labour Department of the Board of Trade to offer conciliation if one side in an industrial dispute requested it, and arbitration if it was expressly sought by both sides. The Act also omitted any provision for a compulsory cooling-off period. Thus it served to underline, rather than undermine, the Conservative Party's voluntarist policy *vis-à-vis* industrial relations.

By the turn of the century, therefore, the Conservative Party had largely come to terms with the existence of trade unionism in Britain. From this time onwards, the acknowledgement of the permanence of trade unions was supplemented by attempts at encouraging 'responsible' trade unionism. The spread of Marxism and syndicalism in Europe, the formation of the Labour Party in Britain in 1906, and the concomitant introduction of the political levy, all led the Conservative Party to posit a distinction between the (legitimate) industrial functions of trade unions, and their (illegitimate) political activities or inclinations.

It was envisaged that industrial and political stability would best be secured by according trade unions a legitimate role in matters pertaining to wages, working conditions, etc., implying their incorporation and integration into the existing industrial-economic order. If this could be achieved, the Conservative Party hoped, then organised labour would be weaned away from any propensity towards the revolutionary doctrines spreading amongst the European working classes at that time.

Obviously, the emergence of the Labour Party as an electoral force strengthened the Conservative Party's desire, or need, to avoid exhibiting or expressing hostility towards trade unions. In other words, electoral expediency continued to play a notable role in informing Conservative attitudes towards organised labour during the early twentieth century.

In fact, a few years before the founding of the Labour Representation Committee, Randolph Churchill had warned the Conservative Party that if, under the existing constitution, the 'Labour interest' found that it could attain its objectives, and secure its own advantage, then labour would be reconciled to the constitution, would have faith in it, and would help to maintain it. But if the 'Labour interest' found that the 'Constitutional' Party was unwilling to hear, and slow to meet, the demands of labour; was stubborn in opposition to these demands; and persisted in the habit of proclaiming unreasoning and shortsighted support of all the existing rights of capital and property, the result might be that 'the labour interest' would identify what it took to be the defects in the 'Constitutional' Party with the constitution itself, and in a moment of indiscriminate impulse might use its power to sweep both away (quoted in Churchill 1906: 458–60).

Yet the attitude of the Balfour government, in response to the Taff Vale decision of 1901, raised questions about the commitment of the Conservative Party to the rights and position of organised labour. A House of Lords decision, in respect of a claim by the Taff Vale Railway Company for compensation for loss of revenue due to strike action by the Amalgamated Society of Railway Servants, established that trade unions were liable for actions carried out in their name, and could thus be sued for damages. Immediately after the decision, Keir Hardie asked Balfour if his government would introduce legislation to restore the protection of trade union funds. Balfour replied in the negative (*HC Debates*, 4th series, vol.98: c.877). Shortly afterwards, T. C. Ritchie, Conservative Secretary of State for the Home Department (Office), rejected calls for an inquiry with a view to subsequent legislation concerning the ambiguity of the financial and legal position of trade unions after Taff Vale. According to Ritchie, if unlawful acts were done, or were authorised by any body of persons, then it seemed obvious that those concerned ought to be financially responsible for any ensuing damage. Consequently, he maintained, he could see no grounds for any inquiry (*HC Debates*, 4th series, vol.108: c.328–9).

Rather than seeking to allay the doubts of trade union officials about his government's commitment to the rights and status of organised labour, however, Balfour showed further ambivalence, by suggesting that a situation had been reached where the combinations of workers could perfectly well hold their own against the combinations of employers, and vice versa; this situation had given rise to the oppression of some sectors of unorganised labour by the bodies of organised labour, and the oppression of small businesses by large, organised capitalists. It was unorganised labour and small businesses who had come to require protection, Balfour alleged, urging an inquiry into the modern system of combinations generally (*HC Debates*, 4th series, vol.122: c.261–4).

Such remarks, allied to a reticence on the part of the Conservatives to support further measures to strengthen the rights of trade unions, particularly in the wake of adverse judicial decisions, were instrumental in creating or, rather, reinforcing the suspicion by organised labour that the Conservative Party was profoundly hostile to trade unions.

THE ADVOCACY OF 'INDUSTRIAL PARTNERSHIP'

Until 1926, Conservative Party attitudes and policies towards the trade unions were characterised by two main features or themes. First, there was strong advocacy by many Conservatives of the desirability or necessity of co-operation and partnership between capital and labour, and between employers and employees, as a means of reducing distrust and disruption in industry. Second, there were repeated criticisms of the political levy, particularly its 'contracting out' provisions.

The advocacy of co-operation and partnership between the two sides of industry was largely derived from the view, held by many Conservatives, that much of the industrial conflict in Britain was attributable to a combination of ignorance and mistrust on the part of many workers; an ignorance both of the functioning of the enterprise in which they worked, and of industry as a whole, coupled with distrust of their employers. According to Balfour, in an address to the Labour Co-Partnership Association, some of the difficulties which had tended to arise between capital and labour were because wage earners had no real, intimate acquaintance with the difficulties which owners of enterprises had to face (*The Times*, 2 December 1908). Meanwhile, Lord Robert Cecil (the former Conservative Prime Minister, the Marquess of Salisbury) acknowledged that the great reproach to the existing system was the antagonism between capital and labour, the remedy for which, he asserted, was to bring the classes together in close co-operation and partnership. This ought to be achieved by allowing workers an intelligent share in the business in which they were engaged. In other words, Lord Cecil claimed, workers should be treated as partners (*The Times*, 26 November 1918; see also *The Times*, 19 January 1920). Similar sentiments were expressed by William Bridgeman, as parliamentary secretary to the Minister of Labour, who argued that the only way in which the suspicion between employers and employees could be removed was by the two sides treating each other with more confidence (*The Times*, 4 October 1917). Such a perspective was widely subscribed to by the Conservative Party, both inside and outside Parliament (National Unionist Association 1924; Andrew Bonar Law, *The Times*, 22 May 1912).

However, in keeping with the voluntarist approach towards trade unions and industrial relations, Conservative proponents of schemes of co-operation and partnership between capital and labour, between employers and employees, repeatedly insisted that such schemes had to be developed by, and within, industry itself, rather than being imposed from above, by government. As Neville Chamberlain (who became Conservative Prime Minister in 1937) argued, it was the businessmen, the managers, and the workers who best knew the difficulties and the possibilities; any suggestions that they could agree among themselves were more likely to command assent, and to prevent friction, than those which might be imposed on them from above (*The Times*, 16 October 1917). In similar vein, Bonar Law (who was to become Conservative Prime Minister briefly in 1922) did not believe that the government could, or should, produce arrangements for co-operation or co-partnership in industry (*The Times*, 22 May 1912). As Arthur Balfour and Arthur Shirley Benn – two of several Conservative MPs to be involved in the National Alliance of Employers and Employed – argued, mutual co-operation in industry, which was essential to national prosperity, could only be attained by the creation of a bond of personal sympathy that arose from working together for a common good (*The Times*, 20 January 1923).

Advocacy of such schemes did not only reflect the predominance of voluntarism in the Conservative Party during the first quarter of the twentieth century: it was equally intended to reinforce voluntarism. The rationale was that co-operation and consultation between employers and their employees would not only reduce the incidence of misunderstandings and mistrust, which often gave rise to industrial action, but would also provide for the machinery through which grievances or disputes which did arise could be resolved without any need for state intervention. Stanley Baldwin (who replaced Bonar Law as Conservative leader in 1923 and became Prime Minister in 1924) provided the most eloquent exposition of such a perspective, insisting that the organisations of employers and workers, if they took their coats off to the task, were far more able than the politicians to work out the solutions to their troubles. He thus urged the two sides of industry to put the state out of their minds, and to try to steer their respective ships side by side, instead of making for head-on collisions, for they were unlikely to get much help from politicians or intellectuals in resolving their differences (*The Times*, 6 March 1925; see also *HC Debates*, 5th series, vol.34: c.956). The theme was developed by Austen Chamberlain (who became Foreign Secretary in 1924) who criticised the 'gradually growing interference' of government departments, and of the government itself, in disputes between capital and labour. One important and dangerous consequence of such 'interference', he pointed out, was that when a significant dispute arose, both sides involved tended to hold back in seeking a solution, because they hoped that they might benefit from what was seen as almost inevitable government intervention (*HC Debates*, 5th series, vol.34: c.73).

Yet Conservative advocacy of greater co-operation and co-partnership between capital and labour was not based solely on the desire for greater harmony in industry; it also reflected wider political considerations. It was envisaged that by encouraging the two sides of industry to work more closely together, organised labour would become more fully integrated into the existing industrial-economic order, as well as being accorded greater legitimacy. Consequently, workers would be less susceptible to radical or revolutionary doctrines and political movements. In other words, Conservative advocates of greater co-operation between capital and labour hoped that the ultimate result would be greater industrial harmony, improved economic efficiency, and increased political stability. Furthermore, in spite of their party's criticisms of various aspects of trade union behaviour, some Conservatives occasionally acknowledged that the unions were actually an important means of securing order and stability in the work-place, particularly as firms and industries became ever larger and more complex. Thus did Bonar Law maintain that trade union organisation was the only thing preventing 'anarchy' in industry (cited in Bagwell 1971: 106; cited in Pimlott and Cook 1982: 4), whilst Balfour proclaimed that ultimately only the effective operation of well-organised trade unions could help to secure peace in industry (*The Times*, 6 October 1910; see also Montagu Barlow, MP, *HC Debates*, 4th series, vol.41: c.3050).

CONCERN OVER THE TRADE UNIONS' POLITICAL LEVY

The second aspect or feature which we earlier noted as a characteristic of Conservative Party attitudes and policies *vis-à-vis* trade unions and industrial relations, during the first quarter of the twentieth century concerned the political levy and, in particular, the 'contracting out' provisions which had been enshrined in the 1913 Trade Union Act passed by Asquith's Liberal government. Opposition to the political levy was largely couched in the vocabulary of 'moral liberalism', emphasising the freedom of the individual, which the political levy was deemed to be at odds with. However, it hardly needs pointing out that Conservative opposition to the political levy – particularly the 'contracting out' aspect – was due to the fact that the levy was the major source of income for the Conservative Party's political opponent, the Labour Party.

Such objections to the political levy were forcefully articulated by Viscount Wolmer, who declared that when men were forced into organisations against their will, and then forced to subscribe to the propagation of political principles which they detested, then the Conservative Party would denounce it as inconsistent with individual and civil liberty. He asked the Labour Party a question: was the minority they were desiring to coerce into paying the political levy a small or a large one? If it was a small minority, he suggested, then the Labour Party would surely have little to fear from that minority being granted the liberty to refuse to pay. On the order hand, if it was a large minority, Viscount Wolmer argued, to the extent that their refusal to pay the political levy would seriously inconvenience the Labour Party, then it seemed to him that that party would be admitting, in effect, to the practice of coercion and intimidation on a very large scale (*HC Debates*, 5th series, vol.41: c. 3035–7).

Backbench hostility to the political levy was such that in 1925 F.A. Macquisten, a backbench Conservative, sought to introduce a Political Levy Bill, which would replace 'contracting out' with 'contracting in'. In so doing, he argued that unions should not have the right to put a man in a position where money was taken from him, so that he had to endure the humiliation of going 'cap in hand' to ask for it back. The political levy, as it stood, was likened by Macquisten to a form of political conscription (*HC Debates*, 5th series, vol.181: c.816 and c.822).

However, elsewhere in the parliamentary Conservative Party, and particularly within the Cabinet, there were reservations about the wisdom of pursuing Macquisten's Bill, in spite of their overall agreement with the sentiments it reflected. A week after the Bill had been tabled, a deputation of Conservative MPs opposed to the measure met the Conservative leader and Prime Minister, Stanley Baldwin, to convey their concerns about such legislation. Yet the two dozen or so Conservative MPs who comprised the deputation were by no means in agreement as to what the alternative to Macquisten's Bill should be. Some were of the opinion that it would be better if the government itself introduced legislation rather than leaving it to a Private Member's Bill, whilst another view was that an independent inquiry should be established to look at the whole issue of political activities by trade unions. Others in the deputation favoured a policy of bringing both parties together 'in an endeavour to reach, by agreement, a fair settlement of a legitimate grievance'.

The point upon which all the MPs agreed, however, was that Macquisten's Political Levy Bill was undesirable, in that it only dealt with one aspect of 'the problem', and said nothing about the conditions in which ballots were taken, or money was transferred from a union's benevolent fund into its political fund. The deputation believed it to be inexpedient to do anything which might appear, to the average man, to be 'not cricket'. In addition to the options put forward, there was still support amongst some Conservatives for a 'voluntary' solution, whereby changes should be initiated by, and within, the trade unions themselves.

Two days later, after meeting the deputation, the Cabinet agreed that Baldwin should intervene, at an early stage, in the second reading of the Political Levy Bill, and reiterate the government's desire for peace in industry. This Baldwin did, by urging his parliamentary colleagues to say:

> We have our majority. We believe in the justice of this Bill, but we are going to withdraw our hand, and are not going to push our political advantage home at a moment like this. We are not going to fire the first shot, for we want to create peace, and create an atmosphere in which people can come together.
>
> (*HC Debates* 5th series, vol.181: c.840).

Shortly afterwards, the Conservative Party's commitment to voluntarism was further underlined when Baldwin reiterated his view that peace in industry could not be directly promoted by the introduction of legislation (*HC Debates*, 5th series, vol.182: c.2445; see also Baldwin, *The Times*, 8 March 1925; Arthur Steel-Maitland, *HC Debates*, 5th series, vol.182: c.820).

Reflecting, at the end of the year, on Baldwin's decision not to proceed with the Political Levy Bill, Lord Salisbury declared that in the realm of industrial affairs no man had illustrated more prominently a policy of goodwill than Stanley Baldwin. Whilst acknowledging the virtue of the Bill in principle, Salisbury entirely approved of Baldwin's decision, insisting that to have pressed ahead with the legislation would have destroyed at the outset any chance of establishing peace in industry, and trust between the Conservative administration and the trade unions (*The Times*, 7 December 1925).

That peace was abruptly shattered by the 1926 General Strike, which arose out of attempts by employers in the coal industry – fully supported by the government – to cut miners' wages, and lengthen the working day. It constituted a climax to numerous industrial conflicts which had taken place during the first half of the 1920s.

However, the involvement of workers from key sectors of industry and the economy, striking in support of the miners, made it qualitatively and quantitatively different from any previous industrial dispute in British history. Furthermore, it was immediately characterised by the Conservative government as a political strike, rather than an industrial dispute. Some Conservatives believed that this provided justification for dealing very severely with the trade unions, with Winston Churchill achieving notoriety for his advocacy of sending troops and tanks into working-class communities, and for other inflammatory remarks.

The General Strike seemed to vindicate those in the Conservative Party who had constantly warned about the growing power of organised labour in Britain, and the threat of Bolshevik-style insurrection. Among the staunchest Conservative critics of trade unionism and voluntarism had been the Home Secretary, Sir William Joynson-Hicks. He had condemned Baldwin's advocacy of peace in industry, claiming that it was no use a statesman crying 'peace when there is no peace'. For Joynson-Hicks, the trade union 'question' would have to be fought out sooner or later, by the people of Britain. They would have to decide whether the country was to be governed by Parliament and the Cabinet, or by a handful of trade union leaders (*The Times*, 3 August 1925).

After the collapse of the General Strike, Conservatives recognised that legislation of some kind was imperative, if only to quell the discontent on the backbenches and among the rank-and-file in the constituencies. Indeed, such was the impatience with Baldwin's conciliatory approach towards trade unions in general that Sir George Younger, the former party chairman, felt compelled to warn the parliamentary leadership that the Conservative Party might be doomed, and replaced by a new 'die-hard' group, if action was not taken against the trade unions (quoted in Middlemas and Barnes 1969: 447). A similar concern was expressed by the party chairman, J. C. C. Davidson (ibid.: 447).

Evidence of the impatience of the Conservative grassroots in the constituencies manifested itself at the 1926 Annual Conference, where strong criticism of the activities of trade unions, and a concomitant desire for a policy of legalism, were accompanied by strong rebukes of the party's parliamentary leadership. Not surprisingly, Baldwin was the focus of much criticism, with one constituency delegate calling on him and his government to 'get on with it or get out' – a call which was greeted with thunderous applause.

Recognition of the need for legislation against the trade unions was one thing; deciding what form that legislation should assume was quite another. As Harold Macmillan was later to comment, the Conservative Party was much divided. The only point upon which there was agreement was that there had to be a Bill of some kind (Macmillan 1966: 225). For some Conservatives, a limited Bill, confining itself to the outlawing of general strikes, would have sufficed. (Indeed, one backbencher sought to introduce an Illegal Strikes Bill himself.) Other Conservatives desired a more comprehensive policy of legal restraint, in the guise of a Bill dealing with a whole range of trade union activities. This was the approach favoured by Conservatives such as Lord Birkenhead, who insisted that whilst it might result in a very bitter parliamentary session and cause 'a great row', such a Bill would be correct.

Such remarks, however, caused considerable concern to those in the Conservative Party who, whilst acknowledging the need for some legislation, were convinced that any Bill ought to avoid an emphasis on repression or 'attacking' the trade unions, including instead some positive, constructive, measures. Thus, according to Lord Robert Cecil, a Bill which emphasised repression rather than reconciliation might make matters worse (Middlemas and Barnes 1969: 447). Similarly, Harold Macmillan (an exponent of One Nation Conservatism on the back benches in the 1920s, to become Prime Minister in 1957) called for any trade union legislation to be accompanied by a progressive programme of social reform and industrial reorganisation, carried out in a constructive spirit (Macmillan 1966: 226). As Steel-Maitland, Minister of Labour, asserted, the government could not wield a sword with one hand, and then convincingly proffer an olive branch with the other (quoted in Wigham 1982: 67; see also Sir Walter Greaves-Lord, *HC Debates*, 5th series, vol.202: c.614).

In the event, the Trade Disputes Act was passed in 1927. Its main provision was to declare illegal any strike which was not in connection with a trade dispute in which the employees were actually directly involved or interested, or any strike which was intended to coerce the government by inflicting hardship on the community. The Act also abolished 'contracting out' of the political levy, and replaced it with 'contracting in'. Although the Act represented a change of industrial relations strategy from voluntarism to legalism, the most notable feature of this period was the extent to which many Conservatives were seeking to encourage a new climate of conciliation and co-operation in industry between capital and labour.

Once the Trade Disputes Act was on the Statute Book, even Joynson-Hicks was among a number of senior Conservatives urging a new era of co-operation and harmony in industry; alluding to others in the party who were eager for the government to deal harshly with the trade union movement, Joynson-Hicks pointed out the need to avoid injuring the legitimate work of the trade unions (*The Times*, 21 July 1927, 29 February 1928). Less surprising was Baldwin's conciliatory stance, emphasising that perpetual strife could only lead to poverty and oppression, two species which could only be removed by peace. He therefore expressed his hope that, before long, more enlightened and statesmanlike minds might emerge amongst the employers and trade unions, so that they could begin the discussions which would put industrial warfare behind them (*The Times*, 14 June 1927). Similar sentiments were expressed by the Minister for Labour, Arthur Steel-Maitland, who, in a speech to the Movement for Industrial Peace, insisted that there could be no lasting efficiency in business without co-operation, although this had to grow from within industry itself (*The Times*, 2 December 1926), a point reiterated by Lord Salisbury (*The Times*, 28 January 1927).

This advocacy of voluntarism was endorsed by the final report of the Balfour Committee on Industry and Trade, published in 1929, which concluded that, in spite of certain shortcomings, the methods of collective bargaining and wage determination which had developed spontaneously in British industry were, on the whole, vastly preferable to any uniform, cast-iron system imposed by law. The Balfour Committee therefore expressed its support for the existing, less formal, more flexible, agreements and understandings, which, it claimed, were in general loyally observed. Furthermore, the Committee claimed, such a perspective was shared by representatives from 'both sides of industry' (Command 3282).

In spite of the Trade Disputes Act, therefore – or maybe because of it – the Conservative Party's discussion of industrial relations was couched predominantly within a voluntarist discourse. It was emphasised that no Act of Parliament could settle the question of who was to control the policy and management of the unions, for that was an internal matter which only the members themselves could solve (National Union of Conservative and Unionist Associations 1926: 18). Indeed, one Conservative MP deemed it statesmanship of the most unsound, jejune, and elementary sort, to try to do for people what they should do for themselves. He therefore looked with the utmost hesitation and distaste on any attempt to interfere, by legislation, with the internal organisation of trade unions, which was a matter for the unions themselves (*HC Debates*, 5th series, vol.202: c.667–9).

Whilst many Conservatives were advocating greater co-operation between the two sides of industry, a new bloc was coalescing in the party which also sought both a more active role for the state in the economy and a partnership between the two sides of industry and government. In the spring of 1927, as the Trade Disputes Bill was going through Parliament, this bloc produced a booklet entitled *Industry and the State* (Macmillan 1966: 223–4). Widely regarded as a manifesto of the Conservative Party's 'progressive' wing, it advocated a middle way between unadulterated private enterprise and socialistic collectivism, whereby broad strategic control of industry would be in the hands of the state, whilst day-to-day operations would be the responsibility of private management. Public and private ownership would operate side by side. More important still, as far as organised labour was concerned, was that such a programme envisaged an enhanced position for trade unions in national decision-making, with government, management, and labour leaders all working much more closely together. This 'middle way' constituted, in effect, an embryonic form of neo-corporatism.

However, it was over thirty years before such a strategy was adopted (in peacetime, at least) by the Conservative Party. In the meantime, the 1930s were characterised by relative industrial peace, accounted for by a confluence of factors, most notably the moderation of the trade union leadership during this time, the conciliatory stance adopted by the Conservative leadership (the Trade Disputes Act notwithstanding), and the mass unemployment of the 1930s, which meant both depleted union membership and a passivity on the part of many of those still members of trade unions. By 1933, trade union membership in Britain had fallen to less than 4.5 million, from a peak, in 1920, of 8 million.

Although the Trade Disputes Act remained on the Statute Book, the emphasis of most senior Conservatives during the 1930s was on the need for (greater) co-operation in industry, with employers and employees being urged to work more closely together. According to Sir Henry Betterton, the Minister of Labour, there were no differences in industry which were not capable of reconciliation, as long as 'both sides' did their best (*The Times*, 13 April 1932), whilst according to Neville Chamberlain, industrial and social progress were dependent on confidence and goodwill. He warned that industry would be crippled if co-operation between employers and workers gave way to distrust and antagonism (*The Times*, 29 April 1937).

By the 1930s, if not before, most Conservatives had come to accept that trade unions were a permanent and important feature of industrial life in Britain. In 1934, for example, Stanley Baldwin acknowledged that trade unions had become an integral part of the machinery of industrial life. Indeed, he believed that in the years ahead, the principle of collective bargaining ought to be extended. The following year, Baldwin claimed that not only were trade unions an integral part of the nation's economic and industrial life, they were also a great stabilising influence. He therefore called upon anyone who had any knowledge of the subject to try and imagine what industry would be like if there were no unions: there would be absolute chaos, Baldwin warned (*The Times*, 15 February 1934, 5 May 1935).

The importance of the trade unions in British economic and industrial life was confirmed by the vital role they played during the Second World War. Maximum co-operation was obviously required for the war effort, and in order to help achieve this, organised labour was incorporated into government and national decision-making, with Ernest Bevin, the leader of the Trades Union Congress (TUC) General Council, being appointed Minister of Labour in 1940. Bevin would only agree to the issuing of orders under the Emergency Powers (Defence) Act if he was satisfied as to the welfare and conditions of the workers to whom such orders were being applied.

The role and influence of labour representatives at the highest levels served to reaffirm the importance of trade unions, and the valuable contribution which they could make to the nation's success, if they were accorded respect and acted responsibly. Many Conservatives fully acknowledged the importance of securing the active involvement of the trade unions in the machinery of government, with Leo Amery, a Minister in Churchill's wartime coalition administration, declaring, in 1940, that: 'The time has come when the organisation and influence of the Trades Union Congress cannot be left outside. It must ... reinforce the strength of the national effort from the inside' (*HC Debates*, 5th series, vol.360: c.1149).

Indeed, barely one month after the start of the war, the Minister of Labour had established a National Joint Advisory Council – comprising fifteen representatives each from the TUC and the British Employers Confederation – whose function was to advise the government on matters pertaining to employment.

Due to the labour shortages which the war engendered competition between employers to recruit the limited supply of skilled labour resulted in strong upward pressure on wage levels, a situation which obviously caused the government and the Treasury considerable consternation. Yet most Ministers, in order to secure the continued co-operation and goodwill of the trade unions, balked at the idea of government intervention to determine wages, upholding, instead, the principle of free collective bargaining. Furthermore, partly in response to trade union demands, the government introduced a system of food subsidies, hoping that this, in turn, would encourage the unions to pursue more moderate pay claims.

The government's desire to establish good relations with the trade unions was also evident in its reluctance to invoke authoritarian measures to curb strike action. In any case, it fully recognised that denying workers the right to strike was incompatible with the maintenance of free collective bargaining. There was also a question of practicability: if Ministers outlawed strikes, would they really be prepared to see workers sent to prison at a time when the country was already experiencing serious labour shortages? The attempted solution to this dilemma was to introduce compulsory arbitration, with the Minister of Labour granted a significant role in referring cases to the especially created National Arbitration Tribunal.

Well before the conclusion of the war – indeed, only one year after it had begun – the government was considering its plans for the post-war period, with particular attention being accorded to industrial affairs. Once again, the themes of co-operation and co-partnership between capital and labour were high on the list of priorities. Viscount Cranbourne, the Secretary of State for the Dominions, believed that there had to be true partnership between the two sides of industry, if private enterprise was to endure in the modern world. Given that Britain had achieved political democracy, he proclaimed, it must not be said that industrial democracy was beyond its powers (*The Scotsman*, 23 October 1943). Meanwhile, the report of the Conservative Sub-committee on Industry, entitled *Work: the Future of British Industry*, published in January 1944, argued that it was essential for the future of Britain that workers should take a greater interest in industrial problems, and that by way of lectures and discussions, knowledge ought to be imparted right down the line, from the manager to the man who swept the floor.

A different aspect of industrial relations was dealt with in an internal Ministry of Labour minute to Sir Frederick Leggett, a senior official in the Ministry, which claimed that the government could not maintain the prohibition on strikes and lock-outs after the war. It was argued that the rank-and-file would not give up the right to strike, and that any attempt to deprive them of it might well be regarded as a departure from the principle for which the war was waged. With regard to post-war wages policy, the Ministry of Labour believed that if adequate steps could be taken to stabilise prices, there seemed to be no reason why the system of collective bargaining should not be permitted to find a solution to the adjustment of wages and conditions in the immediate post-war period. The strength of the collective bargaining system, it was emphasised, lay in its adaptation to the needs and circumstances of particular industries, and to the encouragement it afforded to those with knowledge of practical problems to rely on self-government (Ministry of Labour and National Service 1942: 5).

The pragmatism of voluntary collective bargaining was reiterated, in September 1943, by an internal draft memo for the Ministry of Labour, which emphasised that the value of a voluntary agreement rested upon the fact that the employers and the workers were both able to proceed empirically, in the knowledge that if difficulties should arise, or circumstances change, they were free to negotiate an amending agreement, thus retaining at their discretion the power of determining agreements (Ministry of Labour and National Service 1943: 1).

By the end of the Second World War, therefore, trade unions were widely deemed to have proved their value and viability. Consequently, the Conservative Party fully acknowledged that organised labour would expect, and largely deserve, more respect once the war was over than it had received previously. The war also served to illustrate the merits of state intervention in the economy, and some degree of economic planning, both of which tended to bring governments into closer contact with the trade union movement. In numerous ways, therefore, the war years served to undermine old attitudes and assumptions about government, industry, and trade union relationships. The trade unions were widely perceived as having 'come of age' during the war; they had earned, and would henceforth have to be accorded, an unprecedented degree of respect. The Conservative Party would need to adopt a much more positive attitude and approach towards the unions once the war was over.

3　The search for conciliation, 1945–1964

The profound shock of losing the 1945 general election prompted the Conservative Party to re-examine many of its policies. There was a recognition that, amongst other things, the Conservative Party needed to convince the electorate, especially the 'floating voter', that it had constructive policies, ones which avoided extremism and conflict. Nowhere was this truer than on the party's stance towards trade unionism. Thus, in the wake of the election defeat, there were demands from the Conservative rank-and-file for the parliamentary leadership to clarify and crystallise its policy towards the trade unions. Certainly, the feelings of many Conservatives were expressed at the 1946 Annual Conference by a delegate, Geoffrey Rippon (who became an MP in 1955), when he declared: 'We know our principles. We want a policy.'

THE INDUSTRIAL CHARTER

In response to such demands, Churchill established an Industrial Policy Committee, comprising five members of the Shadow Cabinet (Oliver Stanley, Oliver Lyttelton, Harold Macmillan, David Maxwell-Fyfe, and Rab Butler) and four backbenchers (David Eccles, Derek Heathcoat-Amory, Sir Peter Bennett, and Colonel Jim Hutchinson). The Committee embarked upon a number of discussions with various groups of businessmen, managers, and trade unionists in the industrial regions of Britain, whilst the party chairman, Oliver Poole, solicited the views of senior members of the Conservatives' 1922 Committee.

The outcome, after several Shadow Cabinet discussions, was the publication, in May 1947, of *The Industrial Charter*, the purpose of which, explained Eden (Foreign Secretary in the wartime coalition, Prime Minister in 1955), was to bring government, capital, and labour together in a common partnership, in pursuit of a common objective, and to show what the respective functions and responsibilities of each of the three partners were (*The Times*, 19 May 1947).

The Industrial Charter itself pointed out that the complexity of modern industry, and Britain's position as a debtor country, made it possible to revert to a policy of 'go as you please'; there had to be strong central guidance, with the country's main economic strategy needing to be worked out far more surely than it had been hitherto (Conservative Central Office 1947: 10).

With regard to industrial relations in particular, *The Industrial Charter* stated that the official policy of the Conservative Party was in favour of trade unions, attaching the highest importance to the part they could play in guiding the national economy. It was also claimed that because trade unions depended for their vitality upon a large and active membership, and upon a leadership which enjoyed the confidence of the members, all members of a trade union should be encouraged to participate actively in its affairs. *The Industrial Charter* therefore deemed it right that trade unions should aim to encourage all workers to become members, thereby ensuring that they were fully representative. However, the emphasis remained on voluntary trade union membership, so that the ultimate choice of which trade union to join – if any – rested, ultimately, with each individual employee (ibid.: 21–2).

In the final section of *The Industrial Charter*, entitled 'The Worker's Charter', it was asserted that Conservative policy towards industry was to humanise, not nationalise. This reflected a fundamental feature of Conservative Party thinking during the late 1940s and 1950s, namely that human relations were the key to good industrial relations. The party rejected the notion that there were 'two sides of industry', employers versus workers, who had conflicting and irreconcilable interests, a notion that would produce a 'them and us' mentality in the workplace. Instead, it was emphasised that *all* of those who worked in industry had the same interests (greater productivity, higher profits, etc.) and as such needed to be encouraged to work more closely together. Recognising, however, that employees often felt undervalued or alienated, 'The Worker's Charter' urged that workers be provided with security of employment, incentives to do their work well, and improved status. If these could be provided, it was believed, then workers in industry would begin to feel less suspicious or resentful of management, and thus industrial relations would improve, with employers and employees working more closely together.

However, 'The Worker's Charter' insisted that improved industrial relations could not be secured through an Act of Parliament because the conditions of industrial life were too varied to be brought within the 'cramping grip of legislation' (ibid.: 10). Thus the whole emphasis was on voluntary action and changes to be pursued by those actually working in industry. Government's role was merely to encourage and exhort employers and employees to develop greater trust and tolerance towards each other. Management and workers could not be compelled to work more closely and harmoniously; they could only be encouraged to do so.

At the Conservatives' 1947 Annual Conference, a resolution was debated which offered support for *The Industrial Charter* 'as a basis for discussion', whilst an amendment moved by Reginald Maudling, and seconded by Robert Carr – delegates both elected MPs in 1950 – welcomed *The Industrial Charter* as a clear restatement of the general principles of Conservative economic policy. Rab Butler, meanwhile, spoke of reconciling individual leadership in management with confident participation of the workforce in consultation, partnership, and personal interest in their daily work. Thus they could bring the nation's economic life into tune with the nation's political democracy. Although a couple of delegates denounced *The Industrial Charter* as 'milk and water socialism', the resolution, with Maudling's amendment, was carried by an overwhelming majority.

THE 'HUMAN RELATIONS' APPROACH

Consultation, co-operation, and co-partnership were to become the key themes of the Conservative approach to trade unions and industrial relations from the publication of *The Industrial Charter* until the loss of the 1964 general election. The belief that industrial relations problems were, at root, problems of human relations provided the premise of Conservative policy during most of this time, although by the early 1960s the efficacy and wisdom of such an approach were increasingly being questioned. Certainly during the 1950s, however, the 'human relations' perspective constituted the orthodoxy amongst most senior Conservatives. For example, Anthony Eden proclaimed that when every man felt part of the concern in which he was employed, then men and management would discover that old suspicions, old attitudes, and old practices which held back production were out of date. He referred to the great power of mutual trust and human understanding (Conservative Research Department 1956).

One delegate at the 1949 Conservative Annual Conference went so far as to suggest that closer ties between employers and employees would serve to render trade unions superfluous. However, this view, revealing the delegate's own wishful thinking perhaps, was not shared by the rest of the party; indeed, the overwhelming majority of Conservatives urging co-operation and co-partnership in industry did so partially out of the recognition that trade unions were likely to be a permanent feature of British industrial and economic life. As such, the most that might be hoped for was that closer consultation between the two sides of industry might reduce militancy, and make trade unions more moderate and responsible, as would a concomitant commitment to full employment and the welfare state by the government. Such commitments, some Conservatives evidently hoped, would encourage the trade unions to divert their attention away from political matters, and back towards purely industrial and economic matters directly affecting their members.

The extent to which the Conservative Party seemed determined to avoid confrontation with the trade unions at this time was reflected in Churchill's appointment, in 1951, of Walter Monckton (later succeeded by the equally conciliatory Iain Macleod) as Minister of Labour. Churchill's instructions to Monckton were 'to do my best to preserve industrial peace' (quoted in Birkenhead 1969: 276), which would certainly seem to endorse the view that Churchill 'was determined that there should be no industrial strikes during his term as Prime Minister' (Woolton 1959: 279–80). It is also worth noting the claim that one of the reasons for Monckton's appointment, and the deliberately conciliatory approach to the trade unions, was an ambiguous comment by David Maxwell-Fyfe in the run-up to the 1951 general election. In seeking to emphasise the Conservative Party's new, positive approach to the trade unions, Maxwell-Fyfe – himself tipped at the time to be the next Minister of Labour – declared that a Conservative government would not introduce any trade union legislation without having first consulted the unions themselves. Whilst this was undoubtedly the official policy of the Conservative Party, Maxwell-Fyfe's comment was perceived or portrayed by both the Labour Party and the trade unions as an acknowledgement by the Conservative Party that it would, if elected, introduce trade union legislation after all.

Whilst the Conservative Party still won the 1951 general election, it has been argued that Maxwell-Fyfe's remarks and the response which they engendered

> had four probable outcomes: it may have discouraged trade
> unionists from voting Conservative, helping to explain why the
> Conservatives received a smaller majority in the election than

anticipated; it stiffened Churchill's resolve to avoid trouble with the unions at all costs; it put an end to Maxwell-Fyfe's hopes of becoming Minister of Labour, the appointment going instead to a man thought likely to be 'soft'; finally, it forced the Conservatives to withdraw their active opposition to 'contracting-out' and the closed shop.

(Seldon 1981: 18–19)

The 1950s heard repeated reiterations of the claim that management and workers had the same interests, and that they therefore ought to work together, rather than allow distrust and suspicion to come between them. Thus did Sir Walter Monckton, whilst Minister of Labour, call for a new conception of industrial democracy, one which would lead away from the idea of 'sides' and conflicting interests in industry. He therefore called for the old employer–employee relationship to be developed into something more like a working team (*The Times*, 10 December 1953). A similar call was made by Sir Walter's parliamentary secretary, Harold Watkinson, who declared that the notion of industry consisting of opposing sides was an anachronism (*The Times*, 20 January 1954).

The theme was sustained by Sir Walter's successor at the Ministry of Labour, Iain Macleod, who proclaimed that the true conception of industry was not that of boss and man, or master and servant, or battlefield of class warfare, but one of partnership. It was those who insisted on a conflict of interests between employers and employees, Macleod told Conservative delegates at the party's 1956 Annual Conference, who were the reactionaries looking to the past.

What Conservatives envisaged was the development of institutional channels within industry which would facilitate a regular exchange of views between management and labour. Through bodies such as works committees and councils, employers and employees would be able to communicate and consult with each other. Employees would then be able to articulate their anxieties and grievances to management, whilst employers themselves would be able to keep their workers informed of the decisions being taken concerning their firm or industry, also explaining the rationale and implications of these decisions. As Eden explained, the purpose of phenomena such as joint negotiating machinery was to ensure that management was fully aware of the views of their workers, whilst simultaneously ensuring that the workforce understood the motive and purpose of managerial decisions (Eden 1947). Evidently, many Conservatives during the 1950s were confident that a freer flow of information in both directions would greatly reduce the suspicion and distrust which apparently underpinned much industrial unrest (Clarke 1947: 29).

However, the advocacy of greater consultation and co-operation did not mean any diminution of managerial control. The traditional Conservative belief in authority, hierarchy, and leadership remained firmly intact. Management's right to manage continued to be inviolate. What greater communication between employers and employees was intended to do was make management's task easier by ensuring that workers understood the decisions being taken and felt that their anxieties were being acknowledged. If this led to a reduction in industrial conflict, then management could actually fulfil its tasks more readily and smoothly, free from repeated hostility and opposition from the workforce. As Robert Carr explained, experience showed that when and where management of a company made a conscious effort to inform and consult with its workers about the why and the wherefore of what was going on, smoother and more constructive industrial relations became established (*HC Debates*, 5th series, vol. 568: c.2127).

However, the Conservative Political Centre, in one of a number of related pamphlets on trade unionism, emphasised that joint consultation did not mean that workers should run the firms they were employed in, or even have a say in how their firms were run; instead, it meant that those who worked in an enterprise should be informed about its policies and prospects, should be consulted on matters of concern to them, and should be encouraged to make suggestions. None the less, the responsibility for making decisions had to rest with management; after all, that was what it was there for (Conservative Political Centre 1946: 11). Similarly, Anthony Eden maintained that whilst it was important to seek partnership and mutual understanding between employers and employees, there had to be a clear differentiation of function. A team could not work without a captain, he argued, and in modern industry, the task of leadership had to reside with management (ibid.).

All of this reflected and reinforced the 'human relations' strategy which dominated Conservative approaches to industrial relations throughout the 1950s. If industrial conflict and unrest were largely born of mistrust and misunderstanding between employers and employees, then greater communication and consultation between them would, it was envisaged, result in more harmonious industrial relations. Enlightened employers who took the trouble both to talk and to listen to their employees would, it was emphasised, do much to dispel the 'false consciousness' which many workers allegedly suffered due to the propaganda of 'militants' and 'extremists' in the trade unions. If employers gave their workforce an honest account of the balance sheet of their firms, in plain and straightforward language, Harold Watkinson claimed, they would help to explode many of the false notions about what communist agitators in the trade unions called the 'bloated profits of capitalism' (*The Times*, 20 October 1952).

The constant emphasis on the need for greater consultation between employers and their employees clearly reflected the view amongst the Conservative Party's parliamentary leadership that the majority of industrial relations problems were explicable in psychological terms; that is, workers felt undervalued or neglected by management, and were alienated by a lack of communication and consultation concerning managerial decisions and objectives. Hence the belief of most senior Conservatives at Westminster during the late 1940s and 1950s that better industrial relations could be secured through improving the scope and frequency of dialogue between employers and employees, thereby fostering a sense of partnership and common interests in the workplace. As the 1949 policy document, *The Right Road for Britain*, declared, Conservatives believed that the problems of British industry were, first and foremost, human problems, necessitating constant attention to the personal relations which existed between management and labour (Conservative Central Office 1949: 23).

REFUSAL TO INTRODUCE TRADE UNION LEGISLATION

Throughout this period, the Conservative Party's parliamentary leadership rejected the routine backbench calls for legislation to deal with industrial relations problems and trade union activities. Certainly, the premise that industrial relations problems were mostly derived from psychological factors and lack of communication and consultation between management and workers militated against the efficacy of legislative remedies. Robert Carr, for example, was adamant that 'it is upon voluntary agreement in industry that we must depend for good industrial relations ... good relations cannot be enforced by laws' (*HC Debates*, 5th series, vol.568: c.2127). Indeed, not only was it widely accepted that better human relations in industry could not be achieved merely by passing Acts of Parliament, it was also acknowledged that attempts to do so would actually prove counterproductive, serving to exacerbate, rather than reduce, distrust and conflict between employers and employees. In true voluntarist tradition, the Conservative policy during this period was to rely on encouragement and exhortation in order to improve industrial relations and secure closer contacts between management and labour.

The Conservative Party's avoidance of legislation to regulate the relationship between employers and employees was also extended to the organisation and activities of the trade unions themselves. This did not mean, of course, that the Conservative Party was entirely happy with the behaviour of Britain's trade unions. On the contrary, there were three particular aspects of British trade unionism which most Conservatives found objectionable throughout the 1950s (and beyond), namely the closed shop, the frequency of strikes (particularly those which were unofficial, or called without a ballot), and the 'contracting out' clause of the political levy, which had been restored by Labour's 1946 repeal of the (1927) Trade Disputes Act.

Yet for a number of reasons, the Conservative leadership declined to introduce legislation to deal with these issues. First, the parliamentary leadership was eager to shake off its image, acquired during the inter-war period, of being 'anti-trade union' or 'anti-working class'. Nothing would have been more damaging to the Conservative Party's attempt at building bridges than introducing legislation to regulate the activities and affairs of the trade unions. By avoiding trade union legislation, the Conservatives' parliamentary leadership hoped to gain the trust and confidence of the trade union movement.

Second, the Conservative Party was compelled to accept that the Labour Party was now a major political and electoral force, enjoying substantial working-class support. The resulting need to win votes, particularly from the working class and also from 'floating' voters, meant that policies likely to lead to conflict or confrontation had to be eschewed. Instead, the Conservative Party was at pains to emphasise its acceptance of, and commitment to, free trade unionism and collective bargaining. Thus did Churchill, shortly before the 1951 general election, pledge that if the Conservative Party was elected, it would work with the trade unions on a non-party basis, and consult with them in a friendly manner. Hence his insistence that the Conservatives had no intention of introducing legislation against the trade unions (*The Times*, 10 October 1951).

Third, in seeking to rebuild the British economy after the war, and ensure its competitiveness against other major trading nations, the Conservative Party was eager to avoid policies which might antagonise the trade unions, and thus exacerbate class conflict and industrial unrest. For example, in rejecting demands for action against the political levy, Sir Walter Monckton warned delegates at the party's 1947 Annual Conference that nothing could be more certain to upset the smooth relations between the Conservative government and the trade unions than legislation to curb union donations to the Labour Party. Instead, he suggested that Conservatives should seek to 'educate' trade union members of their right to 'opt out' of political levy payments.

A fourth reason for the Conservative Party's reluctance to introduce trade union legislation was practicability. There was concern amongst many senior Conservatives that certain reforms routinely advocated by backbenchers, and constituency parties via the annual conference, would not be effective in practice. For example, in rejecting perennial demands for the outlawing of strikes which had not been endorsed by a secret ballot of union members, Churchill suggested that the disadvantages of such a measure would greatly outweigh any advantages. He maintained that the government had no intention of departing from the established tradition of leaving the trade union movement to manage its own affairs (*HC Debates*, 5th series, vol.522: 835–6). Similarly, Iain Macleod was also highly sceptical about the value or wisdom of legislating against strikes that had not been subject to a secret ballot of union members. As the majority of strikes were unofficial, he argued, legislation would be quite ineffective (*HC Debates*, 5th series, vol.568: c.1285). Furthermore, Macleod was not convinced that secret ballots would necessarily help to promote industrial peace, suggesting that it was a mistake to believe that workers were less militant than their trade union leaders. He warned delegates at the Conservatives' 1956 Annual Conference that compulsory ballots on disputes normally settled through negotiation might well increase the number of strikes. The same point was reiterated by Conservative barristers (Inns of Court Conservative and Unionist Society 1958: 23–4).

According to Rab Butler, strikes could be divided into three categories. First, there were strikes which occurred when employees withdrew their labour, quite lawfully, in connection with a dispute with their employer. Butler maintained it would be quite wrong for the government in a free society to interfere with the employees' legal right to withdraw their labour in such situations.

The second type of strike identified by Butler was that fomented by 'agitators' for their own ends. When such strikes occurred, he claimed, it was incumbent upon politicians and those trade unionists who opposed such action to rally together to thwart those who sought thus to hold the country to ransom.

Finally, Butler depicted those strikes which arose because of inter-union disputes. These were very difficult for any government to deal with, Butler argued, and in most cases it could do little more than encourage joint consultations. A Conservative backbencher, Sir Cyril Osborne, suggested that one of the reasons for inter-union disputes was simply that Britain had too many trade unions. Indeed, he suggested that one of the major reasons why (West) Germany had enjoyed such a successful post-war economic recovery was that it had fewer than twenty trade unions, compared to Britain's over two hundred. Sir Cyril therefore called on the Minister of Labour to introduce legislation to consolidate and reduce the number of trade unions in Britain (*HC Debates*, 5th series, vol.657: c.143). This proposal was rejected.

In any case, as a Conservative Party committee on industrial relations pointed out, there were forms of unofficial industrial action other than strikes, such as 'go-slows' or 'work-to-rules', which were largely unamenable to legislative proscription. Furthermore, the committee pointed out, a ban on unofficial strikes would imply that only strikes officially called by a trade union could ever be lawful, which would be grossly unfair to workers who were not members of a trade union and who had no wish to join one, yet who might want to withdraw their labour because of a dispute with their employer. It would be a dangerous nonsense, the committee warned, to enact legislation whereby only trade union members had the legal right to go on strike (Conservative Party (Committee on Industrial Relations) 1963: 8).

A fifth reason might be suggested for the Conservative Party's voluntarist policy during this period, namely its traditional laissez-faire philosophy, its belief that government, as far as possible, ought to refrain from intervention in, or regulation of, industrial and economic affairs. Ironically, however, this non-interventionist stance *vis-à-vis* trade unions and industrial relations was in stark contrast to the increasingly interventionist approach of the government to the economy generally, an irony which was not lost on those neo-liberal backbenchers who believed that the Conservative leadership had got its priorities the wrong way round; they wanted less intervention in the economy, but firm action by the government against the trade unions.

ENCOURAGING 'RESPONSIBLE' WAGE BARGAINING

The commitment to full employment and free collective bargaining clearly placed the Conservative government in an awkward situation, particularly from the late 1950s onwards. Growing concern over rising inflation and 'excessive' wage increases meant that the Conservative government was faced with a number of unpalatable or unacceptable options. One of these was to abandon the commitment to full employment, thereby establishing a 'link' between 'excessive' wage increases and rising unemployment. This would put the 'onus' for 'moderation' on the trade unions. However, for political and electoral reasons, the Conservative leadership was not (yet) prepared to abandon its commitment to full employment.

A second option would have been to switch to a legalistic strategy, placing statutory curbs on the activities and power of the unions in order to secure greater responsibility and moderation on the part of organised labour. Certainly some Conservatives envisaged that such a policy would significantly reduce the ability of trade unions to use coercion to achieve unjustified wage increases. Yet as we have recently noted, the parliamentary leadership of the Conservative Party refused to countenance legislative measures, for reasons of principle, pragmatism, and practicability.

A third option, that of a formal incomes policy, was also viewed with considerable reluctance, partly because of the longstanding commitment to free collective bargaining, and also because of the Conservatives' innate hostility towards government determination of wage rates and levels. Wages and salaries were deemed to be for employers and employees to determine themselves, in the context of 'the market' and what firms and employers could afford to pay. Not only was it realised that government determination of wages – and prices too – would have grave implications for the operation of a market economy and the laws of supply and demand, it was simultaneously recognised that once government began to assume responsibility for determining wages it would become the focus of grievances from workers who felt that they had been unfairly treated. The whole issue of wage determination would then become highly politicised.

To all intents and purposes, therefore, the Conservative administration was left with the option which it had been pursuing since 1951, namely voluntarism, but coupled with stronger exhortation that the unions restrain wages. Yet there was mounting concern that the policy was not working with regard to incomes. What was required, many Conservatives believed, was a more concerted effort by the government to 'educate' workers and trade unions, so that they could comprehend the implications and likely consequences of excessive wage demands and pay increases.

Certainly, by the second half of the 1950s, Anthony Eden was convinced of the need for a more intense educational campaign on the subject of wages and prices. To this end, a committee was established by Eden which produced a White Paper on *The Economic Implications of Full Employment*, published in March 1956. According to Eden, the objective of this document was to provide the background to a new approach, to stabilise prices, and to prevent a perpetual upwards spiral in wage claims and the cost of living. Thus, he claimed, the purpose of the White Paper was not to appeal for wage restraint, but to show the need for it.

The publication of the White Paper was followed by a series of informal meetings and discussions between senior representatives from the government, the TUC, the British Employers Confederation, the Federation of British Industries (the latter two merged, along with the National Association of British Manufacturers, to form the Confederation of British Industry (CBI) in 1965), and the chairmen of the nationalised industries. Discussions centred on the general economic situation, emphasising the need to keep prices down and to make wage increases the outcome of increased productivity. Eden was quick to point out, however, that the value of such meetings lay in their informal character, so that it was beyond their scope to make formal arrangements or to seek binding agreements (*HC Debates*, 5th series, vol.550: c.1968 and c.1972.)

The extent to which rising wages and inflation were causing concern in government circles was further indicated by the establishment of the Cohen Council – the Council on Prices, Productivity and Incomes – which the Chancellor, Peter Thorneycroft, set up in 1957. Chaired by Lord Cohen (a judge) and two economists, the Council's brief was:

> having regard to the desirability of full employment, and · increasing standards of living, based on expanding production and reasonable stability of prices, to keep under review changes in prices, productivity, and the level of incomes (including wages, salaries, and profits), and to report thereon from time to time.

Meanwhile, the government found itself simultaneously expressing its support for voluntarism and free collective bargaining, whilst warning that wage increases in the public sector could only be granted if corresponding cutbacks were made in the industries concerned. According to Selwyn Lloyd, speaking as Chancellor of the Exchequer, the government had two sets of responsibilities when seeking to secure a more realistic relationship between increases in wages and increases in national productivity. First, it had responsibilities as an employer; second, it had responsibilities as trustee of, or for, the community as a whole, and as guardian of the national interest. Of these two sets of responsibilities, Lloyd emphasised, the second had to prevail (*HC Debates*, 5th series, vol. 646: c.630).

After its re-election in 1959, the Conservative government began its third term of office with a continued refusal to adopt a formal wages policy. It still relied on exhortation, and still continued to reject the demands for legislative curbs on the trade unions, which emanated at regular intervals from the backbenches and from party activists in the constituencies.

The Minister of Labour, Edward Heath, continued to endorse the voluntarist policy which the party had upheld throughout the 1950s, insisting that good industrial relations were dependent on good human relationships in industry. This meant managers must exhibit greater trust and goodwill towards their employees, Heath argued, thereby helping to eradicate the 'them and us' barriers which ultimately underpinned much of Britain's industrial conflict. Responding to those in the party who urged statutory measures to deal with the problem of strikes, for example, Heath pointed out that whilst strikes annually resulted in the loss of up to 8 million man-days, 18 million were lost through industrial accidents, and up to 220 million days were lost on account of illness. In any case, Heath insisted, the impetus for change in trade union behaviour needed to come from the unions themselves, rather than be imposed from above by the government.

It was this perspective which led him to reject calls from Conservative backbenchers for a Royal Commission on Trade Unions to be established as a prelude to legislation. Instead, Heath called for better joint consultation, better training of management and supervisory staff, and redeployment of employees threatened with redundancy. He thus sought to maintain the 'human relations' approach pursued by his predecessors during the 1950s, according to which much of the disruption afflicting British industry resulted from distrust between management and workers, and was often due to insufficient communication and dialogue between the 'two sides'.

For the voluntarists in the Conservative Party, solutions were not to be gleaned from the Statute Book. On the contrary, any attempt at invoking legislative remedies would serve to exacerbate ill-feeling and hostility in industry. It was essential, therefore, to encourage better methods of consultation and personnel management. The government's role would be to identify problems, make recommendations, and offer advice, whilst leaving the 'two sides' of industry to solve their problems between themselves.

Meanwhile, in the context of a deteriorating economic situation, the Conservative government found itself under pressure, from both the Treasury and the Bank of England, to introduce deflationary measures. Although Harold Macmillan, by now Prime Minister, was 'temperamentally opposed' to such measures, he found it necessary in the circumstances to allow some changes in this direction, such as curbs on public expenditure and higher interest rates. The government recognised, however, that such measures by themselves would not tackle the main problem, namely that wages and salaries were increasing faster than productivity and manufacturing output. This problem required a long-term remedy.

TURNING TO INCOMES POLICY AND TRIPARTISM

The first full step towards finding such a remedy took the form of a 'pay pause', announced by the Chancellor, Selwyn Lloyd, in July 1961. It was intended to remain in force until April 1962, thereby providing the government with 'a breathing space', during which a more permanent wages policy could be formulated. Macmillan was determined to avoid a policy which involved further deflation, as favoured by the Treasury, the Bank of England, and some backbench neo-liberals. Not only did Macmillan disagree with the view that wage inflation could be cured by a general, orthodox policy of deflation, as 'slavishly' followed by successive Chancellors in the inter-war period; he also clearly remembered his early political career, when he was MP for Stockton-on-Tees during the 'Great Depression' of the 1930s. There he had witnessed first-hand the mass unemployment, deprivation, and despair which had been endured. Macmillan's determination to prevent the re-emergence of such conditions bolstered his opposition to a policy of deflation which was predictably being advocated by the Treasury. Consequently, he found himself 'constantly accused ... of being far too much concerned about the personal tragedy of unemployed families' (Macmillan 1972: 218), although some Conservatives were deeply respectful of 'his experience in Stockton which so moulded his subsequent approach to economic affairs' (Maudling 1978: 103).

Yet Macmillan refused to countenance deflation as a solution to Britain's increasing economic problems. Instead, he emphasised the necessity of finding an alternative approach to these problems, using the 'breathing space' of the pay pause to do so. 'We must', Macmillan proclaimed, 'try to work out, during the interval allowed us, some other satisfactory and permanent system' (quoted in Evans 1981: 255). What Macmillan had in mind was the creation of the National Economic Development Council (NEDC), 'drawn from trade unions, management and government, who would participate in central planning advice', although he claimed that 'to Selwyn Lloyd ... belongs the credit for this forward-looking scheme' (Harold Macmillan 1973: 49).

The desire to set up such a body, and thus signal a move in the direction of neo-corporatism, was, not surprisingly, a cause of considerable concern to many Conservatives. As Macmillan himself noted, Cabinet discussion of the proposal revealed 'a rather interesting and quite deep divergence of view between Ministers, really corresponding to whether they had old Whig, Liberal, *laissez-faire* traditions or Tory opinions, paternalists, and not afraid of a little *dirigisme*' (ibid.: 37). It required two lengthy Cabinet meetings before Macmillan obtained formal approval to create the NEDC.

Whilst he was prepared to allow the state to play a much greater role in economic affairs, including the determination of incomes, Macmillan continued to uphold a non-interventionist line with regard to Britain's trade unions. He was hopeful that the incorporation of trade union leaders into discussions concerning economic matters would 'educate' them as to the increasing seriousness of Britain's economic problems, thereby convincing them of the need for lower wage settlements and higher productivity. In any case, Macmillan shared the voluntarist view that greater trust and more responsible behaviour in the realm of industrial relations were unlikely to be secured through legislation.

On the other hand, throughout the early 1960s, the Conservative Party's voluntarists and neo-corporatists (those favouring a closer, permanent partnership between government, trade unions, and employers in order to formulate and implement economic policies) were well aware that failure to reverse Britain's economic decline, and resolve the nation's industrial relations difficulties, would further increase the pressure on the government to introduce trade union legislation. If this were to happen, it was feared, then irreparable damage might be done both to the relationship between employers and employees (thereby exacerbating industrial conflict and unrest), and also to the Conservative Party's own fragile relationship with the trade unions.

Some of the voluntarists in the Conservative Party were also concerned that the adoption of a legalistic policy towards the trade unions might well harm their electoral prospects. Opinion polls indicating increasing public concern over the power and activities of trade unions were one thing; to go to the polls promising a programme of trade union reform which could be perceived, or portrayed, as likely to exacerbate industrial conflict was quite another.

The establishment of the NEDC in 1962 therefore constituted a new long-term approach by the Macmillan government towards productivity, growth, incomes, etc., one which sought to avoid compulsion or coercion. Comprising several Ministers, trade union leaders, industrialists, and senior civil servants from the 'economic' Ministries, and chaired by the Chancellor, the NEDC was expected to assist in the formulation of long-term economic strategy, based to a significant extent on exchanges of information and discussions between its constituent members. More specifically, it was hoped that a growth rate of 4 per cent per annum could be achieved as a consequence of the government, employers, and trade unions working more closely together to secure strong economic growth. According to Maudling, the NEDC reflected a recognition that the three sides were interdependent; without their co-operation, the nation could not prosper (Maudling 1978: 114).

The Conservative's parliamentary leadership envisaged that the NEDC would also constitute an integral part of any successful incomes policy. By bringing trade union leaders into closer, regular contact with Ministers, industrialists, and senior civil servants, the government hoped that the trade unions could be persuaded of the importance of pay restraint, keeping wage increases in line with economic growth and industrial productivity. Or, as Macmillan remarked, the involvement of the TUC in the NEDC 'would at least lead them to greater understanding of the real problems with which the nation was confronted' (Harold Macmillan 1973: 51). Indeed, by this time, some senior Conservatives had become convinced of the necessity of a permanent incomes policy, Macmillan and the Chancellor, Maudling, being two of the most prominent proponents.

The drift towards neo-corporatism understandably alarmed Conservative neo-liberals, many of whom were irked by the 'two sides of industry' assumption inherent in the format of the NEDC, claiming that, in reality, industry was made up of multifarious elements, all of which were important (John Page, *HC Debates*, 5th series, vol.646: c.661). A similar observation was made by the Conservative backbencher who criticised the party leadership's apparent assumption that the country consisted only of the TUC and employers' organisations. She sought to remind the government that 'hundreds of thousands' of people were not associated with any of these bodies (Dame Irene Ward, *HC Debates*, 5th series, vol.649: c.183).

Such criticisms reflected the concern amongst a growing number of Conservatives that the parliamentary leadership was jettisoning the party's traditional principles concerning the supremacy of private enterprise, the market economy, a minimal role for the state in economic affairs, individualism, and the sovereignty of Parliament. In various ways, the creation of the NEDC, coupled with the setting up, in the same year, of the National Incomes Commission to review and give advice on pay settlements, was perceived by those on the Right or neo-liberal wing of the Conservative Party as an attempt at appeasing the trade unions, whilst simultaneously embracing 'socialist' policies concerning economic planning and a greater role for state institutions in the sphere of wage determination. Having drifted with the post-war tide for so long, it seemed, the parliamentary leadership of the Conservative Party had apparently decided to sail full speed ahead into socialist waters.

Yet the most important indictment of the NEDC was simply its failure to help to remedy the industrial and economic problems which had led to its creation in the first place. The year of its inception witnessed both a 120,000 increase in unemployment, and a fivefold increase in the number of workers involved in strikes, virtually doubling the number of working days lost compared to the previous year. Meanwhile, the government's 'guiding light' for pay awards was being exceeded by numerous groups of workers, most notably busmen, dockers, electricity workers, postal workers, and railwaymen.

Not surprisingly, perhaps, an increasing number of Conservatives were coming to the conclusion that some sort of action against the trade unions was essential. Not only were the trade unions increasingly being blamed for many of Britain's economic problems – such as inflation, poor productivity, lack of competitiveness, etc. – but those problems, in turn, served to turn the spotlight on a number of aspects of British trade unionism which Conservatives deemed objectionable or problematic, such as the closed shop, unofficial strikes, overmanning, alleged corruption or intimidation in union elections, and thus in need of legislative remedies. Indeed, throughout the 1960s, unofficial strikes in particular became an increasing cause of concern for both main political parties. This concern was partly attributable to the fact that it was not until 1961 that the Department of Employment began categorising the statistics for strike activity, thereby highlighting the fact that about 95 per cent of strikes were unofficial.

Such was the growing concern over unofficial strikes that Edward Heath was eventually to admit publicly that he had changed his mind over the impact and consequences of such action. Having played down the significance of unofficial strike activity at the beginning of the decade, when he had argued that industrial accidents and illnesses were far more damaging to the continuity and level of industrial production, Heath altered his view towards the middle of the decade: he began arguing that unofficial strikes were actually more damaging to the British economy because they affected whole firms or industries. Industrial accidents and illnesses, by contrast, could normally be covered because they only involved a few workers at any one time (Roth 1972: 189).

There was widespread recognition amongst Conservatives that the high incidence of unofficial strikes was inextricably related to the changing character and structure of British industry. The emergence of large-scale enterprises served to increase the distance, both physically and psychologically, between management and workers, with a detrimental effect on authority in the workplace. However, Conservatives disagreed amongst themselves as to the precise reason why this changing industrial structure resulted in such high levels of unofficial strike activity.

For those in the Conservative Party who still subscribed to a voluntarist perspective, the changing character and structure of modern industry were deemed to reinforce the need for a 'human relations' approach; the prevalence of unofficial strikes was seen as a manifestation of the alienation and anomie experienced by workers in an era of big business and mass production. With management and decision-making appearing ever more remote from the employees on the shopfloor, and workers finding it increasingly difficult to comprehend the value or significance of their individual contribution to the overall production process in an era of assembly lines and automation, it was suggested that unofficial strikes were often the outcome of the frustration and sense of grievance which some working people experienced.

For those Conservatives who continued to subscribe to this perspective, the response was to reiterate the need for closer co-operation and consultation between management and labour. They continued to assume that if workers were kept better informed of managerial decisions, whilst simultaneously being afforded the opportunity of articulating their own concerns and anxieties, then their sense of alienation and anomie would be diminished; this would, in turn, reduce their propensity to participate in unofficial strike activity. Such an analysis clearly precluded support for legislative measures to improve Britain's industrial relations. On the contrary, it was considered that legislation in this sphere was likely to exacerbate distrust and disruption in the workplace. If industrial relations problems were socio-psychological in essence, then solutions were unlikely to be gleaned from the Statute Book.

By contrast, Conservative advocates of legislation against the unions cited the growing gulf between trade union leaders and their rank-and-file membership as the main source of unofficial strike activity. Whilst this was acknowledged to be a consequence of the changing size and structure of modern industry, the prognosis focused on the consequent effect on authority within the trade unions themselves, rather than between managers and workers. It was argued that many trade union members came to view their union leaders as being remote or unrepresentative, by virtue of the organisational and geographical distance from the shopfloor which accompanied their involvement in centralised or national-level bargaining with government or employers. The result, many Conservatives believed, was a vacuum, soon filled by 'militant' shop stewards or union activists at local level. These local-level 'representatives' were often able to command greater loyalty or allegiance among workers on the shopfloor, by virtue of both their proximity and their willingness to pursue wage claims and industrial action in defiance of more modest agreements entered into by the official union leadership at national level.

This problem was deemed to have been exacerbated considerably by the drift towards neo-corporatism and incomes policy, which had served to increase the distance between trade union leaders and their mass membership back on the shopfloor. Whilst union leaders were entering into national agreements to practise wage restraint, their members at local level were deemed to be engaging in unofficial strike activity in support of pay claims which exceeded those being accepted by the official union leadership. It was suggested that whilst the leaders of Britain's trade unions had often shown themselves to be aware of the economic situation and 'the responsibilities of labour', there were grounds to wonder whether the rank-and-file of the trade union movement shared this knowledge or appreciation (Conservative Industrial Department 1963: 60). The implication was that the authority of the official trade union leadership over the mass membership needed to be restored, a belief which was clearly evident in the Conservative Party's trade union and industrial relations policies after 1964.

THE TWILIGHT OF VOLUNTARISM

Certainly, the anxieties amongst many Conservatives about British trade unionism were reflected at the 1961 Annual Conference, which debated a motion calling for an inquiry into the affairs and activities of Britain's trade unions, with a view to introducing legislation. In supporting the motion, one delegate complained vigorously about those in the Conservative Party who 'sat on their backsides and did nothing'. The time had come, it was claimed, for Conservatives to 'grasp the nettle by the hand and take the initiative' in dealing with the trade unions. Following this call, one Conservative backbencher, John Peyton, MP, declared that no inquiry was necessary, for the government already possessed the knowledge and power to deal with the trade union problem. The setting up of an inquiry, he alleged, would merely be an excuse for ministerial inaction. Peyton was adamant that if the unions proved unwilling or unable to eradicate unofficial strikes, and control the activities of 'agitators' within their ranks, then the responsibility lay 'firmly and squarely' with the government itself. In a broadside to the Conservative Party's voluntarists, he alleged that 'exhortation' was a very tainted, overused, and usually disregarded word.

Such advocacy of legislative measures was countered, however, by a number of Conservative trade unionists attending the conference, who emphasised the limitations of what could be achieved by invoking the law. It was argued that no government could operate a law which forbade unofficial strikes, restrictive practices, or the closed shop, for the simple reason that there was no sanction which the government could apply against those involved in a widespread refusal to accept such laws. One Conservative trade unionist also warned the government that interference in trade union affairs would do more harm than good both to the Conservative Party and to industrial relations. A government which legislated against trade unions, it was alleged, would be committing political suicide.

In concluding the industrial relations debate, the Minister of Labour, John Hare (who had replaced Heath in the summer of 1960), reiterated the case for the government's voluntarist approach, insisting on the need for both sides of industry to solve their own problems, and to establish a closer working relationship with each other. Hare emphasised the importance of persuasion and appeals to common interest, which, he claimed, would do more to improve industrial relations than an Act of Parliament. A voluntarist approach might seem painstaking and unspectacular, Hare acknowledged, but it would provide the best remedy for the problems besetting the country's industrial relations.

As the 1960s progressed, however, the voluntarist approach adhered to by the parliamentary leadership appeared less and less plausible. Frustration and impatience increased throughout the Conservative Party. This was only to be expected amongst the advocates of legislative reform, who considered it to be ever more evident that statutory measures were required to curb the power and activities of the unions. Such Conservatives felt vindicated in their advocacy of legislative action to reform the trade unions, and to some extent therefore their exasperation was often directed more at their parliamentary leadership than at the trade unions. Thus did the 1963 Annual Conference hear allegations that there had been far too much appeasement in government thinking *vis-à-vis* the trade unions in recent years.

By this time, however, frustration was no longer confined to the Conservative Party's proponents of legalism; the advocates of voluntarism and neo-corporatism were also experiencing – and expressing – exasperation over the behaviour of the trade unions. The neo-corporatists were particularly frustrated by the unwillingness or inability of the unions to adhere to the government's incomes policy, thereby undermining the incorporationist strategy right from the start. For example, when the dockers received a 9 per cent pay increase in May 1962, after threatening a national strike, Macmillan could not conceal or contain his utter dismay, lamenting that it was difficult to see where the Conservative administration could go next (Harold Macmillan 1973: 66). Indeed, on another occasion, he complained bitterly about 'the utter irresponsibility of labour in some of the new industries and the hopeless conservatism of labour in some of the old industries'. With wild-cat strikes in the former, and restrictive practices in the latter, he lamented, 'our poor economy suffers grievously' (Macmillan 1972: 375).

At the same time, the voluntarists in the party found their faith in the potential for trade unions to reform themselves becoming progressively weaker. Just as the neo-corporatists could see their principles and policies being undermined by the activities of the trade unions, so the voluntarists came – often with reluctance or regret – to recognise the limitations of their approach. The exhortations of a decade for trade unions to be left to 'put their own house in order', free from interference or intervention by the state, now sounded clichéd and banal. For how much longer could they give trade unions the benefit of the doubt? By 1963, their advocacy of voluntarism with regard to the trade unions and industrial relations was subject to qualification. The trade unions were warned that the time for voluntary reform was running out.

In opening the second reading of the 1963 Contracts of Employment Bill, the Minister of Labour reiterated the voluntarist tenet that the most satisfactory way of dealing with industrial relations problems (such as the breaking of agreements, and unofficial strikes) was for the trade unions to 'put their house in order.' By an assertion of leadership and responsibility, he elaborated, the unions ought to see that the agreements to which they were party were honoured. However, alluding to a TUC decision made the previous autumn, to conduct a review of the structure and *raison d'être* of the trade union movement, the Minister insisted that the review be carried out quickly, and be followed by reforms. If the TUC failed to do either, he warned, then the government would have to ask itself whether it could afford to let things continue as they were. The reply, the Minister intimated, would be in the negative. To endorse the government's position, reference was made to 'a strong body of public opinion' which, it was claimed, was demanding legislation to protect the public interest. It would be quite wrong, the Minister argued, for the strength of such feeling to be underestimated (*HC Debates*, 5th series, vol.671: c.1509).

The Minister's hope that the trade unions would carry out their own reforms voluntarily, but without vacillation, was echoed by David Renton, MP. Like the Minister of Labour, Renton alluded to public opinion on the issue, claiming that a stage had been reached where the country would not indefinitely tolerate the unions 'bumbling along' at the pace to which they had become accustomed (ibid.: c.1539). Although some Conservatives, such as the Junior Labour Minister William Whitelaw (ibid.: c.1610–11), continued to espouse a policy of unqualified voluntarism, it was clear that their numbers, and influence, were waning.

The crucial factor in undermining the voluntarist strategy, it would seem, was the failure, rather than the inception, of the neo-corporatist 'experiment' carried out by the Macmillan government. This extremely important point merits further explanation. An analytic distinction can be drawn between, on the one hand, neo-corporatism as the dominant strategy for dealing with trade unions at the macro-level, involving them in national economic policy formulation and decision-making, accompanied by incomes policies, wage restraint, and, possibly, productivity agreements, and, on the other hand, voluntarism as the dominant strategy for dealing with trade unions at a micro-level, the government refraining from directing or determining their internal affairs. With this voluntarist strategy, governments rely on encouragement and exhortation if and when they consider changes within the trade unions are necessary. During the early 1960s, these strategies were pursued simultaneously; the incorporation of trade union leaders into national-level information exchange, policy formulation, and decision-making, coupled with an incomes policy, was accompanied by the continuation of the voluntarist strategy regarding the internal organisation and activities of the trade unions themselves. Certainly, it was hoped that the exchanges of views and information afforded by the NEDC would illustrate to the trade unions the need to become far less defensive and insular, and more adaptable and flexible; to replace restrictive practices with more efficient working methods and greater productivity; and to replace sectional interest with a regard for the 'national interest.' Neo-corporatism and voluntarism were thus pursued in tandem. It was hoped, implicitly at least, that success for the neo-corporatist strategy might assist the trade unions in overcoming their inability or unwillingness to reform themselves, thereby undermining the case for legal restraint. Yet the period was characterised by increasing strike activity (particularly unofficial strikes), 'excessive' pay demands (and awards), and numerous breaches (both procedural and substantive) of agreements secured through collective bargaining.

The combined effect of such events was simultaneously to undermine the Macmillan government's neo-corporatist strategy, grievously weaken the efficacy of voluntarism, and strengthen the claims and credibility of those Conservatives calling for a policy of legalism. Had the neo-corporatist strategy achieved notable success, in terms of resolving industrial difficulties and reversing economic decline, as well as encouraging more 'responsible' trade unionism, then the voluntarist approach to trade union reform would probably have retained its hegemony within the Conservative Party, leaving the advocates of legal restraint to make their routine calls for tougher action against the unions from the Annual Conference platform, the backbenches at Question Time, and their signatures on early day motions. Instead, the responsibility attributed to the trade unions for the failure of the neo-corporatist strategy also served to undermine the case for voluntarism, thereby providing a major fillip to the Conservative advocates of legalism.

However, with only a year or so before the next general election the Conservative parliamentary leadership deemed it both impracticable and inappropriate suddenly to introduce legislative reform of the trade unions, particularly as their preceding four years in office had been characterised by refusal to invoke statutory measures against them. Not only was it recognised that there might be insufficient time to get a Bill through its parliamentary stages and onto the Statute Book before the dissolution of Parliament, it was also acknowledged that the introduction of legislation at such a late stage might weaken, rather than enhance, the Conservative Party's electoral chances. Opinion poll evidence highlighting public concern about trade union power and activities was tempered by recognition that the Conservative Party might suffer electorally from allegations that it was 'declaring war' on trade unions, and promising, in effect, further to inflame industrial conflict. The British electorate might have been concerned about the 'trade union problem', but it was also renowned for wanting a quiet life, with the minimum of disruption. For the voluntarists in the Conservative Party, this consideration was a further reason for avoiding a switch to legalism. By the same token, however, those desirous of a legislative approach to industrial relations interpreted this as yet another example of the parliamentary leadership's pusillanimity and prevarication over the issue of trade union reform.

What the government did promise was a review of trade union law early in the next Parliament. In the meantime, Joseph Godber, who had replaced John Hare as Minister of Labour in the autumn of 1963, suggested the establishment of three-person teams to examine the cause of unofficial strikes. Comprising one employer, one trade union official, and an independent observer, he proposed that these teams should be sent to the scene of unofficial strikes to ascertain the reason(s) for their occurrence. The proposal met with a lukewarm response, and came to naught. This proposal apart, Godber gave priority to improving communications between the two sides of industry, thereby seeking to sustain the voluntarist approach to industrial relations right up until the election defeat in October

1964. With this defeat came another: that of the hegemony of the voluntarists and neo-corporatists in the Conservative Party.

By the time of their general election defeat, therefore – after thirteen consecutive years in office – there had developed a widespread recognition amongst Conservatives that a new leadership, armed with new policies, was urgently required in order to bring Conservatism 'up to date'. For many Conservatives, the late 1950s and early 1960s had been years in which the party had drifted aimlessly, bereft of clear principles or coherent policies. A restatement of Conservative philosophy was deemed necessary. It was only with a period in opposition, however, that this could effectively be pursued. The loss of office, therefore, both underlined the need for, and made practicable, a re-evaluation of principles and a re-examination of policies. As one senior Conservative asserted, the party 'must search its own soul. It must decide its principles anew. The principles of Disraeli, or even of 1951, will no longer do' (Bevins 1965: 150).

Yet the fulfillment of such a task was deemed to require a change of personnel, altering the social composition of the Conservative Party. It was felt that the party needed to be made less exclusive or elitist. The call was thus made for the Conservative Party to 'put its trust in men and women who, whatever their social background, possess character, and an understanding of ordinary people'. This required that the 'rank-and-file of the Party ... speak out loud and clear against the existing composition of the Party hierarchy' (ibid.). Similar sentiments were shared by many younger Conservative MPs who believed that the upper echelons of the party were too much dominated by old patricians and Etonians. This 'old guard' was deemed to have been too concerned with the maintenance of a genial, consensual approach to politics, instead of seeking to tackle problems with courage and conviction. There was a feeling that under such leadership, the Conservative Party had been allowed to drift so far with the tide that it had ended up perilously close to running aground in socialist territory. In the process, pragmatism had replaced principle and compromise had replaced commitment. Neither the 'old guard' leadership, nor its policies were what the Conservative Party – or the nation – were deemed to need in the mid-1960s and beyond.

Such criticisms were not confined solely to younger Conservatives. In late 1963, Conservative Central Office received a letter from a senior industrial manager and 'lifelong Conservative' voter who declared that he was unable to continue supporting the party. Having claimed that there were many people like him, the correspondent proceeded to complain about the Conservative Party's apparent domination by 'too many Etonians', who constituted an out-of-date, out-of-touch establishment within the party. Former Conservative voters like himself, he declared, were 'sick of seeing old-looking men dressed in flat caps and bedraggled tweeds, strolling with a 12-bore' (quoted in Ramsden 1980: 225). Other correspondence received by Conservative Central Office during this time echoed these sentiments.

All of this was to have a profound effect on the Conservative Party after 1964. Its period in opposition was to be characterised by notable changes in both philosophy and policy, as we will observe in the next chapter. These were to have serious consequences for Conservative Party industrial relations and trade union policies, particularly in the context of the recent failures of voluntarism and neo-corporatism. The momentum for a policy of legal restraint was to increase markedly after 1964, so far that even some of those in the party who had hitherto been opposed to legislative measures against the trade unions found their objections dissipating in the wake of their experiences in office.

This was partly because of the failure of the trade union movement to reform itself, in spite of innumerable exhortations and opportunities to do so, and partly because of Britain's continuing – accelerating – economic decline, which meant that trade union activities and practices which might have been grudgingly tolerated during the 1950s could no longer be accepted a decade later. A combination of unofficial strikes, restrictive practices, go-slows, breaches of agreements, and 'excessive' wage increases served to focus attention on the problems of British industry, and render trade unions liable for much of the blame. The voluntarist and neo-corporatist strategies which many Conservatives had originally envisaged as a solution to at least some of Britain's industrial and economic problems came to be viewed as part of the problem. Or, as Enoch Powell wryly remarked, 'The Party came into Office ... without any specific commitment on trade union law and practice, and it faithfully carried that non-commitment out for thirteen years' (Powell 1968: 5). By 1964, an increasing number of Conservatives – particularly newer, younger MPs – were resolved that the same should never be said of the next Conservative Government.

4 Formulating a legalist policy, 1964–1970

A FUNDAMENTAL REVIEW OF PRINCIPLES AND POLICIES

As noted in Chapter 3, dissatisfaction and disillusion had developed amongst a growing number of Conservatives during their final term of office. An increasing number of Conservative MPs and constituency party activists were of the opinion that after thirteen consecutive years in office, the party had lost sight of its principles and purpose. Rather than pursuing specific policies based on clearly defined objectives, it was felt that the Conservative parliamentary leadership had merely drifted with the tide, devoid of any real sense of direction. To pursue the maritime analogy further, one might say that the Conservative Party had simply adopted a 'steady as she goes' approach to steering the ship of state, determined not to rock the boat or make waves.

Two accounts were on offer by way of explanation. First, and more charitably, it was suggested that the parliamentary leadership had been too preoccupied with securing a broad consensus and social harmony as part of the desire to create One Nation. The emphasis, therefore, had lain on the importance of compromise, conciliation, and co-operation, and on abhorrence of anything which might cause conflict or confrontation. This characterisation of the outgoing Conservative government credited it with having been well-intentioned, but ultimately misguided.

The second, and less charitable, explanation of the Conservative Party's recent policies charged the Macmillan and Douglas-Home leaderships with betraying Conservatism and with seeking a consensual approach to problems because of cowardice. Their administrations, it was claimed, had balked at taking 'tough' decisions and pursuing firm, principled, policies for fear of provoking controversy or unpopularity (Coleraine 1970: Chapter 3; Victor Montagu, *The Times*, 16 July 1968; Critchley 1969).

Yet many of the newer, younger Conservatives entering Parliament from the mid-1960s onwards explicitly advocated competition, conviction, and conflict, believing them to be vital to the health of the body politic. The commitment to consensus and compromise, it was proclaimed, had been pursued too far for too long. For new entrants to the parliamentary party, such as Norman St John-Stevas, the Conservatives' duty was to stress freedom and competition rather than consensus (St John-Stevas 1966), whilst David Howell, a backbench MP elected in 1966, was calling for competition to be placed at the centre of the stage (Howell, undated). Not dissimilarly, Timothy Raison, a prospective parliamentary candidate elected in 1970, proclaimed that 'it is not the One Nation spirit that we need today, but willingness to risk the tension that may arise from a greater readiness to root out our weaknesses.' Raison cited industrial relations as a particular area where this new approach might usefully be applied (Raison 1965: 15). With specific reference to the hitherto conciliatory stance adopted towards the trade unions, the perspective of many younger Conservative MPs was reflected in an editorial published in an 'in-house' monthly newsletter, *Industrial Outlook*, which declared that: 'The hard times endured by millions in the twenties and thirties is a poor and inadequate basis for a system of industrial relations relevant to the needs of today and tomorrow. But memories sometimes die hard' (Conservative Central Office 1965: 2).

By the mid-1960s, such views had acquired a much wider currency in the Conservative Party. Even the launch of a major policy review in the wake of the 1964 election defeat, and the election of Edward Heath as Conservative leader the following year, failed to quell the impatience being expressed by many Conservatives both inside and outside Parliament. It was alleged that all over the country, the Conservative Party's grassroots membership was seeking definite promises that public expenditure would be reduced, taxation cut, and 'trade union blackmail' ended, once and for all. Gratitude was expressed that 'a few real Conservatives', such as Lord Salisbury, Lord Coleraine (Bonar Law's son and a Conservative writer), and Major Patrick Wall (a backbench MP), were at last voicing their dismay and disquiet that Conservatism had come to appear virtually synonymous with paternal socialism (letter to *The Times*, 19 January 1966). At the same time, Angus Maude, a backbench MP elected in 1963, was warning that the 'radical wing' of the Conservative Party was becoming restless, adding that there still existed the 'essential task' of differentiating Tory policy from that of Labour (Maude 1966).

The calls for more commitment and conviction, in both the substance and the presentation of Conservative policies, were sustained throughout the period in opposition. A former party chairman, Edward Du Cann, complained that too many Conservatives remained preoccupied with the 'so-called middle-ground' of British politics. He referred to the widely perceived lack of leadership and inspiration, claiming that what was needed was more 'aggression and imagination' in the party's approach (*The Times*, 9 September 1968). Meanwhile, a resolution was passed – by an overwhelming majority – at the 1968 Annual Conference, demanding a more forthright declaration of party policies. Merely 'tinkering with the works' was not enough, it was claimed; there was a need for 'radical, far-reaching changes'. The Conservative leadership was thus urged to be less reticent in its advocacy and pursuit of these changes. Such calls largely echoed former Minister Duncan Sandys's warning at the previous year's conference that 'middle-of-the-road generalities' would get the Conservative Party nowhere.

Yet many of the party's older, senior members were deeply apprehensive about what they perceived to be a swing to the right. They feared that if the Conservative Party adopted the principles and policies which the neo-liberals and younger MPs were advocating, then it would either frighten away voters at the next election or, if returned to office, would come to be seen as a party of class conflict and social division rather than as one of national unity. Thus did Kenneth Lewis, a backbench MP, express his concern at the prospect of the Conservative Party abandoning 'the fulcrum point of the British electorate – namely the centre', in favour of a shift to the Right (letter to *The Times*, 24 April 1965).

Such trepidation was shared by Ian Gilmour, who believed that the Conservatives had lost the 1966 election partly because of the 'heavy emphasis on radical policies'. Whilst acknowledging the case for more competition and greater efficiency, Gilmour warned that a party which received half of its votes from the working class could not make a religion out of the uncontrolled forces of the market (Gilmour 1969: 92). Indeed, it is worth noting, perhaps, that Gilmour had been criticising the nascent neo-liberalism in the Conservative Party several months *before* the 1964 election defeat. To those susceptible to free market ideas, Gilmour pointed out that as the Conservative Party had refused 'to espouse capitalism when she was at her classical and enticing best, to fall in love with her in 1964 would be sheer necrophilia', before suggesting that 'the call to have all economic decisions made by the play of the market ... does not, on the face of it, seem a compelling election slogan' (Gilmour 1964). Party Chairman Anthony Barber, meanwhile, informed the Conservative Party's 1968 Annual Conference that he was a little irritated by the constant calls for a 'more forthright declaration of party policies'. Further concern was expressed by Brendon Sewill and James Douglas, two senior officials at the Conservative Research Department; like Gilmour, they accepted the necessity of changes, but were concerned at the emphasis being placed on them by the party's neo-liberals. Too much talk of more vigorous management, greater profitability, and increased incentives and differentials, Sewill and Douglas feared, might create the impression that the Conservatives were a party of the rich, or of employers; this would be disastrous (quoted in Ramsden 1980: 250).

DRAFTING A NEW TRADE UNION POLICY

Yet with the Conservative Party out of office, and widespread dissatisfaction manifesting itself at all levels of its organisation, a major policy review was announced in the wake of the 1964 election defeat, to be conducted under the overall direction of Edward Heath. This review, he proclaimed, was being carried out 'fundamentally', with the issues of trade union law and practice amongst those policies which 'needed urgent attention' (*The Times*, 23 April 1965).

The review entailed the establishment of twenty-one advisory groups, each examining a specific aspect or sphere of policy, although within a few months the total number of groups had risen to thirty-six, due to the creation of fifteen subgroups. By July 1965, 248 Conservatives were involved in the deliberations of these policy review groups: 120 MPs, ten peers, and 118 extra-parliamentary Conservatives. Occasional advice and assistance were also forthcoming from sympathetic individuals working in industry, finance, commerce, and academia.

In addition, there were 300 other groups, involving 3,000 people, contributing to the deliberations on future party policies, via the Conservative Political Centre's 'Two-Way Movement of Ideas' network in the constituencies. Not surprisingly, it was the review of trade union and industrial relations law which was to produce some of the most notable discussions in the Conservative Party during the years in opposition. Indeed, the debates amongst Conservatives over the issue of trade union and industrial relations reform were to be sustained right up until the 1970 election – and beyond.

The Policy Review Group on Trade Union Law and Practice was one of the first to commence work, under the auspices of Lord Amory. Its membership was comprised of: Joseph Godber, Sir John Hobson, Geoffrey Howe, Ray Mawby, Richard Wood, Iain Macleod, Dudley Smith, David Clarke, and Aidan Crawley, the latter also serving on the Conservative backbench committee on industrial relations. Selected to ensure a cross-section of views, the backgrounds of those serving on the Group meant that a wide range of experience was brought to its deliberations. Godber had been Minister of Labour during the final two years of the Conservative administration, whilst Macleod had held the same post during the 1955–9 period. Both had therefore played an integral part in the party's attempt at sustaining a voluntarist policy towards the trade unions. Prior to his political career, Godber had been a chairman of the National Farmers Union, whilst Ray Mawby had formerly been both a shop steward and the first President of the Conservative Trade Unionists (CTU) National Advisory Committee.

By contrast, Sir John Hobson and Geoffrey Howe were both barristers, and were to play an important part in influencing and framing the party's subsequent legalist strategy towards the trade unions. Indeed, Conservative policy in this area became prone to repeated criticism that it was too legalistic, devised by men who lacked experience and understanding of the day-to-day functioning of both industry and trade unions. Neither did the remaining members of the Review Group on Trade Unions have backgrounds which suggested intimate knowledge of life on the shopfloor: Dudley Smith had been a journalist; Richard Wood an officer in the King's Royal Rifle Corps; and David Clarke an insurance broker. Aidan Crawley, meanwhile, had been a company director, and, through numerous business trips to the United States, had become greatly impressed by certain aspects of American industrial relations, for example that collective agreements were legally enforceable for a fixed period.

As expected, the Group developed a policy which broke with the voluntarist strategy hitherto pursued by the Conservative Party, and committed it, instead, to a policy of legalism. However, this shift was tempered by caution and care, with the supporters of a tough line on industrial relations having to moderate some of their demands or desires. This was partly due to the 'cross-section' of views held by the members of the Group on Trade Union Law and Practice, which almost inevitably led to some compromises, and also by the intrusion into the Group's deliberations of 'reality' and 'practicability', whereby certain limits on what was actually feasible were recognised – albeit grudgingly in some quarters. Thus, for example, Sir John Hobson, Geoffrey Howe, and Aidan Crawley, the supporters of a robust legislative approach to industrial relations reform, were countered by the voluntarist sympathies still held by Conservatives such as Joseph Godber (who even circulated a paper to the Group stating the case for *avoiding* significant changes in trade union law) and Iain Macleod (Macleod 1965).

In connection with the second factor encouraging a 'moderation' of demands and proposals, namely the need to recognise what was actually feasible or practicable, the Group made several amendments and revisions to its proposals during the course of its numerous meetings. For example, having agreed at its very first meeting that the 'number one problem' in British industrial relations was unofficial strikes, and that collective agreements ought to be legally enforceable, the Group had to grapple with the problem of reaching agreement on measures which would be effective and enforceable, a task which was to prove less straightforward than the proponents of legalism had envisaged. Thus, even by early 1966, they had accepted that any legislative changes had to be enforceable in practice, otherwise both the law and a (future) Conservative government would be brought into disrepute.

This was by no means the only compromise that the more 'hard-line' members of the Group felt obliged to accept; an earlier decision 'that it was, in theory, desirable to remove the existing immunity against actions for tort' was countered with recognition that 'such a step might well be impracticable, and, politically, unwise'. The Group also decided to defer a decision on the issue of legally imposed 'cooling-off' periods prior to a major strike, preferring instead to await the outcome of the Royal Commission on Trade Unions and Employers' Associations, being conducted under Lord Donovan.

None the less, within a few months of its formation, the Group on Trade Union Law and Practice had developed a body of proposals which was subsequently adopted, albeit with a few modifications, as official Conservative Party policy, and which was to culminate in the introduction of the Industrial Relations Act a few years later. The policy proposals of the Group included the creation of a new Industrial Court, along with the establishment of a Registrar of Trade Unions. Also, in spite of the serious reservations of some of its members, the Group pressed ahead with the recommendation that all collective agreements be enforceable in law.

Yet discussion – and disagreement – continued as the Group continued to meet up until early 1970, long after most of the other policy review groups had ceased functioning. Furthermore, the Conservative Shadow Cabinet declined to support the Group's proposal on the enforceability of all collective agreements, declaring, instead, that only certain types of collective agreements ought to be made enforceable, especially those on procedure. By the time that a modified set of proposals had been submitted to the Advisory Committee on Policy, in September 1965, the section on trade unions, according to Brendon Sewill, constituted a 'very careful compromise between Sir Keith Joseph [who had by this time taken over as chairperson of the Group on Trade Union Law and Practice] and Joseph Godber' (quoted in Ramsden 1980: 244).

In the same month, the Conservative Party published a policy document, *Putting Britain Right Ahead*, which reflected some of the proposals and changes advocated by various policy review groups. The publication included the recommendations on industrial relations and trade union reform referred to above. One pro-Conservative journal commented that whilst the section on trade unions was 'a trifle delphic', it was 'perhaps, none the worse for that'. It was not the flat-out attack on the trade union leaders 'which some Tories wanted, and some Tories feared'. None the less, the commentary continued, it still represented 'a major departure from traditional bipartisan policies in this field' (*The Spectator*, 8 October 1965). Yet with the Labour government itself edging towards industrial relations reform, commentators at the time might have been forgiven had they prophesied the emergence of a new 'bipartisanship' in this particular area of policy.

REJECTION OF INCOMES POLICY

Further evidence of a change in Conservative Party policy was intimated, through the publication of *Putting Britain Right Ahead,* on the issue of incomes policy. Whereas the party's 1964 Election Manifesto had insisted that an incomes policy was 'crucial to the achievement of sustained growth without inflation', *Putting Britain Right Ahead* made only slight allusion to the issue, preferring instead to emphasise features such as competition, efficiency, and incentives. Economic planning, *à la* NEDC, received no mention whatsoever.

The issue of incomes policy was inextricably linked to the Conservative Party's development of a new trade union policy. After its 1964 election defeat, the Conservative Party steadily moved away from any commitment to incomes policy, although a few senior figures continued to hanker for one, thereby helping to ensure that the subject remained a bone of contention. The criticisms of incomes policy, which emanated mainly from neo-liberals in the Conservative Party, such as Enoch Powell, Sir Keith Joseph, John Biffen, Norman St John-Stevas, Richard Body, and Jock Bruce-Gardyne (to name but a few), were both economic and political in nature.

At the economic level, two main objections were advanced. First, much was made of the notion that an incomes policy distorted or destroyed the natural mechanisms of the market economy, and prevented the effective, unfettered operation of the laws of supply and demand. In a market economy, neo-liberals maintained, wages and prices would find their 'natural' level. Any attempt by Westminster or Whitehall to establish wage levels according to such criteria as 'justice', 'fairness', or 'merit' would grievously undermine the operation of 'the market', and thereby seriously exacerbate, rather than solve, Britain's industrial and economic problems (Bow Group 1965: 4). In response to the party's remaining advocates of incomes policy, Powell called upon those who realised 'that the nation lives by price and profit ... to band together to protect, defend, and champion price and profit, from whatever quarter they are attacked' (Powell 1969: 161).

The other 'economic' objection raised against incomes policies by an increasing number of Conservatives from 1964 onwards was targeted at the orthodox view that 'excessive' wage increases were responsible for inflation. Due to the prevalence of this view, it had been widely assumed that the key to holding down inflation was to hold down wage increases, through an incomes policy. Again, Powell expressed the view of an increasing number of Conservatives when he vigorously attacked this orthodoxy and the premise upon which it had been based. According to Powell, the root cause of inflation was government expenditure, when this was sustained through the printing of more money rather than via increased productivity and a rise in national income sufficient to cover the governments' expenditure. Because of this, Powell was emphatic that there was no mystery about inflation; it was willed by governments. Inflation was 'politician-made', he argued, arising of government thriftlessness and unwillingness to face the economic facts of life. Thus if inflation was the consequence of excessive government expenditure, sustained through the printing of more money, Powell, and the growing number of neo-liberals in the Conservative Party, deemed it 'a nonsense' for the politicians responsible to seek a reduction in inflation by holding down prices and incomes. Indeed, Powell deemed the whole concept of an incomes policy a fraud, and an irrelevance to the problem it purported to solve (ibid.: 173, Chapter 9).

Not surprisingly, Powell was also the Conservative Party's leading neo-liberal exponent of the 'political' objection to incomes policy, arguing that such a policy invariably had corporatist implications or consequences, for it meant the TUC and the CBI attempting to 'manage' or 'coerce' their memberships, in order to ensure the success of the government's policy. Instead of wages being determined by the laws of supply and demand in a free market, incomes policies meant that the government sought to determine wage levels, using the 'representative' organisations of capital and labour to administer their decisions, and, in effect, control their members on behalf of the government. Powell warned that Britain was in

> imminent danger of slipping unawares into that form of State socialism which is known as fascism, whereby the control of the State over individuals is exercised largely through corporations which purport to represent the various elements of society, and particularly the employers and employees.

> (ibid.: 164)

Disagreement in the Conservative Party over the issue of incomes policy was highlighted by the Labour government's introduction of a Prices and Incomes Bill, which sought to provide statutory enforcement of a six-month pay freeze, to be followed by a longer period of stringent restraint. The introduction of this Bill, in the summer of 1966, lent urgency to the ongoing debate in the Conservative Party over its own position concerning incomes policy. The Shadow Cabinet was divided on the issue. Powell was clearly opposed to incomes policies generally, and to the Labour government's Bill in particular. Yet Edward Boyle (Shadow Cabinet Minister and former Treasury Minister), Reginald Maudling, and Iain Macleod were proponents of incomes policy, and believed that the Labour government's response to the balance of payments crisis of July 1966, and the continuing rise in both wages and inflation, lent some merit to the Prices and Incomes Bill. A meeting of the Shadow Cabinet prior to the second reading therefore secured an agreement to table a 'reasoned' amendment to the Bill, expressing qualified acceptance of the principle of an incomes policy, but opposing the compulsion and coercion enshrined in the government's measure. This amendment evidently constituted a compromise between the members of the Shadow Cabinet, with both Powell and Maudling agreeing to it after they had publicly expressed widely different views on the concept of incomes policy (*The Times*, January 1966, *passim*). (Maudling's consent to the amendment was secured by a phone call to Moscow, where he was on business at the time of the Shadow Cabinet meeting, from the Conservative Chief Whip.)

However, the amendment failed to endear itself to all of the neo-liberals on the Conservative backbenches; Geoffrey Hirst resigned the Conservative whip as a consequence of the party's decision not to vote against the second reading of the Prices and Incomes Bill 'in a straightforward manner'. In accounting for his action, Hirst pointed out that an incomes policy had not worked in any other country, and would not work in Britain. Instead, he warned, such a policy merely provided a 'slippery slope' to an ever increasing infringement of personal liberty (*The Times*, 11 July 1966).

Other Conservative backbenchers echoed Hirst's concern, with Thomas Iremonger also alleging that the Bill represented 'the first step down the slippery path of total socialistic control of processes which were best left to the operation of the immutable laws of supply and demand' (*HC Debates*, 5th series, vol.731: c.1742). Meanwhile, Norman St John-Stevas claimed that there were two indictments against the Bill; first, that it was economically irrelevant; and, second, that it constituted a threat to the freedom of British society (ibid.: c.1830), and Enoch Powell reiterated his concerns about the 'ominous ring of the Corporate State' sounding from the proposal that (Labour) government, the TUC, and the CBI should attempt to enforce a Prices and Incomes Bill (Powell 1969: 164).

Whilst Conservative neo-liberals were unequivocal in their opposition to incomes policy *per se*, a number of backbenchers continued to believe that some form of incomes policy was unavoidable. Like Sir Cyril Osborne, they were adamant that there could not be a return to 'the bad old days', when the economic machine was allowed to grind its way, regardless of the social consequences of its actions. The nation's conscience would not stand for a free-for-all, Sir Cyril argued, hence there had to be some political control of the economic machine (*HC Debates*, 5th series, vol.731: c.1783–4). Indeed, two weeks previously, he had sought an assurance from the Labour government that it would not abandon its prices and incomes policy, because he believed it to constitute Britain's only hope of economic salvation *(HC Debates*, 5th series, vol.730: c.2171).

Such disagreement continued to manifest itself in the Conservative Party during the committee stage of the Prices and Incomes Bill. Kenneth Lewis abstained in parliamentary divisions on several of the clauses, which the rest of his party voted against. He justified his refusal to join his colleagues in the 'No' lobby by insisting that if there was no incomes policy in the full employment situation which existed at that time, then there would be inflation. The alternative, he argued, would be a very high level of unemployment (*HC Debates*, Standing Committee B, 1966–7, vol.3: c.274–5).

Lewis's stance was not shared by his colleagues serving on the standing committee, however. John Biffen proclaimed that Tory governments did not engage in 'this kind of interventionist nonsense' (ibid.: c.62), whilst Sir Keith Joseph reiterated the neo-liberal view that it was disastrous for the efficiency of the economy to attempt to regulate the movement of prices and pay, for these needed to respond to all kinds of pressures of supply and demand (ibid.: c.263). These different perspectives received further expression during the third reading of the Bill, with Kenneth Lewis and Terence Higgins (opposition spokesperson on Treasury and Economic Affairs) arguing that the Conservative Party ought to favour a voluntary incomes policy, whilst John Biffen insisted that 'the market should establish the pattern of wages' (*HC Debates*, 5th series, vol.733: c.1765, c.1821, and c.1807).

The Conservative Party's response to the Labour government's Prices and Incomes Bill thus served to sustain its own internal debates and disagreements concerning the issue of incomes policy. With neo-liberalism acquiring increasing credence and credibility in the party after 1964, some Conservatives felt compelled to restate the case for incomes policies. Amongst them was former Treasury Minister Sir Edward Boyle who was emphatic that an incomes policy had a part to play in restraining the wage-cost spiral. That no incomes policy could ever be 100 per cent effective, he argued, was no reason to give up all attempts to establish one (Boyle 1966: 26–7). Reginald Maudling also remained committed to the need for an incomes policy, due to the monopoly power of the trade unions which ensured that the free market model assumed by 'liberal economists' did not exist. In this situation, therefore, Maudling advocated an incomes policy as the means to secure expansion without an increase in inflation, and to ensure that wage increases took account of factors such as 'fairness' and 'justice', rather than being solely determined by the 'brute force' of monopoly power in industrial bargaining (*The Times*, 5 January 1966; *HC Debates*, 5th series, vol.731: c.1760 and c.1765). Meanwhile, the former Postmaster General, Reginald Bevins, urged the Conservative Party to 'have the courage and the sense' to go for an incomes policy (*The Times*, 16 November 1965), a call which was endorsed by Eldon Griffiths, a new MP, elected in 1964 (Griffiths 1966). Indeed, just after the 1964 election defeat, but before neo-liberalism had gained wider currency in the Conservative Party, a founder member of the Bow Group went as far as to suggest that the time to argue the case for an incomes policy had passed; the question now was about the detailed ingredients of such a policy, and its actual implementation (Driscoll 1965: 46).

Yet it soon became clear that such an assertion was presumptuous and premature. With the party re-examining its principles and policies, the 'old guard' and their neo-corporatist inclinations being displaced by a newer, younger breed of Conservative MP, and the Labour government experiencing increasing difficulty in maintaining statutory wage restraint, the proponents of incomes policy found themselves diminishing in numbers, and declining in influence. By virtue of these factors, the neo-liberals in the party were becoming increasingly influential in their insistence that the Conservatives should avoid advocacy or adoption of a formal incomes policy. According to Duncan Sandys, government in a free society had no business to fix wages; consequently an incomes policy was wrong in principle and unworkable in practice (*The Times*, 18 March 1968). Similarly, Jock Bruce-Gardyne proclaimed that to seek to restrain or control wages by legislative means was to engage in 'the pursuit of the unattainable' (Bruce-Gardyne 1969: 678; see also James 1972: 48–9).

Thus did the the Conservative Party's move away from incomes policy proceed *pari passu* with its move towards a legalist policy on industrial relations and the trade unions. Whilst analytically separate, the abandonment of an incomes policy and the adoption of legalism were inextricably linked in practice, for both were deemed essential in enabling a future Conservative government to resuscitate the market economy. Not only were incomes policy and trade union power perceived to be obstacles to the successful operation of a market economy, they were also deemed to prevent the creation or restoration of a market economy in the first place. Hence, neo-liberals simultaneously sought a radically reduced role for the state in the spheres of wage determination and income distribution, and a significantly enhanced role for the state in the realm of industrial relations and trade unionism – a freer economy but a stronger state.

One commentator has suggested that the development of Conservative industrial relations policy up until 1970 – and after – can best be interpreted as an attempt to answer two sets of questions: what was the most desirable way of solving the problems of industrial relations, and which possible solutions would be most likely to gain acceptance by 'interested parties', namely employers and trade unions (Moran 1977: 62).

Whilst this is a reasonable characterisation, two points must be emphasised: first, beyond nebulous intentions about 'tackling the trade union problem', there were, in the Conservative Party, different perceptions about what precisely the problem was, meaning that different remedies were being advocated; second, there was an increasing belief amongst Conservatives that there had been far too much 'appeasement' of 'interested parties' (i.e. trade unions) hitherto; hence there was rather less concern about ensuring that the solutions were acceptable to those 'interested parties'. With hindsight, for example, Shadow Labour Minister Robert Carr admitted that the Conservative Party ought to have introduced trade union reforms during its period in office, but had not done so due to its hope that the two sides of industry would act voluntarily to solve Britain's industrial relations problems. The Conservative Party had, he believed, waited for too long, but had 'learnt its lesson', aided considerably both by its experience in office, and its 'studies' in opposition (Conservative Political Centre 1967: 479).

IDENTIFYING BRITAIN'S INDUSTRIAL RELATIONS AND TRADE UNION PROBLEMS

With regard to the differing – though by no means mutually exclusive – perceptions about the particular problems of British industrial relations and trade unionism, a distinction can be posited between those features or aspects of industrial relations and trade unionism which had traditionally been a source of concern to Conservatives, and those features and aspects which became 'problematic' from the late 1950s onwards, as a consequence of structural changes in British industry and the problems afflicting the economy. Although this distinction is somewhat arbitrary, it ought none the less to provide a starting point in enabling us to delineate the main problems identified by Conservatives during the 1964–70 period, which informed the party's discussions concerning trade union reform, culminating in the adoption of a legalistic approach towards the trade unions. Of the 'traditional' criticisms about trade unionism, the closed shop and the political levy were accorded renewed attention, yet still failed to yield agreement amongst their Conservative critics as how best to deal with them.

The closed shop

The issue of the closed shop continued to highlight the tension between two of the fundamental tenets of Conservatism: liberty and order. This meant that whilst the closed shop was widely condemned as constituting a negation of individual liberty (as well as reflecting and reinforcing the alleged drift towards corporatism), there was a recognition by some Conservatives that the 100 per cent trade union membership secured via the closed shop could assist in making collective bargaining more efficient and effective, thereby contributing to the maintenance of order and stability in industry. For this reason, the closed shop was often approved of by some large employers, as well as some Conservatives.

The Conservative leadership initially saw the solution to this dilemma as lying in the notion that maximum membership of a trade union ought to be attained voluntarily, by persuasion and recruitment campaigns, rather than through compulsion or coercion. Indeed, many Conservatives were fond of arguing that a trade union which did a good job for its members would be able to win recruits anyway, thereby obviating reliance on 'conscription'. Norman St John-Stevas was amongst Conservatives who renewed calls for legislation to outlaw the closed shop (*HC Debates*, 5th series, vol.731: c.130). Elsewhere, the Inns of Court Conservative and Unionist Society, in its written evidence to the Royal (Donovan) Commission on Trade Unions and Employers' Associations, accepted 'unanimously' the principle of maximum trade union membership, provided that it was achieved by peaceful persuasion and discussion. The notion that 100 per cent membership should be secured by statute or compulsion was strongly rejected. This view was echoed by the CTU National Advisory Committee in its written evidence to the Commission, when it declared that 'with regard to union membership, we are in favour of 100 per cent trade union membership, but we feel that this must be achieved on the basis of recruitment and example. We are utterly opposed to making trade union membership a condition of employment.'

The political levy

With regard to the political levy, the Conservatives began placing increasing emphasis on the concept of 'educating' trade unionists of their right to contract out. The Shadow Labour Minister, Robert Carr, in his written submission to the Donovan Commission, suggested that there existed a strong case for making all trade union membership application forms provide information on the right to 'contract out', and be accompanied by an attached 'contracting out' request form. This was a popular approach to the political levy problem in the Conservative Party, with Anthony Grant – a backbench MP, elected in 1964 – having already sought to introduce a Bill (supported by Sir Edward Brown – a senior figure among Conservative Trade Unionists – Thomas Iremonger, David Mitchell, and John Page) to provide that all trade union membership application forms should specifically refer to the applicants' right not to pay the political levy. Although a signatory to Grant's Bill, Iremonger remained convinced of the need to go further by replacing 'contracting out' by 'contracting in'. Without this change, he argued, the 'negative forces of inertia' would continue to operate in favour of a particular political candidate (*HC Debates*, 5th series, vol. 737: c.1362–3).

Concern over the political levy was clearly increasing amongst the Conservative rank-and-file; between 1967 and 1969, the number of motions submitted to Annual Conference calling for 'contracting out' to be replaced by 'contracting in' more than trebled. Yet by 1970, proposals initially agreed upon by the Policy Review Group on Trade Union Law and Practice to reform the political levy system had been quietly dropped. In addition to the concern which some Conservatives still felt about antagonising the trade unions, there was a realisation that an attack on the political levy might provide the Labour Party with the opportunity to claim that the Tories were seeking to destroy them financially.

**The increasing remoteness of trade union
leaders from their members**

The 'traditional' Conservative concerns about the closed shop and the political levy were supplemented during the the 1960s by newer concerns and issues, which arose by virtue of changes taking place in the structure and operation of British industry and the economy.

The late 1950s and 1960s had been characterised by an increasing trend in industry and the economy towards centralisation and monopolisation. The increasing size and scale of firms and industries gave rise to new industrial relations problems, not least because the structural and organisational changes in industry led to corresponding changes in the trade unions themselves. Thus, as firms and industries became ever more centralised, hierarchical, and bureaucratic, so too did the trade unions within those firms and industries. The decision-making activities and procedures of both had become increasingly removed from the local or plant level, with both management and trade union leaders appearing ever more remote, both organisationally and geographically, from those working on the shopfloor.

Neo-corporatism and incomes policies had both reflected and reinforced this trend. As noted in the previous chapter, the outcome was a vacuum at local or plant level, a vacuum which was increasingly being filled by shop stewards and local trade union officials *in situ*. By virtue of their proximity to, and closer contact with, the workers on the shopfloor, these local-level officials and shop stewards were often able to command greater loyalty and support than the official, national union leadership. This was particularly true when shop stewards or local-level officials were able to win better wage increases or benefits for the rank-and-file union membership than were being achieved by the official national leadership, which was increasingly being expected by the government to secure the membership's compliance in wage restraint.

From the Conservative Party's perspective, this development not only exacerbated wage drift, but also led to the problem of 'unofficial' strikes. The problem was clearly identified by the CTU National Advisory Committee, whose evidence to the Royal Commission on Trade Unions and Employers' Associations (the Donovan Commission) referred to the trend whereby more and more power had been diverted from the central executives of trade unions to unofficial bodies, such as shop steward committees, industrial liaison committees, etc. The Committee identified the emergence of two systems in British industry: one in which trade union leaders negotiated with employers at national level, and adhered to agreements on procedures; the other, at the local level, where there was plant bargaining, often entailing the use of militancy to short-circuit procedural agreements. For some Conservatives, it was these breaches of agreements which constituted the main problem of British industrial relations in the second half of the 1960s.

Unofficial strikes

Other Conservatives, however, were more concerned about a related problem, namely 'unofficial' strikes. Indeed, for Robert Carr, unofficial strikes were the outstanding feature which distinguished industrial relations in Britain from those of other advanced countries. Such strikes were an urgent problem, he emphasised, and as such, action needed to be taken to deal with them. It was not simply the number of unofficial strikes which constituted the problem, Carr explained – even though they accounted for 95 per cent of all strikes in Britain – but the effect on industry and the economy. In a modern economy, with highly 'capitalised' production methods, and a large degree of interdependence between one company and another, stability was becoming ever more important. In consequence, Carr emphasised, the frequent and unpredictable interruptions in production which the country suffered because of unofficial strikes were particularly damaging (*HC Debates*, 5th series, vol.807: c.633–4; see also Abbott 1966: 8; Conservative Political Centre, undated, circa 1966: 4–5; Conservative Central Office 1971: 5). Elsewhere it was pointed out that the statistics on unofficial strikes failed to illustrate the ways in which enterprises and their employees were themselves affected as a consequence of unofficial strikes elsewhere. The effects of unofficial strikes permeated far and wide, often in subtle and unseen ways. Indeed, it was alleged that 'The indirect effects of strikes in Britain can do far more damage to our economy than the strikes themselves' (Conservative Central Office 1968).

Furthermore, these strikes were almost invariably in breach of either contractual or procedural agreements, and were widely seen to be a consequence of the widening gap between the official trade union leadership at national level, and the rank-and-file at local level where 'unofficial' representatives became active, and were more readily able to gain the allegiance of those on the shopfloor than was the 'remote' national leadership. Thus, although there were always Conservative backbenchers ready to ascribe the incidence of unofficial strikes to 'foreign-inspired' attempts at sabotaging British industry and destroying the economy, more rational Conservatives located their cause in the changing structure of both British industry and the trade union movement itself. According to future Conservative MP John Spence, speaking at the party's 1966 Annual Conference, it was at workshop level that all the haggling took place over piecework rates, overtime, bonuses, etc., and it was disagreement at this level, he argued, which very often resulted in unofficial strikes. It was here also, Spence pointed out, that trade union officials were seen at their weakest, and 'irresponsible' shop stewards at their strongest.

Restrictive practices

A further particular problem identified by some Conservatives during the course of the 1960s was that of restrictive practices. Indeed Sir Keith Joseph suggested at the Conservative Party's 1965 Annual Conference that restrictive practices were at the heart of Britain's economic problems. Certainly, some Conservatives deemed them to be more damaging to Britain's industrial and economic performance than unofficial strikes. Edward Heath, for example, had become convinced that of all the obstacles in the way of Britain's pursuit of economic growth, restrictive labour practices were the most insidious and difficult to shift (*The Times*, 15 September 1967). Similarly, a prominent Conservative backbench critic of trade unions, Ronald Bell, declared that restrictive practices were among the main causes of the nation's poor economic performance. With regard to a solution to this and other problems (such as overmanning), he complained that Conservatives had 'waited 10 years too long' (letter to *The Times*, 5 February 1968).

The elimination of restrictive practices was thus accorded an important place in the Conservative Party's proposals for the reform of trade unionism and industrial relations, particularly because of the need for greater competition, efficiency, and steady economic growth. It was therefore envisaged that the Prices and Incomes Board, set up by the Labour government in 1966 as an integral part of its incomes policy, would be reconstituted as the Productivity Board, and would have the power to initiate investigations into specific employment practices and working methods if and when they were unjustified or harmful to the economy. Furthermore, it was intended that higher wages would be linked to increased productivity and agreements by the trade unions to eliminate restrictive practices. Other Conservative proposals for dealing with restrictive practices included the possibility of enabling an Industrial Court to issue an injunction against those engaging in restrictive practices, and removing legal immunity for strikes called to defend restrictive practices (Conservative Political Centre 1966: 5–6).

'FAIR DEAL AT WORK'

These proposals were part of a wider set of recommendations on industrial relations and trade union reform, which had been included in the Conservative Party's 1966 Election Manifesto, *Action Not Words*. Amongst them had been pledges to: make certain agreements legally enforceable, most notably procedural ones; establish a registrar of trade unions and employers' associations and ensure the fairness of their internal rules; establish a new Industrial Relations Court to deal with disputes; and introduce measures providing workers with protection against 'unreasonable' activities or behaviour by trade unions.

The Conservatives sought to clarify and restate the case for legislative reform of trade unionism, and industrial relations generally, with the publication of *Fair Deal at Work* (Conservative Central Office 1968). This document both reflected and contributed to the ongoing debate in the party over industrial relations and trade union reform. Described as 'a comprehensive policy document explaining and extending the policies to which the Conservative Party has been committed for two-and-a-half years' (Conservative Research Department 1969: 83), *Fair Deal at Work* clarified the party's policies towards various aspects of industrial relations, such as restrictive practices, definitions of what actually constituted a trade dispute (and even a trade union), enforceability of collective agreements, and the closed shop. It was proposed that trade unions 'should be re-defined in law, as properly constituted bodies, with rules approved by a new Registrar'. *Fair Deal at Work* proposed that upon registration, a trade union would be granted 'corporate legal status', which, among other things, would enable it to sue, and be sued, in connection with any agreement that had been made, and also to become liable for torts committed by cither itself, its servants, or its agents, except in connection with a lawful trade dispute (Conservative Central Office 1970: 18–19). On this last point, *Fair Deal at Work* proposed that the definition of a 'trade dispute' be narrowed, so as to exclude: sympathetic strikes, and the 'blacking' of goods and services of an employer elsewhere who was not in dispute with his employees; inter-union disputes; and strikes aimed at the enforcement of a closed shop. Any of these activities would constitute an 'unfair labour practice', for which the union(s) involved would be legally liable (ibid.: 30).

The section on the enforceability of collective agreements indicated the continuation of the problems that the issue had posed for the Policy Review Group on Trade Union Law and Practice and, indeed, the Shadow Cabinet. The original compromise of making only procedural agreements enforceable was replaced by a pledge to make all collective agreements legally enforceable, unless the parties to an agreement specifically stated that it, or any particular part of it, was not to be considered legally binding on them. Not every MP serving on the Group was in favour of rendering all collective agreements legally enforceable, hence the attachment of a proviso giving the parties to an agreement the opportunity to 'contract out' of making it enforceable in law. This proposal was another manifestation of the disagreement which permeated Conservative policy-making in the sphere of trade union and industrial relations reform. It also illustrated the fact that those most committed to a policy of legalism still needed, on occasions, to make concessions to those in the party who were uneasy about invoking too many legislative measures, or who convincingly pointed out the practical difficulties of certain legal remedies.

Fair Deal at Work proposed that when an 'enforceable' agreement was breached, the individual or the trade union deemed responsible for breaking it would be liable to be sued for damages, with the case being heard by a specially constituted Industrial Court. However, trade unions would not be deemed liable if they could prove that they had done everything in their power to prevent the breach of agreement.

The legal enforceability of agreements, and the concomitant liability for damages of those who breached them, was advocated by the Conservative Party on four specific grounds. First, it would provide a strong incentive to both sides of industry to consider more carefully the actual content and consequences of collective agreements, whilst simultaneously encouraging union officials to explain them more carefully to their members. Second, and following directly on from this, it would provide a strong incentive to trade union leaders to maintain much closer contact with those whom they purported to represent, and to be quicker in identifying problems. Third, it would encourage clarification of the precise functions and status of shop stewards. Fourth, it would assist in the removal of a major deterrent to management taking just disciplinary action against those guilty of breaching agreements. This was because if a trade union intervened in support of those being disciplined, it would be deemed to be condoning the breach of agreement, and thus become liable itself (ibid.: 32–4).

Fair Deal at Work also indicated a modification of the Conservative Party's traditional opposition to compulsory trade union membership and the closed shop. The strand of 'moral individualism' in Conservative attitudes towards this issue, which emphasised the denial of individual liberty that the closed shop constituted, was countered by a recognition – by some Conservatives at least – of the practicalities of daily industrial life, of which the closed shop was so often a feature.

Juxtaposed to the defence of the rights and liberties of the individual was the concept of majoritarian rule, which constitutes a key principle of western democracy. In this context, the Conservative Party had to recognise, however reluctantly, that in many instances and industries, trade union membership was compulsory because an overwhelming majority of the employees wished it to be so. More important, perhaps, was cognisance of the fact that total trade union membership could be a stabilising influence in industrial relations, whilst greatly assisting the process of collective bargaining.

In an attempt at resolving the tension between the principle of 'individualism', and the practical advantages of 'industrial collectivism', *Fair Deal at Work* posited a distinction between what it called a 'closed shop' and a 'union shop'. The former was defined as one whereby a person could not obtain employment in a particular firm or industry unless already a member of an appropriate trade union. As well as being deemed a denial of a person's freedom to work for any employer prepared to employ him or her, the 'closed shop' was also alleged to usurp management's right to manage, and an employer's right to employ, for it enabled trade unions to act virtually as recruitment agencies. 'Union shop' agreements, on the other hand, were those where non-unionists were expected to join a trade union after commencing employment.

Having posited this distinction, and having acknowledged that 'this emotive and complex problem' involved questions of principle which were by no means one-sided, *Fair Deal at Work* suggested that 'union shop' agreements 'need not be discouraged' when and where it could be shown that the majority of employees wanted them, and that 'adequate safeguards' existed for individuals who held strong convictions against trade union membership. It was, however, suggested that those who cited religion, or other reasons of principle, as a justification for refusing to join a trade union ought to pay a sum equivalent to the union subscription fee to an agreed charity. (This was to counter the possibility that some individuals might seek to avoid joining a trade union merely because they did not want to pay the membership fee, not on grounds of deeply held principle.) Existing employees who had not joined a trade union would be exempt from any requirement to do so (ibid.: 24–5).

DOUBTS OVER THE DIRECTION OF POLICY

Fair Deal at Work reflected – and refuelled – the discussions which had taken place in the Conservative Party over trade union and industrial relations reform since the 1964 and 1966 election defeats. Thus it partially sought to respond to the concerns and reservations of those Conservatives who had expressed doubts about pursuing 'legislative' solutions to industrial relations problems. Whilst recognising the problems which existed in this area, some Conservatives had always remained sceptical about the wisdom of an apparent solution which relied too heavily on the Statute Book. Both Edward Boyle and William Whitelaw recognised the danger of introducing an Industrial Relations Bill which attempted to do too much (letter to *The Times*, 11 February 1975), whilst John Biffen had doubts on two grounds. First, he was concerned at the possibly damaging effect which such a Bill might have on the Conservatives' electoral prospects, wondering how 'the Tory penchant' for trade union reform would be received by working-class voters, particularly those who were actually in trade unions (Biffen 1965). Second, Biffen referred to 'the most authentic of all Tory traditions', namely that of a healthy scepticism of both government itself and public regulation of social and economic affairs. It was in this spirit, Biffen suggested, that a Tory would have serious doubts as to whether altering trade union law would produce a new spirit in industrial relations, or lead to the abandonment of restrictive practices (Biffen 1968: 9–10).

Further concern was expressed by David Madel, himself an industrialist, who was apprehensive about 'bringing agreements between employers and employees into the framework of the law', not least because of the danger that the party would pass a law which could not be made effective. To do so, he warned the 1967 Conservative Annual Conference, could be a danger to democracy. Madel was fearful that unless the Conservative Party had 'really thought out all the implications' of its policies, it would be 'in danger of triggering off the greatest industrial unrest of the century'. Concern about the party leadership's apparent faith in legislative solutions to industrial relations problems was also expressed by the CTU whose National Advisory Committee warned that 'to legislate directly against the unofficial strike is impossible, and would bring the law into disrepute' (CTU (National Advisory Committee) 1966: 6). The most outspoken criticism, however, came from Pressure for Economic and Social Toryism (PEST) which upheld the voluntarist banner in the party, urging the Conservatives to leave the trade unions alone, so that they could carry out the necessary reforms without interference from politicians. Indeed, according to PEST, it was actually the Conservatives who had too often thought in terms of 'them and us' (PEST circa 1967).

Such concerns were not entirely placated by the publication of *Fair Deal at Work*; indeed, the specificity of its proposals and pledges provided scope for further unease amongst some Conservatives, and instilled doubts in the minds of a few others. The emphasis on legislative measures, and the possibility that the Conservative Party might suffer electorally, were two of the most commonly cited anxieties amongst those Conservatives who were less than whole-hearted in their support for a policy of legalism. A prospective Conservative candidate expressed both of these concerns simul-taneously, complaining that the philosophy of the party's industrial relations strategy was 'overridingly legal' and thus failed to show sufficient recognition of the fact that there was much more to the whole complex issue of trade union modernisation than the mere establishment of an operational framework within recognised rules of law. In addition, he noted, there was a danger that 'invoking the majesty of the law will frighten off many trade unionists' who were, to some extent, 'amenable to Tory ideas' (Dykes 1968: 32).

The commitment to a legislative policy, confirmed by *Fair Deal at Work*, led to a restatement of the case, in some quarters of the Conservative Party, for a voluntarist industrial relations strategy. Some Conservatives repeated that most of the problems on the shopfloor were the outcome of alienation and anomie, and other such socio-psychological maladies, which therefore necessitated a 'human relations' solution, coupled with closer co-operation and consultation between the two sides of industry. For such Conserva-tives, the party's proposals concerning the restoration of managerial authority, trade union discipline, and the construction of a frame-work of law were an indication that the nature of Britain's industrial relations problems had been misunderstood, for what was needed was a conciliatory approach, not recourse to authoritarian measures. Paradoxically, it was a Conservative neo-liberal who provided the most succinct expression of such concerns, pointing out that when a handful of men on strike could paralyse whole industries, the vulnerability of industry was too great for the Tory Party to be able to rely primarily on discipline. What was needed was the active co-operation of the whole workforce in any given enterprise (Ridley 1969: 21).

The Conservative Party's final Annual Conference in opposition, in 1969, provided further evidence of the ambivalence and anxiety in some quarters over policy towards the trade unions and industrial relations. The motion on industrial relations included the claim that the TUC had to play 'a major part in the control and disciplining of its members', and although it was carried by a large majority, three of the seven speakers from the platform expressed their opposition to it. A significant element in this opposition was deeply concerned about the TUC being called upon to act as 'watchdog' over its members. It was deemed wrong, both in principle and in practice, for the TUC to be given such a duty, and surprise was expressed that Conservatives should be advocating such an approach which, it was explained, would entail placing great power in the hands of the TUC. A prospective Conservative candidate expressed opposition to a policy which gave the TUC 'responsibility to police its members', pointing out that if the TUC 'failed' in discharging this responsibility, it would be brought into further disrepute, whilst if it succeeded, it would lose the confidence and support of its rank-and-file membership. The conference also heard a reiteration of the voluntarist approach from a delegate who called on the Conservative Party to remember that industrial problems were human problems, and therefore to recognise that it 'must not put complex law on the statute book'.

In spite of such criticisms, or maybe because of them, Robert Carr declared that the Conservative Party knew what it was doing, and had made it clear. Consequently, he proclaimed, its will was strong and would not be broken. Yet Carr's clarion call was belied by an increasing sense of apprehension within the parliamentary Conservative Party, an apprehension which had been compounded by the manner in which the Labour government had been forced, in 1969, to abandon its own programme of industrial relations reform (known as *In Place of Strife*), in the face of fierce trade union opposition. Whilst it certainly illustrated to Conservatives the necessity of trade union reform, the whole affair also exacerbated the fears of those in the party who felt that the leadership was treading a dangerous path in pursuing a policy of legalism. That the Labour Party had come to recognise the need for industrial relations reform was certainly seen by many Conservatives as vindication of their own Party's decision to tackle the issue. For others, however, the fact that the Labour Party's 'special relationship' with the trade unions had counted for naught in gaining the TUC's consent to industrial relations reform did not augur well for the Conservative Party's own proposals. If the unions had forced the Labour Party to abandon its efforts, then what sort of response awaited a Conservative government attempting legal reform of trade unionism?

In attempting to allay such anxieties, the Conservative leadership's response was twofold. First, further measures were proposed which would be added to those already included in the proposed Industrial Relations Bill. These measures pertained to the 'rights' of employees *vis-à-vis* their employers, and the concomitant obligations which employers were to have conferred upon them. It was proposed that every employee in an enterprise above a certain size should be provided with a written statement of his or her basic rights and obligations when commencing employment. At the same time, the party suggested that employees in larger firms ought to be entitled to as much information about the company's affairs as the shareholders were. Finally, it was recommended that employers might be placed under an obligation to inform and consult their employees on important matters pertaining to their employment. These proposals were clearly intended to placate those critics and 'faint-hearts' in the Conservative Party who feared that the existing policies were too authoritarian or legalistic, whilst simultaneously serving as a small olive branch to the trade unions.

The second aspect of the Conservative leadership's efforts to overcome both the reservations which existed in the party, and the anticipated opposition of the trade unions with regard to a policy of legalism was increasingly to cite public opinion, and the mandate that the party would have for a programme of trade union and industrial relations reform if it won the next general election. To soothe the fears of some of his colleagues, and to warn the trade unions at the same time, Heath emphasised that the party's policies on industrial relations would be in the Election Manifesto for everyone to see, so that people would know what they were voting for. He did not believe that the trade union leadership, or its members, were going to 'challenge the verdict of the electorate in this democracy' (BBC Television, *Panorama*, 2 February 1970). Heath evidently underestimated the degree of union opposition which the Industrial Relations Bill would arouse.

5   The experiment with legalism, 1970–1974

INTRODUCING THE INDUSTRIAL RELATIONS BILL

In the 'foreword' to the Conservative Party's Election Manifesto in June 1970, Heath declared that if elected, his government would 'seek the best advice and listen carefully to it. It should not rush into decisions . . . it should be deliberative and thorough.' Such a worthy approach did not seem to apply to the Industrial Relations Bill, however. Admittedly, the groundwork had been conducted during the years in opposition, but there was still considerable surprise, and some foreboding, when the newly elected Heath government immediately published a 'consultative paper' which only allowed for one month of discussion and feedback on the imminent industrial relations legislation. In any case, the Employment Secretary, Robert Carr, made quite clear to the TUC that the central features of the forthcoming Industrial Relations Bill were 'non-negotiable'.

The Industrial Relations Bill received its first reading at the end of 1970. The main provisions – the 'eight central pillars' which Carr insisted were not negotiable – were: (i) the statutory right to belong, or not to belong, to a trade union; (ii) registration of trade unions and employers' associations with a new Registrar of Trade Unions and Employers' Associations; (iii) enforceability of collective agreements; (iv) the limitation of legal immunities; (v) the right of a trade union to be recognised; (vi) machinery to define bargaining units; (vii) the selective enforcement of procedural agreements; (viii) emergency provisions, whereby the Secretary of State for Employment could apply to a newly instituted Industrial Court for a sixty-day 'cooling off' period, if and when industrial action was deemed likely to injure the economy or lead to serious public disorder. These provisions also empowered the Employment Secretary to apply to the Court for a strike ballot on the same grounds.

Carr declared that the Industrial Relations Bill was to be judged by four main principles. First, that of collective bargaining, freely and responsibly conducted. Second, the principle of developing and maintaining orderly procedures in industry for the peaceful settlement of industrial disputes. This was to be achieved through negotiation, conciliation, or arbitration, with due regard for the interests of the community. Third, the principle of free association for workers, in independent trade unions, which were to be organised in a manner conducive to being representative, responsible, and effective bodies, for regulating relations between the 'two sides' of industry. Fourth, the principle of freedom and security for workers, protected by adequate safeguards against 'unfair' industrial practices.

Speaking in support of the Industrial Relations Bill, Tom Normanton referred to the changed structure of British industry: the growth of large firms had tended to make it essential that detailed variations of wages, working practices, and physical conditions at the workplace be increasingly resolved at, or near, the place of employment. This, however, had led to a weakening of basic trade union authority and responsibility, thereby enabling irresponsible and disruptive individuals and groups in industry to acquire power on the shopfloor. As the law then stood, Normanton alleged, those engaged in disruptive activities in industry were able to shelter under legal immunities enshrined in previous trade union legislation, and it was for these reasons that responsible trade union authority needed to be restored to the official leadership (*HC Debates*, 5th series, vol.808: c.1007 and c.1009). Not dissimilarly, Derek Coombs spoke of the apparent inability of trade unions to control their own extremists, requiring that the law had to do it for them (ibid.: c.1016–17), whilst another Conservative backbencher, Albert Cooper, graphically suggested that the trade union leadership had become so afraid of exerting authority over its members that the tail was wagging the dog (*The Times*, 2 February 1971).

Yet the introduction of the Industrial Relations Act was accompanied by repeated Conservative claims that, far from constituting an abandonment of voluntarism, the Bill represented a strengthening of it. Government spokesmen were emphatic that a predominantly voluntarist system of industrial relations required a clearly defined framework of law within which to operate. When this framework proved inadequate, then the government was obliged to bolster it, so that voluntarism could once again function effectively. This, the Conservative leadership repeatedly insisted, was the purpose of the Industrial Relations Bill. The party apparently came not to bury voluntarism but to praise it. Yet even this image of the Bill failed to calm the unease of some Conservatives over the degree of legislation being prepared.

As was noted in the previous chapter, the move towards a legislative industrial relations policy did not enjoy unanimous or unequivocal support in the parliamentary Conservative Party; reservations were harboured in some quarters over the wisdom of seeking legislative remedies to Britain's industrial relations problems, and these doubts were compounded by anxieties over the efficacy of some of the specific proposals entailed in the programme of reform. Therefore the introduction of the Industrial Relations Bill occasioned a continuation of the debates within the Conservative Party itself over the issue of trade union and industrial relations reform. Indeed, the differences of opinion which had manifested themselves during the opposition years were refuelled as the Bill proceeded through Parliament.

At a general level, there remained different perceptions or explanations by Conservatives as to the root causes of the problems besetting British industrial relations, notably the problem of unofficial strikes. Three main interpretations continued to be advanced to account for the incidence of unofficial strikes and breaches of collective agreements.

First, there was the belief that the development of large-scale national or multi-national industries and firms had led to a growing gap between management and workers on the shopfloor, resulting in a breakdown in communication. This development was clearly identified by Philip Holland, when he referred to the remoteness of managers from their employees. This problem, he argued, arose because of the rapid growth in the size and complexity of industrial undertakings. Consequently, Holland – himself a former personnel manager – believed that the remedy was to be found in the pursuit, by employers and managers, of far more enlightened policies, involving better communication and consultation between the two 'sides' of industry (*HC Debates*, 5th series, vol.807: c.719 and c.721–2).

The second, but clearly related, explanation preferred by some Conservatives to account for the problems of British industrial relations suggested that the labour process itself served to engender a feeling of alienation and anomie amongst workers on the shopfloor. The alleged outcome was that minor grievances or discontents were prone to 'flare up' into more serious industrial disputes. For example, Barney Hayhoe, a backbench MP elected in 1964, noted how poor working conditions, coupled with dull, frustrating, or repetitive work, could lead people to take action which was less wise than they might normally envisage. He emphasised that good industrial relations could only be based on good human relations, and could only be attained by 'fair' and 'reasonable' behaviour by all concerned (ibid.: c.667–8).

Third, there was that hardy Conservative perennial, the claim that Britain's industrial relations problems were caused by 'extremists', 'wreckers', 'militants', 'subversives', etc., who constantly fomented unrest as part of a concerted effort to sabotage British industry. Thus did William Clark, a backbencher, allude to 'disruptive forces in industry', 'Reds under the bed', and 'a hooligan element' at work in British industry. Clark was adamant that it was 'militants' in the trade union movement who had largely 'precipitated the opening of the floodgates of wage demands' (ibid.: c.685–7). Meanwhile, Dudley Smith inveighed against 'wildcat strike leaders' and 'Communist agitators'. He believed that the transfer of power to the shopfloor in the trade union movement had not been accompanied by a transfer of responsibility (*HC Debates*, 5th series, vol.808: c.1075–6).

Continued controversy over the closed shop

Meanwhile, the closed shop (and agency shop) continued to be a source of controversy amongst Conservatives debating the Industrial Relations Bill in Parliament. Initially, the Bill provided workers with a right not to belong to a trade union if they did not wish to do so, something which was seen as a landmark in the 'libertarian' attempts at outlawing the closed shop. Conservatives such as Dudley Stewart-Smith were jubilant that 'mercifully', the closed shop and its tyranny would be 'killed off' by the Bill. However, such joy was significantly tempered by the Bill's 'agency shop' provisions (stipulating that in certain cases workers would be expected to join a trade union after commencing employment, or else pay an equivalent of the union subscription fee to a charity; failure to do either would render employees who lost their job as a consequence ineligible to claim unfair dismissal). Stewart-Smith considered the 'agency shop' provisions to be 'indefensible', effectively constituting 'a continued form of closed shop, plus or minus a few days'. In believing this to be 'intolerable', Stewart-Smith made a special request to Robert Carr to delete all reference to the agency shop from the Bill (*HC Debates*, 5th series, vol.808: c.1024–7).

In sharp contrast, David Mitchell asked Carr whether, having 'cleaned up some of the dustier corners of the trade union movement', it would be so daring for the Conservative Party to accept the idea of a 'post-entry' union shop, which would enable all employees to have an influence on the affairs and activities of their union (*HC Debates*, 5th series, vol.807: c.711).

Yet it was during the committee and report stages of the Industrial Relations Bill that it became evident just how problematic the closed shop and the proposed 'agency shop' were for the Conservative Party. As ever, there was a tension between the emphasis on the liberty of the individual, entailing the right to choose whether or not to join a trade union, and the desire for greater discipline and order in industry and industrial relations. As John Boyd-Carpenter noted, trade unions and employers often supported the closed shop for reasons of practicality in day-to-day industrial relations. None the less, he was adamant that an even more important consideration was involved than the practical convenience of those in industry, namely the rights and freedom of the individual. Having alleged that the closed shop itself was 'a bad thing', because it constituted a form of compulsion of the individual in aid of a private organisation which was unaccountable to the rest of society, Boyd-Carpenter declared himself to be 'very unhappy' about the clause proposing to permit 'agency shop' agreements. Such a clause constituted a contradiction of the Conservative principles of liberty and individual freedom of choice, he argued. Indeed, such was Boyd-Carpenter's concern that he warned his party leadership that he might 'find it impossible to support' the clause in the lobbies (*HC Debates*, 5th series, vol.813: c.944–6).

Such an interpretation of Conservative principles earned Boyd-Carpenter a mild rebuke from his fellow backbencher, Sir Harmar Nicholls, who pointed out that another principle of Conservatism was that its adherents should not allow themselves to become slaves to dogma, but, instead, should be members of 'a practical party', which could recognise exceptions to the rule (ibid.: c.945).

Meanwhile, Nicholas Scott, a vice-chairperson of the Conservative backbench employment committee, was going so far as to argue that society ought not to be completely neutral about the right to join, or not to join, a trade union. Whilst desiring an adequate safeguard for those employees who genuinely wished to refrain from joining a trade union, Scott wanted the Industrial Relations Bill to make it clear that people ought to be members of trade unions. What he certainly did not want was a Bill whose provisions served to encourage apathy, non-involvement, and non-participation (*HC Debates*, 5th series, vol.810: c.625).

Another argument in favour of the agency shop was proffered by David Mitchell when he referred to the resentment felt by trade unionists when they witnessed 'free-riders' enjoying benefits gained by the unions whilst refusing to make any contribution themselves. Mitchell believed that the agency shop provision constituted a compromise between those who upheld the rights of individuals who did not wish to become trade union members, and those who acknowledged the 'tensions and embittered feelings' which union members felt towards 'free-riders'. In supporting the agency shop provisions, he alleged that 'the vast majority' of employees refusing to join a trade union did so, not on grounds of conscience or conviction, but because of a wish to avoid paying the subscription fee (ibid.: c.641–2).

Mitchell then proceeded to adumbrate yet another reason for avoiding measures which would encourage, or make it easy, for employees to leave, or refuse to join, a trade union, namely that they might provide 'an incitement to the silent, but responsible and politically disinterested, not to join a trade union'. Whilst opposed to compulsion, Mitchell pointed out that not only did people have a social and industrial duty to join a trade union but that the Bill's own professed objective of strengthening collective bargaining in British industry logically required that as many employees as possible belong to a trade union. Furthermore, he claimed, the oft-repeated references to encouraging 'responsibility' in industrial relations surely meant that the government ought to be encouraging the 'silent, responsible, and politically disinterested, to join, and play an active part in, their trade union, to counterbalance the hot heads'. For this reason, Mitchell was somewhat concerned that the Bill provided an equal right to be, or not to be, a trade union member 'as if they were one and the same thing', which he believed they were not (ibid.: c.643). Further support for an 'agency shop' was given by Barney Hayhoe, who believed that the objections of some of his colleagues were sometimes overstated (ibid.: c.666).

Partly through acknowledgement of industrial reality, and partly in response to proposals urged by backbenchers speaking on behalf of particular occupations, the government introduced a new clause during the report stage, allowing for 'approved closed shop' agreements which would permit the operation of a closed shop in certain industries or sectors of employment when it could be proved to be justifiable and necessary. It was envisaged that the clause would only

be applicable in a small number of instances. However, the introduction of the clause immediately caused consternation amongst
some Conservative backbenchers who feared that the measure might
'knock a large hole in the general principle against the closed shop'
(*HC Debates*, 5th series, vol.813: c.931). Yet Carr was emphatic that
the community had an interest in having good order in industry; this
entailed the maintenance of strong, stable, collective bargaining
machinery, coupled with the democratic right to respect, and give
effect to, the wishes of the majority, provided that adequate safeguards were provided for the minority. Carr also emphasised that
the right to join a trade union was of a different order to the right
not to join (ibid.: c.945).

The introduction of the clause permitting 'approved closed shop'
arrangements was warmly welcomed by Peter Emery, a Junior
Minister, who believed that it would prove to be of great value in
helping to secure industrial discipline. However much Conservatives
might abhor the fact, he argued, there were some industries where
management had become so remote from the workers on the
shopfloor that the maintenance of industrial discipline and order had
become the *de facto* responsibility of the trade unions themselves.
Consequently, Emery suggested that the operation of a closed shop
would enable a trade union to exert more control over militants or
other workers who failed to adhere to agreed procedures or collective bargains. Referring explicitly to the principle of individualism
subscribed to by neo-liberals such as Boyd-Carpenter, Emery insisted
that an individual's right to work was not the individual's right to
be able to disrupt an industrial organisation. Indeed, in this context,
Emery suggested that as the Industrial Relations Bill was primarily
concerned with obtaining a greater degree of industrial order and
discipline, the closed shop could go a long way towards securing
this objective (*HC Debates*, 5th series, vol.813: c.956–60). Not
surprisingly, Emery's somewhat enthusiastic endorsement of the
closed shop caused considerable consternation amongst his neo-
liberal backbench colleagues (ibid.: c.958).

The tension between the principle of individual liberty and the
pursuit of industrial order was also apparent in the debate over a
clause proposing that workers be permitted to belong to 'any such
trade union as he may choose'. John Page, a vice-chairperson of
the Conservative backbench employment committee, was concerned
that a completely free choice in this respect might result in the
fragmentation of British trade unionism, thereby increasing the
number of unions with which employers had to deal. Page thus

attempted – unsuccessfully – to introduce an amendment permitting workers to join 'an appropriate trade union'. Page's concern was shared by Philip Holland who also failed in his efforts to introduce a similar amendment.

A further source of disagreement within the Conservative Party concerned the clause in the Industrial Relations Bill stipulating that all collective agreements between employers and employees, management and unions, should be deemed legally binding on both parties, unless both expressly and explicitly stated otherwise at the outset. The Labour opposition proposed an amendment suggesting, instead, that all collective agreements should not be considered legally binding unless the parties stipulated otherwise. Whilst one Conservative lawyer, Raymond Gower, opposed this amendment, believing it 'absurd' that collective agreements should not be legally enforceable, another Conservative lawyer, Robert Awdry, expressed some sympathy for Labour's amendment. Awdry acknowledged that whilst, at the time of the general election, he had also been in favour of making collective agreements between the two sides of industry legally enforceable, he had since developed considerable doubts about the wisdom of such a measure. He therefore urged the government to give sympathetic consideration to Labour's amendment (*HC Debates*, 5th series, vol.810: c.1300–1).

Concern over a different issue was expressed by Christopher Woodhouse, a former CBI official who was unhappy about the prospect of individual trade union members, rather than unions as corporate bodies, being deemed liable for breaches over the Industrial Relations Bill. This was 'one feature of the Bill which seems bound to lead to trouble', he warned, for if an individual was really obstinate, then in the last instance the result would be imprisonment. If this stage was reached, Woodhouse feared, then 'martyrs' would be created, to whose support the unions and public opinion might rally, whilst at the same time the law itself might be brought into disrepute. Indeed, this was part of a more general concern which Woodhouse harboured, namely that the tenor of the Industrial Relations Act was overly legalistic, and thus likely to exacerbate Britain's industrial problems even further (*HC Debates*, 5th series, vol.808: c.1051 and c.1048). Such fears were very soon to be vindicated.

THE ISSUE OF INCOMES POLICY

The Heath government hoped that the restoration of 'responsible' trade unionism would in turn contribute to a concomitant moderation in wage demands and pay settlements. This would obviate the need for a formal incomes policy. The reform of industrial relations, and the rejection of incomes policies, were thus intimately and inextricably related. One leading backbench critic of the trade unions, Ronald Bell, had previously opined that the strengthening of 'responsible' trade union leaders would lead to moderation in the realm of wage demands and determination (*HC Debates*, 5th series, vol.706: c.47).

The rejection of formal incomes policy reflected the Heath government's view that wage increases had to be earned through higher productivity and efficiency. It was not the state's role to determine levels of pay. Yet the government was clearly responsible for wage determination in the public sector where it was, ultimately, the employer. As such, the approach of the Heath government was to 'stand firm' when faced with 'excessive' pay claims from public sector trade unions. This, in turn, was intended to set an example to the private sector, and encourage British management in general to follow suit. As one senior Cabinet Minister at the time, Reginald Maudling, explained, the government acted according to the premise that 'the main cause of wage inflation arose from the demands in the public sector', and it was assumed therefore that if these demands could be restrained, then a solution would have been found to the problem of wage inflation (Maudling 1978: 191).

Yet Maudling himself 'became more and more convinced that this was not an acceptable way of proceeding'. Given that the government was faced with the 'newly conscious monopoly power of the trade unions', and challenges from groups of workers such as refuse collectors, railwaymen, electricians, miners and local government employees, Maudling became convinced that 'a single coherent policy was required'. Consequently, late in the summer of 1971, Maudling sought to submit a paper (published – over one year later – in *The Times*, 12 September 1972) to the Cabinet in which he presented the case for greater government intervention in the realm of prices and incomes. The monopoly power of the trade unions, he argued, served to invalidate orthodox economic solutions to inflation, to the extent that neither greater competition nor the linking of the money supply to national output any longer provided remedies to inflation. If the government did attempt either of these approaches, Maudling claimed, the result would be that 'the socially powerful' would be able to increase their incomes at the expense of others. Furthermore, he pointed out, a competitive economy tended to enhance the power of stronger trade unions, whilst in a period of economic downturn, many employers were likely to accede to union wage demands because they could not afford to 'ride out' industrial action and disruption. Either way, the old, classical economic solutions were no longer relevant to the wholly new political situation which had developed by the 1970s.

Following on from this analysis, Maudling concluded that the Heath government (indeed, any government) was faced with two options concerning incomes. The first option was to pursue a policy of conflict, of 'fighting it out', and thereby defeat inflationary forces. The second option was to encompass the main social forces in modern society, thereby bringing them into the sphere of economic policy-making. As policies based on conflict would no longer work, Maudling insisted, the government had little alternative but to accept that 'in modern political circumstances', a capitalistic economy had to be prepared to accept a far greater degree of systematic control over prices and incomes than had hitherto been considered desirable or acceptable.

Maudling found himself isolated within the Cabinet, however, as his colleagues maintained their opposition to a formal incomes policy. Indeed, Maudling's paper was the subject of a sharp disagreement between him and Heath, who requested him to refrain from circulating his paper, a request with which he complied. The prevailing view amongst Cabinet Ministers during this time was neatly encapsulated in a pamphlet published by the Conservative Political Centre, in which it was claimed that incomes policies constituted an attempt by government to determine wages and prices in domains in which they had no direct responsibility. Furthermore, such policies had always failed in the past, degenerating either into meaningless verbiage or into a form of totalitarian economic control (Conservative Political Centre 1971: 1). The Heath government's official policy therefore remained one of non-intervention in private sector wage determination, whilst applying an 'N minus 1' formula to the public sector, whereby each year's pay increase was to be 1 per cent less than that of the previous year.

THE FAILURE OF THE INDUSTRIAL RELATIONS ACT

The introduction of the Industrial Relations Act presented the Heath government with a paradox, for whilst trade union members as individual citizens and voters expressed their overall support for industrial relations reform, many of them were none the less readily mobilised against the Act by their union leaders. Whilst this opposition was expressed through marches, rallies and demonstrations as part of a campaign to 'Kill the Bill', the main, and by far the most effective, tactic pursued by the TUC was to ensure that most affiliated unions refused to register with the newly appointed Registrar of Trade Unions and Employers' Associations, a policy which did much to undermine the legislation. The Industrial Relations Act was further undermined by the reluctance of many large employers to instigate proceedings against their employees in accordance with the Act's provisions, for fear of exacerbating distrust and conflict between the two sides of industry. However, what ultimately undermined the Industrial Relations Act was a series of court cases and verdicts during the spring and summer of 1972, leading a number of commentators to describe the events leading to the Act's downfall as 'a farce' (Dorfman 1979: 58; Stewart 1977: 127; Taylor 1993: 199).

In March 1972, dockers on Merseyside refused to handle the goods of the container company, Heaton's, because of the firm's employment of non-dock labour. The Industrial Relations Court (established under the Act) instructed the Transport and General Workers' Union (TGWU), to which the dockers belonged, to order them to cease their action. In accordance with the TUC's policy of non-compliance with the Industrial Relations Act, the TGWU refused both to appear before the Court and to instruct the dockers concerned to stop their boycott of Heaton's. The Industrial Relations Court thus imposed a fine of £5,000 on the TGWU, which was soon increased to £50,000 when the action by the dockers continued unabated.

At this point, the TUC suspended its policy of non-recognition, in order to enable the TGWU to challenge the case in the Court of Appeal. There the union argued that it could not be held legally responsible for the unauthorised actions of individual members. The Court of Appeal upheld the TGWU's appeal, thereby highlighting the tension inherent in the Industrial Relations Act between enhancing the freedom of individual trade union members on the one hand, and strengthening the power of union leaders on the other. The Appeal Court's decision was subsequently overturned by the Law Lords in July 1972, but by this time two other similar cases had been brought before the courts.

In the first, three dockers in east London, who were also 'blacking' a container firm because it employed non-dock labour, were threatened with imprisonment. In this case, the Industrial Relations Court acted in accordance with the Appeal Court's verdict in the Heaton's case, thereby declaring that if a trade union could not be held liable for the unauthorised actions of its members, then the members themselves had to be deemed legally responsible. The threatened imprisonment of the dockers was countered by the threat of a national dock strike, whereupon the Solicitor-General miraculously appeared to intervene on behalf of the dockers, and ensure that the case against them was quashed.

The final nail in the coffin of the Industrial Relations Act once again involved dockers who were 'blacking' a firm for employing non-dock labour. When the dockers involved refused to halt their action as instructed by the Industrial Relations Court, five shop stewards deemed responsible for organising the action were found guilty of contempt of court, whereupon they were sent to Pentonville Prison. This led to an immediate national dock strike, as well as sympathy stoppages by various other groups of workers. The situation was resolved when the Law Lords delivered their verdict in the Heaton's case, for this reiterated that it was the trade union, not its individual members, who were liable in such cases. This served to exonerate the 'Pentonville five' (as they had become known), who were released, on 1 August 1972, to a hero's welcome from many other trade unionists. The Industrial Relations Act was in tatters.

Trade union hostility towards the Industrial Relations Act was by no means the only source of industrial conflict with which the Heath government had to contend during the early 1970s. There was also a number of strikes, particularly in the public sector, in response to the government's 'N minus 1' pay policy. The most serious of these strikes was that pursued by the miners during the winter of 1971–2.

The National Union of Mineworkers (NUM) had commenced an overtime ban in November 1971, in support of a pay claim which was five times the amount being offered by the National Coal Board, the latter claiming that it could not offer any more because of the Heath government's public sector pay policy. Following a ballot of its members, the NUM began a national strike in January 1972, one which acquired considerable notoriety because of the 'mass picketing' which accompanied it. This picketing was by no means confined to the pits themselves; ports and power stations were also picketed. The effects permeated the whole of British society, with electricity cuts and black-outs being imposed in order to conserve dwindling coal supplies.

Eventually, the NUM secured a settlement which was considerably in excess of the Heath government's official figure, the miners' case having effectively been vindicated by an inquiry headed by Lord

Wilberforce. The episode grievously undermined the government's stance on pay, thus adding to the problems it was already encountering over the Industrial Relations Act. It was in this context that Heath embarked on a major policy U-turn, and laid 'Selsdon Man' (see p. 103) to rest.

HEATH'S U-TURN

By the beginning of 1972, therefore, Heath was offering to sit down with trade union leaders and employers, in an attempt at finding 'a more sensible way' of dealing with the problems of inflation and industrial relations. A number of particularly conciliatory statements emanated from Heath and some of his ministerial colleagues, all intended to prepare the ground for a new rapport between the Conservative government and the trade unions. Thus whilst Heath himself was proclaiming that the Industrial Relations Act was no longer a barrier to good contacts between the government and the trade union movement, a Cabinet Minister, Peter Walker, was talking of a partnership between the government, the trade unions, and the employers' representatives, which would thereby establish a 'trialogue'. This sudden change of strategy and stance, a senior Conservative was later to explain, was born of the realisation by the Cabinet that the party could not prosper by setting class against class – however many warlike telegrams its supporters might send (Hurd 1979: 105).

The Conservative government now proclaimed its objective of developing a fast-growth economy, with a high level of employment and a steady rise in real earnings. This was to depend, however, on the ability to contain price rises and avoid further social division, raising difficult questions about collective bargaining and methods of settling disputes, questions for which, Heath admitted, the government had no easy or readily available solutions. He none the less emphasised that the government was not impressed by Britain's experience of incomes policies. He referred to its desire to commence discussions with trade union leaders and employers, so that they could together examine possible methods or solutions. This change in approach was warmly welcomed in some quarters of the Conservative Party, where it was suggested that the implementation of 'tough, long-term legislation' during the first two years in office ought to be followed by the adoption of a more conciliatory approach (Bow Group 1972: 5).

Government spokesmen remained adamant, however, that the Industrial Relations Act would remain on the Statute Book. Indeed,

Carr was convinced that Britain 'would never again be without some framework of industrial relations law, which would include many of the provisions of the present Act.' Yet whilst ruling out any possibility of repealing the Act, Heath intimated a willingness to discuss with the TUC some of their specific objections to the measure. If a convincing case was made that changes to the Industrial Relations Act were necessary, he promised, then the government would respond (*HC Debates*, 5th series, vol.840: c.74 and c.207). This pledge was condemned by Jock Bruce-Gardyne as an indication that the Conservative leadership was in the mood for 'industrial appeasement' (Bruce-Gardyne 1974: 88).

Yet with both unemployment and inflation increasing during 1972, it became clear that the Conservative government's room for manoeuvre was restricted. The party leadership veered towards a policy of voluntary wage restraint, to be secured through the estab-lishment of a 'concordat' between the government, the TUC, and the CBI. The alternative to a voluntary agreement, it was reckoned, was either further legal intervention, renewed confrontation, or continuing inflation. None of these options was deemed desirable or acceptable by the Conservatives' parliamentary leadership.

Neither was the strategy, advocated by neo-liberals, of simply restricting the growth of the money supply. At the Conservatives' 1972 Annual Conference, the Chancellor, Anthony Barber, warned that the consequences of such a strategy would be less economic growth, less investment, less modernisation, less industrial activity, lower living standards, and even higher unemployment. This was not a price he was prepared to pay. Barber acknowledged that the Government's approach involved some interference with the free and untrammelled interplay of market forces, but he pointed out that if rampant inflation ensued, then this itself would play far greater havoc with market forces than a prices and incomes policy. Barber thus called on those 'latter-day laissez-faire liberal theorists' in the Conservative Party to recognise that the government's policies were in the interests of the whole country, which was what ultimately mattered.

By the summer of 1972, therefore, three general options were being canvassed in the Conservative Party with regard to the issues of incomes policy and tripartism. First, the neo-liberal proposal of much greater reliance on market forces, restriction of the growth of the money supply, and the abandonment of tripartite decision-making and incomes policy. Proponents of such a strategy, such as Enoch Powell and John Biffen, recognised that unemployment would significantly increase, but believed this to be unavoidable anyway, due to the inevitable failure of any incomes policy.

Second, there was advocacy of a voluntary agreement, between the government, the TUC, and the CBI, to limit, or even freeze, wage and price increases for a given period of time. With inflation at 8 per cent, this was the course pursued by Heath, and many of his senior colleagues, during much of 1972. Not only was the consequent interference with market forces deemed justifiable, as emphasised by Barber, it was also feared that a continued rise in unemployment might threaten social stability, and even the legitimacy of the British political system itself.

The third option canvassed in some quarters of the Conservative Party during 1972 was the imposition of a statutory prices and incomes policy. Advocacy of such a measure was often made with reference to the inability, or unwillingness, of trade unions to adhere to a voluntary pay policy. In a situation where a few powerful trade unions could create or sustain inflationary pressures, it was argued, statutory measures were a regrettable necessity, for such inflationary pressures could not be contained by fiscal or monetary policies alone. Thus, according to a Bow Group publication on the issue, the contemporary labour market was so imperfect that the 'economic' objections to an incomes policy no longer carried much conviction. Indeed, it was alleged that those who sought salvation in the 'solution' of fairy-tale economics were engaging in 'a form of economic masturbation' (Nelson-Jones/Bow Group, circa 1972).

As already intimated, it was the second of these options which the Heath government pursued throughout the summer of 1972. A meeting in July, between Heath and the General Council of the TUC, to discuss both the Industrial Relations Act and the economic situation was followed a few days later by a meeting between Heath and a deputation from the CBI. During the latter meeting, employers' representatives made clear their willingness to participate in tripartite talks, although they emphasised their opposition to statutory controls on prices and incomes. Soon afterwards, the first 'trialogue' took place, following which Heath announced that the government, the TUC, and the CBI had reached 'general agreement on the aim of achieving a steady rise in real earnings, and on the need to approach the problem of inflation by working out sensible arrangements on a voluntary basis' (*HC Debates*, 5th series, vol. 841: c.163).

NEO-LIBERAL ANGER ON THE CONSERVATIVE RIGHT

Having seen their party elected on a programme which had promised to reduce trade union power, and had eschewed incomes policy in favour of a return to 'the market', Conservative neo-liberals were filled with disgust and disbelief as their leadership enacted a swift U-turn, and began holding regular discussions with the TUC in order to formulate a voluntary incomes policy. Indeed, the rapid reversal of the government's original policies prompted the formation of the Selsdon Group, which sought a return to 'those true Conservative policies' which the party had adopted at its Selsdon Park conference prior to the 1970 election. In advocating a restoration of the free market, the Selsdon Group described itself as composed of 'classical liberals', who believed that only 'a policy of economic freedom can give the individual the degree of choice and independence essential to his dignity' (*The Times*, 8 October 1973).

Not for the first time – or the last – Enoch Powell proved to be the Conservative Party's most trenchant and eloquent critic of incomes policy and of the direction in which the Heath government was moving. Having reiterated his well-known thesis about the relationship between inflation and the money supply, and the concomitant irrelevance of incomes policy, Powell insisted that government hopes of ending inflation without accompanying economic dislocation or unemployment were a 'will-o'-the-wisp', which tempted political travellers onto the quicksand of incomes policy (quoted in *The Times*, 28 October 1973).

By 1972, however, Powell's economic arguments had acquired a wider audience in the Conservative Party, particularly amongst newer and younger MPs who had no real recollection of the 'Great Depression' and mass unemployment of the 1930s, and who therefore had little sympathy with the post-war commitment to Keynesian economics, consensus politics, and the concomitant priority accorded to the maintenance of full employment. Richard Body, for example, called upon the Right to re-examine its principles, whilst simultaneously urging every government Minister and most backbenchers to read Hayek's *The Road to Serfdom* (Body 1972: 8). Meanwhile, a backbench finance committee meeting during the early summer warned that if the government were to end up introducing a statutory prices and incomes policy, it would be opposed in the lobbies by several of its backbenchers. The warning had been issued in response to a call by a backbench MP, Peter Tapsell, for a statutory freeze on wages, prices, and dividends, a measure which, he claimed, enjoyed support in the party (*The Times*, 13 June 1972).

Other Conservative critics of incomes policy emphasised the inability of the trade unions to adhere to any such agreements. According to John Biffen, the reality of shopfloor power in the trade union movement made the idea of enticing a tame set of union moguls to 10 Downing Street or Chequers, where they would answer on behalf of their members, 'a proposition of the greatest potential delusion' (*HC Debates*, 5th series, vol.845: c.927–8). Wyn Roberts, a Parliamentary Private Secretary, was also sceptical about the ability of the TUC to enforce a voluntary incomes policy, presciently predicting that the failure of a voluntary agreement would almost inevitably be followed by the introduction of a statutory incomes policy, which was a very dangerous route to pursue (*HC Debates*, 5th series vol.840: c.99–100).

Further objections were raised by Teddy Taylor. Referring to the allegedly increasing support in the Conservative Party for a statutory freeze on prices and incomes, Taylor warned that such a 'crazy and impractical' policy would be a recipe for industrial chaos. In any case, he argued, a freeze on wages and prices was not a viable proposition in a country which was so dependent on imported goods and commodities, the prices of which were determined by world markets (Taylor 1972). Supporters of a wages freeze were also strongly criticised by backbencher Robert Taylor (no relation), who believed that such Conservatives were putting short-term electoral considerations before the long-term national interest (quoted in ibid.).

Following on from these 'economic' objections to incomes policy, either voluntary or statutory, were concomitant 'political' objections to tripartism, with which incomes policy was inextricably connected. John Biffen expressed particular concern at the role allocated to the TUC and the CBI, in both national decision-making and in enforcing the resulting agreements. He warned of the danger of 'subcontracting authority away from the House', a move which would, he alleged, undermine respect for Parliament and the democratic process. If the government were to be tempted by such a policy, Biffen proclaimed, it would inevitably be dragged back to the 'simple realities of economic life' (*HC Debates*, 5th series, vol.845: c.927–8). Jock Bruce-Gardyne expressed similar concern about the 'diminution of the sovereignty of Parliament', which might arise from attempts to involve the TUC and the CBI in economic management and decision-making (ibid.: 1974).

Yet for proponents of incomes policy and tripartism, it was *their* perception of the 'simple realities of economic life' which played a major part in their rejection of neo-liberalism. For Conservative neo-corporatists, the 'reality' of trade union power (and the political unacceptability of high unemployment) made reliance on, or reversion to, unfettered free market forces an impracticable proposition. The most realistic approach for such Conservatives was to incorporate trade unions into political and economic decision-making, in the hope that their power would thereby be channelled in more constructive directions; the consent of the unions for policy decisions to which they themselves had been party would also be obtained. For one Conservative industrialist, a policy such as more trade union participation in industry would go a long way 'towards removing the idea that a union should be in a permanent state of conflict with an employer' (*HC Debates*, 5th series, vol.840: c.119). There was also a belief that an 'incorporatist' strategy would play a major part in the creation of One Nation, giving organised labour an important stake within the existing socio-economic order. According to Conservative neo-corporatists, this would prove a far more effective strategy for sustaining freedom and democracy than a return to atavistic neo-liberalism.

With both inflation and unemployment increasing, the Conservative leadership spent the summer, and much of the autumn, of 1972 meeting TUC and CBI representatives, in an attempt to gain a voluntary agreement on the restraint of prices and incomes. After some reticence and suspicion on the part of a few union leaders, talks with the CBI and the government became more involved and detailed, with a number of working groups being established to look at the issues of pay and prices in more detail. By the early autumn, it seemed that the issue was no longer one of whether to agree to a voluntary incomes policy, but what the specificities of such a policy were to be.

Towards the end of September, the Conservative leadership proposed a policy whereby pay rises would be limited to £2 per week, and price increases would not exceed 5 per cent per year. On this basis, the government promised to pursue a 5 per cent annual rate of growth during the next two years. However, the TUC demanded far stronger – perhaps statutory – measures on prices, something which Heath and his colleagues were not willing to concede if agreement on pay were to remain voluntary (see Dorfman 1979: 79–86 for a fuller account). Once again, the Conservative leadership found its room for manoeuvre severely limited. As critics had pointed out, a voluntary incomes policy would fail because of trade union inability or unwillingness to 'deliver the goods'. By the autumn of 1972, therefore, only one option remained.

A STATUTORY PAY FREEZE

On 6 November 1972, Heath announced a ninety-day freeze on prices, pay, rent, and dividends, to be enforced by a Counter-Inflation (Temporary Provisions) Bill. It was envisaged that this measure would constitute a short-term response to the problem of inflation, in lieu of a long-term concordat between the government, the TUC, and the CBI. As such, Heath hoped that the 'freeze' would not be permitted to stand in the way of resumed tripartite discussions concerning economic policy and management.

Heath's announcement outraged many Conservative neo-liberals, who felt that the principles and policies on which the party had fought and won the last general election had now been completely abandoned. Their exasperation was compounded by the fact that the suspension of market forces entailed in the pay and prices freeze was to be a prelude to a permanent incomes policy. Seen from the neo-liberal perspective, the government's pursuit of a 'freeze', to be followed by a move towards neo-corporatism, constituted both a betrayal of the Conservative principles of individualism, the free market, and minimal government intervention in social and economic affairs, and also a rejection of Conservatism's traditional respect for the lessons learnt from historical experience.

The announcement of the ninety-day freeze led Powell to enquire whether Heath had taken leave of his senses in introducing a policy which was in direct contravention of the party's deepest commitments. So strong was his opposition to the measure that Powell was to vote against the government at the end of the second reading of the Counter-Inflation (Temporary Provisions) Bill. Before doing so, however, he once again reiterated his argument that inflation was the outcome of the rate of increase in the money supply exceeding the output of goods and services. As such, he insisted, inflation could only be controlled by government action to restrict the increase in money supply: an incomes policy was thus an irrelevance (*HC Debates*, 5th series, vol. 845: c.885–91).

Similar arguments were advanced by Nicholas Ridley, a back-bencher, who believed the attempt to control inflation through a statutory prices and incomes policy, rather than via a curb on the increase in the money supply, was to indulge in 'economic Canutism'.

Unlike Powell, however, Ridley was prepared to support the government in the lobbies, but urged it to use the following three months to adjust the money supply (ibid.: c.1039 and 1043). Unlike his fellow neo-liberals Jock Bruce-Gardyne, John Biffen, Neil Marten, and Anthony Fell, Ridley did not abstain during the division on the second reading.

To some extent, therefore, there was disagreement among Conservative neo-liberals over whether the government's policy was totally undeserving of their support, or whether qualified support could be proffered on the grounds that the policy would provide a 'breathing space', during which time the government would be able to develop or implement more 'acceptable' policies. Neo-liberal supporters of this latter perspective also suggested that the prices and incomes freeze might at least provide a 'psychological' shock to the electorate, by indicating the seriousness of the economic situation which faced the country. A considerable number of neo-liberals were thus prepared to give the government qualified support in the circumstances, even though this invariably conflicted with their opposition to incomes policies in principle.

Other Conservatives were far less reticent in proffering their support for the government's policy on prices and incomes. For some of them, such as David Knox, secretary of the Conservative back-bench finance committee, inflation was as much a social problem as an economic one, due to the rising expectations which many people had acquired during the 1960s. During this period, it was argued, living standards had stabilised, but expectations remained high. An important consequence of this had been the emergence of more militant trade unionism, as people sought to satisfy their expectations through higher wages. According to Knox's analysis, economic growth was an absolute prerequisite of reducing cost inflation to tolerable limits. Such growth could not be achieved through a strict control of the money supply, because this would serve to depress demand. The necessary alternative, it was thus argued, was to have an incomes policy, voluntary if possible, but statutory if necessary (ibid.: c.1107–10).

Reginald Maulding also emphasised his continued support for an incomes policy, arguing that the monopoly power of the trade unions made such a policy essential. In an era of increasing competition and interdependence in industry and the economy, coupled with the increased specialist skills attained by many workers who could no longer be easily replaced by volunteers in the event of an industrial dispute, Maudling was emphatic that the power of the trade unions could not be dealt with through legislation. Neither could conflict or confrontation offer a solution, he insisted, for any such attempt would do great damage to the nation, causing Britain to become a deeply and bitterly divided society.

Maudling also rejected the policies of the 'monetary enthusiasts', arguing that the effect of attempting to compress the money supply would be to ensure that those with powerful organisations behind them would continue to press home their demands at everyone else's expense. At the same time, unemployment would rise, the economy would stagnate, and investment would wither, he warned. Consequently, Maudling supported the government's prices and incomes freeze, believing that it would provide a breathing space during which time a voluntary prices and incomes policy could be formulated. Without such a policy, he claimed, Britain's future prospects would be disastrous (ibid.: c.1065–6). Not dissimilar arguments were advanced elsewhere in the Conservative Party, one example being the claim that without an incomes policy Britain was unlikely to remain a capitalist democracy (Nelson-Jones/Bow Group, circa 1972: 19), whilst Peter Tapsell alluded to the 'unacceptable social and economic costs' in terms of bankruptcies, unemployment, postponed investment, and loss of production that would be incurred if the Conservative Party sought a drastic tightening of the money supply instead of an incomes policy (*HC Debates*, 5th series, vol.845: c.878). Similar support for an incomes policy was offered by David Knox (ibid.: c.1107).

Against such claims, the neo-liberals in the Conservative Party found it necessary to argue that social stability would be jeopardised by continuing inflation, unchecked by restrictions on the money supply. Powell explained that by attributing inflation to wage increases, supporters of incomes policy might inadvertently encourage one group of citizens to blame another group for the country's economic problems. The outcome, he warned, would not only be increased conflict in industrial relations, but also increasing tension and bitterness in social relations. Following on from this line of thinking – which was endorsed by Timothy Raison (ibid.: c.1087) – Powell insisted that recognition of the true monetary causes of inflation was the essential key to restoring national unity and social harmony (Powell 1969: 168–92; *HC Debates*, 5th series, vol.845: c.890).

The Conservative government's introduction of a prices and incomes freeze also caused some disagreement within party 'factions' such as the Monday Club. Thus one senior official urged the Monday

Club to support the government on this issue, arguing that however distasteful it might find a statutory prices and incomes policy or 'freeze', the alternative of 'economic anarchy and vaulting price rises' would be even more unpalatable. It was claimed that the introduction of the 'freeze' was not the occasion for rigid adherence to theory; the situation had become so parlous that action had to be taken to allow the government to tread water whilst seeking a better means of ordered economic progress (*Monday News*, November 1972). The economic policy group of the Monday Club, however, was less sympathetic, complaining that the 'freeze' marked an important stage in the deliberate abandonment of the economic policy upon which the Conservative Party had fought and won the 1970 election (ibid.).

The chairman of the Monday Club, Jonathan Guinness, meanwhile was advocating both an incomes policy and a reduction in the money supply. He was convinced that Powell without Heath spelt social tension leading to revolution, whilst Heath without Powell meant a futile attempt at using incomes policy alone as a method of reducing inflation. The main advantage of an incomes policy, it was alleged, was that it would provide for some semblance of 'fairness' and 'justice' in the battle against inflation (*The Times*, 17 November 1972).

This last perspective also had its advocates outside the Monday Club, for there were Conservative MPs who wanted the government to pursue a dual strategy of incomes policy and money supply reduction, rather than see them as 'either/or' strategies. Thus did Sir Robin Turton, a backbench MP, argue that a prices and incomes policy could only succeed if the nation's money supply was linked to the output of goods and services. Such a policy, however, needed to incorporate notions of 'social justice' and 'fairness', he insisted (*HC Debates*, 5th series, vol.845: c.868).

In spite of the disagreements which manifested themselves in the Conservative Party in the wake of Heath's announcement of a statutory prices and incomes freeze (including a call by one back-bencher for Heath to be replaced as Conservative leader and Prime Minister), the Counter-Inflation (Temporary Provisions) Bill passed its second reading with a majority of thirty-five votes. However, the parliamentary support given to the Bill by Conservative back-benchers derived from differing expectations about what the measure was to be followed by. For the neo-liberals, the Bill was envisaged as a breathing space, during which the money supply could be dealt with, to be succeeded by a return to 'the market'. For others, it constituted the prelude to a welcome return to neo-corporatism.

Having succeeded in passing the Bill, the Heath government entered 1973 faced with the task of introducing the Counter-Inflation Bill proper, a measure which would inevitably fuel further the disagreements manifesting themselves within the Conservative Party. Indeed, a few days before the second reading, Anthony Barber was sent to explain the government's position to a meeting of the party's backbench finance committee. About twenty-four MPs made their dissatisfaction with the government's approach clear to Barber, with Timothy Raison reminding him of the party's election pledges, and Norman Lamont (a former merchant banker) offering the Chancellor an exposition on the paramount importance of the money supply. None the less, most of the backbenchers present promised to give the government their support in the lobbies, albeit grudgingly in several cases, whilst continuing to maintain their objections in principle. However, at least six backbenchers made it apparent that they intended voting against the government on the second reading, with a further twelve MPs intimating that they might abstain.

Certainly some of the public comments and statements made by various neo-liberals did not augur well for the government. On the eve of the second reading, Richard Body was warning Heath that the government policy was doomed because it failed to identify excessive government expenditure as the root cause of inflation (*The Times*, 24 January 1973). A few days previously, backbencher Ronald Bell, after having expressed serious doubts about just how transitional the statutory controls would actually prove to be, insisted that prices and incomes policies of any kind were incompatible with the British way of life. As such, Bell argued, they were not, and could never be, genuine Conservative policies (*The Times*, 29 January 1973). Meanwhile, Nicholas Ridley was reiterating the view that whilst the measure might have a beneficial psychological effect, the battle against inflation needed to be fought with a 'proper' economic policy (*The Times*, 19 January 1973).

During the second reading of the Counter-Inflation Bill, Powell yet again denounced the government's approach, accusing his colleagues of contriving to pursue one of the 'hoariest futilities' in the history of British politics, namely the use of coercion to prevent the laws of supply and demand from expressing themselves (*HC Debates*, 5th series, vol. 849: c.977). Powell thus voted against the government on the second reading of the Bill, just as he had done with its predecessor.

On this occasion, however, he was not accompanied by any of his neo-liberal colleagues. Instead, critics of the government's policy, such as John Biffen, were prepared to support the Bill on the basis that it had 'a strong psychological element involved in it', which might serve to raise awareness about the need to overcome inflation. Even so, Biffen openly admitted that the basis on which he offered his support was not one which he found intellectually convincing (ibid.: c.1044).

During the committee stage of the Counter-Inflation Bill, however, Biffen and Nicholas Ridley tabled amendments which sought to reduce the period of the government's statutory prices and incomes policy from three years to one, thereby making it subject to annual re-examination and renewal. In spite of pleas from the government's Chief Whip, Biffen and Ridley pressed a division, whereupon they joined the opposition in the lobbies, thereby ensuring that their amendments enjoyed a majority of two, and that the government was defeated (for a more detailed account, see Norton 1976). However, the government was adamant that the three-year provision should remain part of the Bill, and therefore declared its intention of seeking to reverse this defeat during the report stage – which it subsequently did, in spite of abstentions by Ronald Bell, Richard Body, Jock Bruce-Gardyne, John Page, and Enoch Powell.

Whilst these neo-liberals were highly and vociferously critical of the government's approach, most Conservatives acknowledged that the parliamentary leadership's room for manoeuvre was severely limited, and that for the time being at least it needed to be given support. At the same time the supporters of neo-liberalism had not yet acquired sufficient influence in the Conservative Party to be able to spearhead an abandonment of the party's commitment to incomes policy.

Yet their numbers and influence on the backbenches had increased significantly since the mid-1960s, and by the second half of 1973 some of them were admitting that they had only refrained from launching a sustained attack on Edward Heath's leadership and policies because they had recognised that he was 'on probation'. According to one Conservative critic, backbenchers were waiting to see if any success would follow the government's measures, warning that 'if he [Heath] does not come up with the goods, then he is in very real trouble' (*The Times*, 19 October 1973). It was clear, therefore, that many Conservative MPs were extremely unhappy about the direction of the government's policies, and that in some instances patience with the party's leadership was wearing thin.

In the meantime, in the wake of the prices and incomes freeze, Conservative MPs became reluctant to deliver speeches in their constituencies because they feared that they would find themselves contradicting virtually everything they had previously proclaimed. Thus in the four months following the announcement of 'the freeze', the number of Conservative MPs making speeches relating to economic policy fell by half.

Whilst Conservative critics of the prices and incomes freeze constantly reiterated the thesis that it was excessive increases in the money supply, rather than wages and incomes, which were the root cause of inflation, the government's statutory pay policy also prompted a forceful restatement of 'political' objections. For some Conservatives, the pursuit of a statutory prices and incomes policy constituted a fundamental betrayal of Conservatism's free market principles. Indeed, one critic alleged that the Heath government was taking both the party and the country closer to the fascist state of Mussolini (Bevins 1973: 136). Not dissimilarly, it was claimed that Britain was being presented with the biggest policing operation ever conducted although it was the 'chief of police' (i.e. Heath) who had committed the crime. The outcome of the government's policy, it was warned, would be an ever increasing totalitarianism (letter in *The Times*, 23 January 1973). The allegedly grave implications for Britain's liberal democracy were also referred to by Harvey Proctor, who spoke ominously of 'dictatorial powers' being assumed, and of 'Government by Ministerial Decree'. Proctor wondered just how long Britain's parliamentary democracy could withstand the apparent aggrandisement of power by the executive (*Monday News*, February 1973).

That the Heath administration envisaged 'the freeze' being succeeded by a long-term voluntary agreement on economic issues, particularly incomes, between the government, the TUC, and the CBI, was of no comfort to neo-liberal critics of the statutory incomes policy. On the contrary, it was perceived as a further example of Heath's inability to recognise the true cause of inflation, whilst also apparently representing a further capitulation to the trade unions who were yet again to be given a prominent role in policy discussion and decision-making at national level. Ronald Bell thus echoed the sentiments of many neo-liberals when he deemed it quite wrong for the trade unions to be made part of a 'triumvirate', along with the CBI and the government (cited in ibid.).

Indeed, for the neo-liberals, the whole attempt at pursuing tripartism was itself part of the problem, for such a strategy was largely concerned with the notion of 'economic management'. Such a concept was viewed with grave concern by Conservative neo-liberals, conjuring up as it did visions of price fixing and wage determination by government and dominant producer groups, with scant regard for the laws of supply and demand, increases in the money supply, or the interests of consumers. For the neo-liberals, strict control of the money supply was what 'economic management' ought primarily to be concerned with, coupled with the removal of obstacles to the free play of market forces. The mode of economic management which the Heath government's move towards neo-corporatism entailed was thus perceived by neo-liberals as itself constituting much of the problem.

TROUBLE OVER TRIPARTISM

Apparently oblivious to the disagreement in the Conservative Party, Heath followed the enactment of the Counter-Inflation Bill with an invitation to the TUC to resume the negotiations which had broken down in autumn 1972. The objective of such discussions was to lay the foundation for a government–TUC–CBI partnership in economic management, which would include agreements on prices and incomes. According to James Prior, Cabinet Minister and Deputy Chairperson of the Conservative Party, the government was offering the trade unions an unprecedented share in the running of the British economy (*The Times*, 7 May 1973). At the Conservatives' 1973 Annual Conference, Trade and Industry Secretary Peter Walker explained that the government was seeking a means of creating a new sense of partnership in industry, which would serve to eradicate from the capitalist system any trace of the historic relationship of baron and serf, and the laissez-faire concept of master and servant.

Even before the invitation to the TUC to resume negotiations, there had been indications that the Conservative leadership was anxious not to offend or alienate the trade union leadership in lieu of a move back towards neo-corporatism. A call the previous November for social security payments to be refused to strikers was quashed by the government, on the grounds that introducing such a measure would kill, once and for all, any hopes of a voluntary agreement being reached between the Conservative government, the TUC, and the CBI. In other words, it was emphasised, this was not the best time to be acting on such an issue (*The Times*, 23 November 1972). A few months later, the government resisted strong backbench pressure for a change in the law relating to picketing, arguing that the existing law was adequate if properly enforced.

Yet at the same time, those Conservatives most reluctant to intervene or legislate further in the sphere of industrial relations were often the staunchest proponents of the government's move towards neo-corporatism, with all the 'interference' which that entailed by the state. For Conservative neo-corporatists, no conflict or contradiction was involved in this stance. Faced by charges from the party's neo-liberals that Conservative principles were being betrayed, the proponents of tripartism and incomes policy retorted that the Conservative Party had always been interventionist, from the Corn Laws onwards. This, it was pointed out, was because they had never accepted the sacrifice of ordinary Britons to a nineteenth-century liberal theory of the 'free market'. The rejection of such a 'theory' was justified by the insistence that economics and politics could not be separated (Nicholson 1973: 15). Thus did the debate in the party over incomes policy, industrial relations, and trade union reform draw upon differing historical interpretations of Conservative principles and policies, and the extent to which they were relevant or applicable to contemporary circumstances.

The Conservative Party's most recent experiences were also invoked as obvious justification for a more interventionist industrial and economic policy by the government. As Fred Silvester (a prospective parliamentary candidate elected in February 1974) baldly explained, the reason why the Conservative leadership changed its non-interventionist policies was because they had failed. To have continued with the pursuit of such policies, he argued, would have necessarily offended against the older and deeper traditions of the Conservative Party. Individual freedom and liberalism, Silvester emphasised, had to be weighed against the need for obligations towards the community, and the protection of the nation as a whole. This required that bounds had to be set to 'the competitive thrust' of both industrialists and trade unions, in order to protect other citizens. Silvester believed that if it was carefully executed, greater government intervention could be 'an effective, intelligent, humane and above all Tory thing to do' (Silvester 1973: 15–16).

Important though they were, principles and practicability were not the only factors to manifest themselves in the debates over the direction of Conservative policy during 1973. As always, electoral considerations were also of prime importance. In addition to Heath's concern over the potential political and electoral repercussions of unemployment remaining at the one million mark which had been reached in the winter of 1971–2, a number of backbenchers were concerned that the Conservative Party would suffer in the next general election if it were to readopt the same sort of policies that had been campaigned upon in the 1970 election, as some of their backbench colleagues were urging the leadership to do. Not the least of those Conservatives concerned about calls for a return to 'right-wing' policies were those MPs who would be defending narrow majorities in their constituencies. For them, success was to be found by aiming for the 'middle ground' (*The Times*, 12 July 1973).

This increasing tension between neo-liberals and neo-corporatists in the parliamentary Conservative Party was reflected amongst the constituency delegates at the 1973 Annual Conference. Although an economic policy motion calling on the government, the TUC, and the CBI to work together was carried by an overwhelming majority, it was attacked by several delegates, largely because of the corporatist connotations which were entailed. The government was criticised for assuming that the CBI represented all employers' interests and the TUC all workers' interests. It was called upon to pursue a policy for the benefit of all, rather than just for the advantage of dominant producer groups.

Inextricably linked to such criticism was the expression of concern for the 'little man' and the *petite bourgeoisie*, who, it was claimed, were being squeezed by larger firms. A number of factors were cited to explain this predicament. First, it was pointed out that whilst domestic prices had been restrained by the government's statutory policy, world prices had continued to rise. This made it more profitable for larger manufacturers to give priority to foreign trade and exports, rather than to concentrate on the domestic market.

Second, and directly related to this factor, small businesses found themselves having to import many of their supplies and materials; this exacerbated their financial difficulties, not merely because of the increased prices they had to pay on the world market, but also because they were subsequently prevented from passing on these increased costs to domestic customers through correspondingly higher prices.

Third, a recent upturn in business activity was alleged to have occurred and to have resulted in some shortages of materials and manpower. In this situation, suppliers were deemed to be giving priority to their larger customers. At the same time, it was argued that in a period of statutory wage restraint, larger firms were more capable than small businesses of offering their employees fringe benefits. Such difficulties and inequities, it was claimed, would not exist if free market forces were once again permitted to operate.

Such calls for a return to 'the market' were echoed at the Conservatives' 1973 Annual Conference by prospective Conservative candidate Anthony Marlow, who outlined his vision of a socio-economic order in which public expenditure was properly cut, and in which both the money supply and trade union power were curbed. Against such calls, however, the delegate from the Conservative Political Centre's National Advisory Committee enquired whether the advocates of neo-liberalism had adequately considered the fact that the million plus unemployed which would inevitably result was politically unacceptable.

The conference also heard strong criticism of the industrial relations motion, which alleged that many of the problems afflicting British industry arose from the unnecessary alienation of the workforce by outdated concepts of capitalism, and therefore called for increased worker participation and involvement in industrial decision-making. The motion also argued that Britain's industrial relations had been detrimentally affected by government legislation, not least the Industrial Relations Act itself. Although carried by a large majority, the motion was criticised by some delegates for being 'trendy' and for constituting 'woolly-minded idealism ... a recipe for industrial anarchy'. Yet the government employment spokesperson, Maurice Macmillan (son of Harold), remained adamant that workers should not be left at the mercy of economic forces. This stance, it was alleged, was consistent with both the old Tory tradition and the new Conservative desire to make enterprises fair as well as efficient.

What proved to be the final six months in office for the Conservative government was marked by increasing tension between the neo-liberals and the neo-corporatists in the party over its policies *vis-à-vis* industrial relations, wages, trade union reform, and tripartism. Such was the concern and anger of Conservative neo-liberals at the government's pursuit of an incomes policy, and its concomitant move towards neo-corporatism, that Patrick Jenkin, Chief Secretary to the Treasury, found himself heckled at a Bow Group meeting when he sought to defend the Heath administration's strategy by claiming that the Conservative Party had never been, and hopefully would never become, a party of unfettered laissez-faire liberalism. By contrast, the same meeting warmly welcomed John Biffen's reiteration of the 'Powellite' perspective on economic policy. Biffen claimed that he could not see 'any long-term future for the Conservative Party if it is committed in perpetuity to this kind of policy' (*The Times*, 11 October 1973).

Further disquiet over the government's strategy was expressed at a meeting of the 1922 Committee immediately after the 1973 Annual Conference, where Edward Heath found himself less than favourably received by Conservative backbenchers as he defended his government's approach to economic affairs and industrial relations. Having explained the administration's approach, he was subjected to some critical questioning by a number of backbenchers, including Ivor Stanbrook and Julian Ridsdale (*The Times*, 19 October 1973). Meanwhile, Teddy Taylor was calling upon Heath to readmit Enoch Powell to the Cabinet so that his economic views could be discussed more fully at the highest level. Far from being a 'lone and isolated renegade', Taylor warned, Powell's views had widespread support in the Conservative Party (*The Times*, 16 October 1973).

Yet with a general election imminent, the Heath government was even more anxious to pursue a conciliatory approach towards the trade unions. Whilst ruling out actual repeal of the Industrial Relations Act, it expressed its willingness to consider any amendments which were proposed and offered to listen to 'constructive proposals' concerning the future of the Act.

There was also a renewed emphasis by the Conservative leadership on the issue of employee participation in industry, with a concomitant reiteration of the notion that much of the unrest and disruption in industry arose from feelings of alienation and exclusion on the part of workers (Macmillan 1973; Oppenheim 1973; Conservative Political Centre 1973–4). Indeed, Heath informed delegates at the party's 1973 Annual Conference that the Conservative government's development of ideas and proposals for extending employee participation in industry would 'demonstrate once again, our belief that co-operation is a better policy than conflict'.

THE 1973–4 MINERS' STRIKE

However, debates in the Conservative Party were dramatically overtaken by events elsewhere. A massive increase in oil prices, due to military conflict in the Middle East during the autumn of 1973, posed immense economic difficulties for many western nations, particularly in the context of the fight against inflation. Yet with oil prices greatly increased, the importance – and, hence, the bargaining position – of miners and electricity workers was significantly enhanced. That engineers in the electricity industry had successfully pursued a pay claim in excess of the third stage of Heath's incomes policy 'norm' was problematic enough for the Conservative administration; however, it was the invoking of an overtime ban by the NUM, in pursuit of a wage increase well above the Phase Three limit, which was to prove most traumatic for the Heath government, and was to make trade union 'power' the issue of British politics and of the imminent general election.

Faced simultaneously with an oil crisis, industrial action by electricity engineers, and the miners' overtime ban – which was soon to become a full-scale strike – the government imposed a state of emergency, with the introduction of a three-day working week and systematic power cuts, in an attempt at conserving Britain's energy supplies.

For Conservative neo-liberals and advocates of trade union legislation, the industrial action by both electricity workers and miners, along with another dispute involving train drivers (which was seriously inconveniencing commuters in the south-east of England as well as hindering the transportation of coal supplies), was not merely a clear manifestation of trade union power, it was also deemed to illustrate the folly of seeking to implement an incomes policy, particularly a statutory one. Thus did Enoch Powell refer to the 'grim satisfaction' being experienced by neo-liberals as they saw their warnings being vindicated. The only viable solution, Powell reiterated, was the same as there had been all the time – a return to free collective bargaining, in the context of market forces, where the price of labour, like the price of anything else, would be determined by the laws of supply and demand (*HC Debates*, 5th series, vol. 867: 214–20).

According to such a perspective, the government was largely to blame for the situation it found itself in during the winter of 1973–4. Or as John Page argued, the government was in a mess with the miners because it had insisted on pursuing a statutory prices and incomes policy, which had subsequently left it 'boxed in' (*HC Debates*, 5th series, vol. 868: c.1305), whilst another backbencher, Anthony Fell, could not resist caustically commenting that 'chickens have a way of coming home to roost' (*HC Debates*, 5th series, vol. 864: c.725–7).

Yet the Heath government's statutory incomes policy, and the subsequent industrial disputes which arose, also served to win new converts to neo-liberalism in the Conservative Party. Most notable of these were Sir Keith Joseph, Margaret Thatcher, and Geoffrey Howe, who became fully converted to the concept of a free market economy in the wake of their experiences as Ministers in Heath's Cabinet. This 'conversion' was to have immensely important implications for

Conservative policies in the wake of the February 1974 election defeat.

Meanwhile, the proponents of neo-corporatism and incomes policy were claiming that the events leading up to the miners' strike served to underline the necessity of a policy on prices and incomes, which ought to be based on agreement between the government, the unions, and the CBI. Christopher Woodhouse, for example, was convinced that sooner or later it would be necessary to arrive at a multilaterally agreed system for vetting and controlling prices and incomes, within the limits of what was practicable and reasonable. It would have to include everyone involved in industry and government, he emphasised (*HC Debates*, 5th series, vol.868: c.1298).

For David Knox, meanwhile, the miners' strike 'highlighted one of the most important questions confronting any government in Britain today', namely whether to pursue full employment policies and to restrain price and wage increases through an incomes policy, or to deflate the economy to the point where insufficiency of demand would keep inflation under control. Knox expressed his unequivocal support for the former of these two alternatives, arguing that 'in a full-employment situation, a prices and incomes policy is absolutely essential ... indispensable' in order 'to prevent people using to the full the bargaining power that a full-employment economy gives them'. In other words, an incomes policy was the means by which to prevent certain workers from 'fully exploiting their market position' (ibid.: c.1255–60).

Whilst the government's experiences were encouraging some Conservatives to turn to neo-liberalism, those who maintained that incomes policy remained absolutely essential were also winning converts. Hence, William Shelton, a Parliamentary Private Secretary, admitted that whilst he had been doubtful about government pursuit of a prices and incomes policy in 1972, by the winter of 1973–4 he had come to believe that such a policy offered the only solution, because the government's initial free market 'solution' had failed (ibid.: c.1327). Such were the differences of opinion in the Conservative Party over the issues of free collective bargaining and incomes policy, particularly in the context of the industrial and economic situation which had developed by the winter of 1973–4, that an argument took place on the government backbenches in the House of Commons between Enoch Powell and Patrick McNair-Wilson (*HC Debates*, 5th series, vol.867: c.125). Neo-liberals and neo-corporatists alike thus cited the miners' strike as evidence of the efficacy of their respective policies.

The miners' strike also brought other themes to the fore on the backbenches, not the least of these being the claim that the dispute was the work of 'militants' and 'extremists'. This hardy Conservative perennial was assiduously cultivated by Ralph Howell, who alleged that the conflict was 'to do with Communists, Anarchists and Maoists who are determined to wrest power from the House of Commons' (*HC Debates*, 5th series, vol.868: c.1320), whilst William Clark was emphasising that Britain's economic situation could not be improved 'unless, somehow, we stop the militants in some trade unions'. This could best be achieved, he claimed, by alerting the moderates – 'the silent majority in the trade union movement' – who had been silent for too long. Certainly, Clark was of the opinion that the government 'must stop pussyfooting with the Communist element' (*HC Debates*, 5th series, vol.867: c.73). Following on from this, Wilfred Proudfoot, a backbench MP, called on the unions to organise their electoral systems better, for this would result in a more moderate union leadership (*HC Debates*, 5th series, vol.868: c.1320). In the meantime, backbench MP Frederick Burden was proclaiming that 'it is a question of Government or Communism' (*HC Debates*, 5th series, vol.867: c.270).

The miners' strike also afforded some Conservatives the opportunity of repeating the call for social security payments to strikers to be curbed. It was claimed that such payments meant that the taxpayer was subsidising those who went on strike. This, one neo-liberal complained, was 'utterly absurd', and constituted 'a misappropriation of public funds'. Indeed, the very availability of social security payments to strikers was deemed to be a factor which in itself encouraged 'extremism' and 'irresponsibility' on the part of trade unions and their officials (*HC Debates*, 5th series, vol.868: c.1321–2; see also Lawrence 1973: 6).

In the context of the miners' strike, many Conservatives were of the opinion that the government should call a general election as an alternative to giving in to the miners and their use of industrial power to break the incomes policy. In effect, the election would be fought on the question of 'Who Governs Britain?' – the government or the trade unions? Certainly, this was the issue underpinning Heath's decision – supported by his Cabinet colleagues – to call an election at that time. Yet a number of backbenchers failed to comprehend the point of a general election when the government had a majority of fifteen and up to eighteen months in office remaining. For these backbench critics, the decision to call an election under such circumstances seemed an act of cowardice, and suggested that Heath and his colleagues lacked the resolve to 'stand up' to the miners. Indeed, Enoch Powell declined to stand as a Conservative candidate, partly on the grounds that it was 'an essentially fraudulent election'.

Meanwhile, the Director-General of the CBI called for the repeal of the Industrial Relations Act, alleging that it had worsened relations between trade union officials and employers' representatives. In its Election Manifesto, the Conservative Party pledged itself to 'maintain the essential structure of the Industrial Relations Act', but at the same time promised to amend it 'in the light of experience, and after consultation with both sides of industry'. One of the amendments specifically promised 'to provide more effective control for the majority of union members', through the introduction of postal ballots for trade union elections. The Manifesto also contained a pledge to 'amend the social security system' to ensure that the unions themselves, rather than the taxpayer, 'should accept their primary responsibility for the welfare of the families of men who choose to go on strike'.

With regard to incomes policy, the Conservatives' Election Manifesto pledged to renew the offer to the TUC and the CBI to join a Conservative government in 'working out an effective voluntary pay and prices policy' to replace the existing statutory policy. At the same time, the Conservatives were adamant that if necessary, the existing pay and prices policy would be stiffened 'in the light of the developing economic situation'.

THE FEBRUARY 1974 ELECTION DEFEAT

The February 1974 election did not produce a clear-cut victor. If the question underpinning the election had been 'Who Governs Britain?', then the electorate's response was ambiguous. The Labour Party won just four more parliamentary seats than the Conservatives, whilst receiving a quarter of a million fewer votes. Initially, Heath sought to form a coalition with the Liberal Party, which had fourteen seats in the Commons, but the Liberals rejected this proposal, arguing instead for a 'government of national unity to be formed to include members of all parties'. The Conservative Cabinet dismissed this counter-proposal, thereby leaving Heath no alternative but to resign. On the same day, 4 March 1974, Harold Wilson and the Labour Party replaced Heath and the Conservatives in office.

Had the Conservative Party won the February 1974 election, then it is quite possible that Heath's neo-corporatist strategy would have been continued and consolidated. Heath could have claimed a mandate from the people, and thus ascribed greater legitimacy to such an approach. Even if, in such circumstances, a re-elected Conservative government had felt it necessary to concede to the NUM's demands, this would not in itself have precluded the continued pursuit of a neo-corporatist strategy more generally. All of this, however, is mere conjecture. The fact of the matter is that the election defeat not only signalled the imminent demise of Heath's leadership of the Conservative Party but also sounded the death-knell for the party's neo-corporatist approach to industrial relations and the trade unions.

Once the election had been lost – followed by another defeat in October of the same year – Conservative advocates of neo-liberalism in economic policy and legalism in trade union policy felt free to seek a fundamental change in party policies in these – and other – areas. For such Conservatives, the fate which had befallen Heath and his policies was vindication of their criticisms, whilst simultaneously serving to enhance the credibility of their 'alternative' approach to economic affairs and industrial relations.

It was not only among Conservative backbenchers that support for neo-liberalism increased in the wake of the Heath government's experiences. Some of those who became converted to, or convinced of, the alleged virtues of the free market had themselves served as Ministers in Heath's Cabinet. As noted earlier, Margaret Thatcher, Sir Keith Joseph, and Geoffrey Howe were three of the most obvious examples. Indeed, in Howe's case, it was partly impatience with the unwillingness or inability of the trade unions to adhere to agreements which led to his disillusionment with neo-corporatism and incomes policies (Keegan 1984: 73), although during the early years of opposition, he continued to moot the idea of some kind of tripartite forum in which economic policy and wages could be discussed.

Once the Conservative Party was in opposition, the advocates of neo-liberalism and legislative reform of the trade unions felt free to speak out and set a new agenda for the Conservative Party. Hitherto, when the party had been in office, many backbenchers had felt constrained by obligations of loyalty to the leader, even though they disliked or distrusted Heath's post-1972 policies, whilst those who had served in a ministerial capacity had effectively been silenced by the doctrine of collective responsibility. It was in opposition from 1974 to 1979, therefore, that the Conservative Party was, once again (as between 1964 and 1970), able to develop a new set of principles, priorities, and policies. Integral to this was the formulation of yet another approach towards trade unionism.

6 Back to the drawing board, 1974–1979

DECIDING ON A NEW APPROACH
TO THE TRADE UNIONS

Those who subscribed to the view that 'bashing the unions is indeed the task that lies before the Conservative Party' (Shenfield 1975: 37) were likely to have been disappointed by the circumspection shown by much of the parliamentary leadership over the issue of trade uniom reform during the latter half of the 1970s. After the 1974 election defeats, senior Conservatives recognised that if the party's response to the experiences and problems of the Heath government was to declare 'all-out war' on the trade unions, and pledge to seek revenge, then it was highly unlikely to win the support of the electorate or the consent of ordinary trade unionists. The experiences of the Industrial Relations Act, and the lessons learnt as a consequence, permeated Conservative thinking and policy-making concerning trade union reform throughout the opposition years.

Some Conservatives were ever fearful that a future Conservative government once again seeking to legislate against the trade unions might find itself merely provoking yet more class conflict and social division. Neither the party nor the country, it was maintained, could risk such an outcome. If the Conservative Party were to embark upon such a course, it was believed, then it would forfeit its claim to be a 'national' party. Those Conservatives subscribing to this perspective upheld the One Nation tradition in the party, maintaining that the power of organised labour was best dealt with through co-operation and incorporation. Such a strategy was not only deemed more likely to yield positive results but constituted a far more virtuous, worthy approach in principle (Gilmour 1974b).

Yet for many, if not most, Conservatives, this strategy had been irreparably damaged and discredited during 1972–4. Those neo-liberals who had opposed the policy right from the start felt their case had been vindicated, whilst many of those in the party who had proffered their support – often reluctantly or sceptically – for Heath's post-1972 strategy became convinced that such an approach was no longer tenable (Mount 1978: 4).

Following the 1974 election defeats, therefore, opinion in the Conservative Party hardened considerably against voluntarism and neo-corporatism. The dominant issue was not so much whether to pursue voluntarism/neo-corporatism or legalism; it was more a question of what the form and content of a legalist policy would be. As one former senior member of the Conservative backbench employment committee explained to this author, there was a widespread 'demand to do something . . . a cry for reform'. So the question was not whether the Conservative Party should seek to reform the trade unions in future, but 'how far and how fast we should go'.

THE OPTIONS AVAILABLE

Three general strands or perspectives were thus discernible in the Conservative Party with regard to trade union policy during this time. First, there was that segment of the party which continued to support a predominantly neo-corporatist strategy, favouring the involvement of representatives of organised labour in tripartite discussion and decision-making, coupled with agreement on some form of incomes policy. Such Conservatives continued to hope that the reform could be effected voluntarily, with the trade unions being persuaded through exhortation and encouragement to carry out the process themselves. Such an approach was deemed to be in the best tradition of One Nation Toryism, based on paternalism, conciliation, and national unity. The abandonment of such an approach by a future Conservative government, it was feared, would probably undermine industrial harmony still further, whilst simultaneously serving to jeopardise social and political stability. Warning against a tough policy towards the trade unions, one Conservative commentator suggested that 'any attempt to interfere with their domestic procedures by Act of Parliament will provoke another orgy of collective defiance. Change will have to be brought about by persuasion rather than by legislation' (Grigg 1976: 3). Yet this perspective was marginalised in the Conservative Party from 1974 onwards, not least because it was widely seen as having finally been discredited by the experience of the Heath government.

The second perspective which was identifiable in the Conservative Party after the 1974 election defeats was that which combined support for legislative reform of the trade unions with caution born of the lessons learnt from the Industrial Relations Act of 1971. Many of the Conservatives endorsing this perspective had been closely involved in the introduction of the Act, or had, at least, been in the parliamentary Conservative Party during the early 1970s, often in ministerial positions, and had subsequently recognised that the comprehensive and legalistic character of the Industrial Relations Act had been a mistake (a point confirmed to this author by both a former Employment Secretary in the Thatcher governments, and by a former senior member of the Conservative backbench employment committee). Whilst they were therefore convinced of the need for at least some legislative reform of the trade unions, they also recognised that the substance, tone, and pace of any new legal measures would have to be rather more modest and moderate than the Industrial Relations Act had been.

There remained a third strand of opinion in the Conservative Party, however, which brooked no criticism of the Industrial Relations Act, and believed that the party should have pledged its continued commitment to it. In a letter to *The Times*, one constituency Conservative Party member claimed that One Nation Tories like Ian Gilmour were 'completely out of touch with grass roots opinion in the Conservative Party, and in the country, in regard to the trade unions'. What was required, it was suggested, was 'a renewal of the battle to bring the trade unions within the rule of law' (*The Times*, 10 May 1974; see also Boyson 1978: Chapter 3). According to this perspective, the Conservative government had made a shameful capitulation to organised labour by virtually abandoning the Industrial Relations Act after 1971, and simultaneously promising to amend it in the light of criticisms made by the trade unions. For such Conservatives, the failure resolutely to enforce or maintain the Industrial Relations Act implied a lack of political will-power on the part of the parliamentary leadership. There could be no excuse, it was felt, for abandoning such an important, and necessary, policy when the weight of public opinion was behind it. This perspective commanded only limited support in the parliamentary Conservative Party, however.

PREPARING TO TACKLE THE TRADE UNIONS BY STEALTH

It was thus the second perspective which predominated on the opposition benches after 1974. The experiences of the 1971 Industrial Relations Act made many Conservatives even more convinced that a legalist policy towards the trade unions was needed, whilst simultaneously inducing an awareness that greater care would be required in implementing it. There was a widespread recognition in the Conservative Party that the policy pursued by the Heath government had been too confrontational and heavy-handed, however laudable its objectives might have been. The views of many such Conservatives were reflected in the acknowledgement by Douglas Hurd, Edward Heath's political secretary, that, with the benefit of hindsight, it had been unrealistic of the Heath government to impose the Industrial Relations Act (Hurd 1979: 105; see also Prior 1977b; Clarke 1974: 24). Certainly, Ian Gilmour was claiming that had the Conservative Party been re-elected in February 1974, there would have been a 'substantial amendment' of the Industrial Relations Act, an assertion endorsed by the shadow employment spokesperson, James Prior (Gilmour 1974a; Prior 1977c).

Therefore, a former Bow Group official, David Mahony, suggested that if it was determined to reform the trade unions, the Conservative Party had two options available to it. Either it could declare all-out war on a broad front, or it could carefully analyse the strengths and weaknesses of the trade unions and then adopt a 'guerrilla warfare' approach. A key aim of the latter strategy was to ensure, as far as possible, that control of union bureaucracies was gained by Conservatives or/and other non-Left elements. The former of these two options, Mahony explained, had the advantage of satisfying the emotions and frustration of those exasperated by the way in which the unions had thwarted previous attempts to curb their power. The major drawback, however, was deemed to be that such a policy was 'very risky', and the cost of failure very high. For this reason, Mahony reckoned that the probability of success was not sufficient to justify the gamble of pursuing the policy. Consequently, he advocated the second of the two options, on the grounds that, whilst it was more subtle, it was less likely to fail. Furthermore, Mahony added, the approach had the additional advantage that, if necessary, it could be used as a 'softening-up' stage for 'confrontation' – should this become necessary (Mahony 1976: 15–16).

It soon become clear that most Conservatives in Parliament were thinking along the same lines. In cautioning the party against the future introduction of legislation which could be construed as an attack on the basic operations of the unions or as detailed interference in their internal affairs, Leon Brittan, elected in

February 1974, spoke of the fear of confrontation which had been expressed to Conservative candidates on doorsteps throughout the country during the election campaigns. Whilst the political objective of bringing about a fundamental shift in the balance of industrial power might well be highly desirable, he elaborated, the trade unions would almost inevitably see it as partisan in character, and therefore likely to lead to massive and organised opposition. If this happened, the electorate might fear to vote Conservative because of the potentially disruptive outcome. Brittan therefore urged the Conservative leadership to pursue legislation which was less direct in motivation, but based instead on a clear and popular principle, namely that of 'individual rights'. By supporting the 'individual underdog', rather than pitting itself against the trade union movement, the Conservative Party would be best placed to win 'the crucial battle for public opinion'. If the trade unions did seek a confrontation, Brittan argued, the answer would not be found in passing more industrial relations legislation, but in a resolute combination of economic and administrative measures whose success would be entirely dependent on the degree of public support which they could command (Brittan 1976).

Similarly, Nicholas Scott advised a future Conservative government to take small, evolutionary steps to alter the law governing the trade unions. He endorsed the view that the party had been mistaken in attempting to implement wholesale comprehensive industrial relations reform in 1971. A wiser alternative, Scott suggested, would have been to introduce a series of smaller measures which would have been more likely to gain the gradual confidence and support of the trade union movement itself (*The Times*, 3 February 1976).

Meanwhile, eight senior Bow Group officials produced a publication entitled *Lessons for Power* in which they expressed reservations about the possibility of legislating *vis-à-vis* trade union rulebooks, elections, and secret ballots. In view of 'the present climate', they argued, it was questionable whether the benefits of supervision would outweigh the disruption which would probably arise. Consequently, it was urged that the party's industrial relations policy be permissive rather than prescriptive, thereby avoiding the likelihood of a head-on confrontation with the trade unions. For these reasons, the authors endorsed the party leadership's pledge not to reintroduce the Industrial Relations Act, which had recently been repealed by the Labour government.

FURTHER FACTORS ACCOUNTING
FOR CONSERVATIVE CAUTION

In addition to the Conservative Party's recognition of the problems incurred by the Industrial Relations Act, and the degree of union opposition it had provoked, three other factors accounted for the party leadership's efforts at formulating an industrial relations policy which, in effect, constituted a highly cautious form of legalism.

First, there was reaffirmation of the Conservative Party's traditional opposition to excessive legal regulation of social and industrial affairs. This was derived both from the party's philosophic belief that the state should refrain, as far as practicable, from detailed interference or intervention in the internal or private affairs of individuals and institutions, and also from recognition – revealed or reiterated by the experience of the Industrial Relations Act – that in some spheres, statutory measures were extremely difficult to enforce. To legislate in such instances, it was widely recognised, merely served to bring the government, Parliament, and the law itself into disrepute. The need for the Conservative Party to avoid the Heath government's 'mistake' of passing comprehensive and detailed industrial relations legislation was acknowledged, however grudgingly, by many senior party figures, particularly those who had held ministerial posts under Heath.

The second consideration which tempered any emotional inclination that some Conservatives might have felt for an unadulterated policy of legal restraint was an electoral one, and as such constituted something of a paradox for the party. It was universally recognised that the trade unions were highly unpopular amongst the electorate, with numerous opinion polls revealing that most people considered the unions to be too powerful. Yet precisely because of the excessive power of the trade unions, there was considerable agreement amongst parliamentary Conservatives on the need to avoid a 'confrontational stance', for whilst the electorate was deeply concerned about trade union power, it was also anxious about the possibility of further conflict between a future Conservative government and the unions.

This clearly posed something of a dilemma for the Conservatives. The adoption of a fully-fledged legalist policy might well strike a sympathetic chord with many voters, yet at the same time the electorate was fed up with industrial conflict and disruption, and so might actually hesitate to vote for the Conservative Party if it pledged a confrontation with the trade unions. As one commentator had noted prior to the October 1974 election, with the miners long since back at work, and the three-day working week a fast-fading memory, the Conservative Party could not go to the country promising a resumption of hostilities (Wood 1974; see also Butler and Kavanagh 1975: 61).

It was this consideration which, to a considerable extent, accounted for the appointment of James Prior as Shadow Employment Secretary. Part of his role had been to pursue a conciliatory approach, in order to 'help bridge the credibility gap' in the minds both of Conservative politicians and of voters who feared that a future Conservative government would again be obstructed or brought down by the trade unions (Cabinet Minister in Thatcher government to this author).

The third factor which served to encourage a less 'aggressive' or 'confrontational' stance by the Conservative opposition concerning the issue of trade union reform was the increased importance of neo-liberal economic policy, and the avowed objective of creating a social market economy. This had important implications for the party's industrial relations policies, although again a paradox could be discerned. When, at the beginning of the nineteenth century, trade unions had been perceived as a fetter on the operation of the market economy, severe legislative curbs had been deemed necessary to prevent organised labour from obstructing the 'natural' processes and mechanisms of 'the market'. Some legal restraint was still deemed necessary over 150 years later, but for many neo-liberals in the Conservative Party, it was envisaged that the operation of 'the market' itself would serve to reduce much of the power of the trade unions. In this sense, trade union 'power' was to be restrained as much by the operation of market forces as by legislation.

The caution which characterised the Conservative Party's legalistic policy after 1974 was vindicated by a secret inquiry conducted by a small group of former Ministers and party advisers, under the auspices of Lord Carrington, a Shadow Cabinet Minister. This inquiry into the Conservative Party's relations with the trade unions, particularly in the light of the events and experiences of the Heath government, culminated in the presentation of a report to the party's leader, Margaret Thatcher. This report insisted that in the modern era – characterised by strong trade unions, their members often operating advanced technology – no government could hope to win a major industrial dispute in the same way that Stanley Baldwin's government had in 1926. Certain trade unions, the report warned, had the power to throttle the physical and economic life of the country if they chose to confront the government. In such a situation, a Conservative government would be unable to defeat the trade unions, not least because it was no longer possible to deploy troops to break a strike: their numbers were insufficient, certain tasks and occupations required a high degree of expertise or technical knowledge, and using troops in such a manner would permanently damage the fabric of British politics (*The Times*, 18 April 1978).

Not surprisingly, the report attracted some criticism for its 'defeatism'. It was suggested in some quarters that 'a number of shell-shocked casualties of 1973–4 have no enthusiasm for going over the top again.' They were likened to men who, not wishing to fight a battle, were likely to say that the battle was bound to be lost anyway (*The Spectator*, 22 April 1978: 3).

The 'defeatism' of Lord Carrington's report was also rejected by Nicholas Ridley, who drafted another report prophesying that within a year or two of being elected, a Conservative government might be faced with a challenge from a major – possibly public sector – trade union seeking a substantial pay increase or opposing redundancies. Consequently, Ridley suggested a five-part strategy for dealing with such a challenge. First, figures indicating the return on capital should be 'rigged', so as to enable the government to meet an 'excessive' wage claim if it was not completely ready and able to confront the union concerned. Second, the government should determine which 'battle' to fight, and on which terrain, so that it could retain the initiative, rather than be forced into defence. Third, on the assumption that any challenge might well emanate from the coal industry, Ridley recommended that the next Conservative government should: build up coal stocks (particularly at power stations), make contingency plans for importing coal, and encourage the recruitment of non-union lorry drivers by road haulage firms (to assist in the transportation of coal supplies). Fourth, Ridley called for the next Conservative government to cut off social security payments to strikers, so as to force unions to support them from their funds. Fifth and finally, Ridley emphasised the need to ensure that the police were numerous enough, and sufficiently equipped, to deal with mass picketing, and also to protect 'good, non-union drivers' crossing the picket lines (*The Economist*, 27 May 1978: 21–2). The extent to which the Conservative leadership acted upon Ridley's proposals was only to become evident with the 1984–5 miners' strike.

THE EMPHASIS ON 'INDIVIDUAL RIGHTS'

A key feature of the Conservative Party's approach to trade union reform after 1974 was the emphasis placed on protecting and enhancing the 'individual rights' of trade unionists *vis-à-vis* their union and its leaders. In the context of a renewed emphasis by the Conservative Party on the principle of individualism generally, the concept of promoting 'individual rights' was to have profound implications for party policy regarding industrial relations and trade unionism in particular. Much of the Conservative Party's approach to trade union reform was based on the premise that if ordinary members were given a greater say in the affairs of their union, then it would be far more likely to pursue 'moderate' or 'responsible' policies and activities. Underpinning this premise was the assumption, clearly stated in the 1979 Election Manifesto, that 'too often trade unions are dominated by a handful of extremists who do not reflect the commonsense views of most union members'.

In line with this perspective, the Conservative Party formulated a set of proposals which purported to provide ordinary trade unionists with a much greater say in the affairs of their union, advocating secret and/or postal ballots to elect trade union officials and to gauge support for industrial action, and trade union political levies or funds, and increased opportunity for employees to refuse membership of a closed shop union, coupled with enhanced compensation for those whose employment suffered as a consequence of such refusal. All of these proposals were advocated on the grounds that they would significantly increase the 'individual rights' of trade union members. Furthermore, it was confidently envisaged that virtually all rank-and-file trade unionists would themselves approve of such measures, thereby overcoming the problem of consent.

'Individual rights' and the trade union closed shop

The avowed objective of enhancing the rights of individuals within trade unions, as opposed to explicitly legislating against the trade unions themselves, was most evident in the Conservative Party's approach to the closed shop – an issue which acquired renewed significance during the second half of the 1970s. Conservatives had traditionally harboured a number of objections to the closed shop. First, there were those circumstances where individuals were denied employment because they chose not to join a trade union. This was deemed to be a fundamental and unacceptable denial of individual liberty. Second, there were occasions when employees applied for trade union membership, but had their application turned down, which effectively meant that they could not be employed in that particular firm, trade, or industry. Conservatives not only condemned such practices on grounds of individual liberty, but also saw them as denying management's right to manage, because the trade union was, in effect, determining whether or not a particular individual could be appointed. Third, and following on from this last point, it was alleged that in certain circumstances, employees might have their trade union membership revoked, usually as a disciplinary measure when they had incurred the displeasure of their union (maybe by ignoring a strike call, for example). Again, the consequence might well be termination of employment. It was therefore argued that 'in a closed shop, a man has two bosses, and he can lose his job by offending either of them; he's in double jeopardy' (Cabinet Minister in Thatcher government to this author).

Recognising that the Industrial Relations Act had not so much eliminated the closed shop as driven it underground, however, the Conservative leadership sought to come to terms with it by adopting a policy which would enhance and protect the rights of employees detrimentally affected by compulsory union membership schemes. This entailed permitting a closed shop only when a ballot of employees had indicated an overwhelming majority in favour, whilst simultaneously seeking to ensure that any employee who had strong reasons, on grounds of conviction or conscience, for not becoming a trade union member would be exempt from compulsion to do so.

Furthermore, the Conservative Party proposed that employees whose employment was affected by refusal to join a trade union, or by a trade union refusing them membership, would have the right of recourse to an independent appeals procedure. In addition, generous compensation was urged for employees who lost their employment by virtue of not belonging to a trade union. Many Conservatives clearly believed that this 'individual rights' approach would prove both far more practicable and far more popular than another direct attempt at outlawing the closed shop entirely (Hayhoe 1977; Brittan, *HC Debates*, 5th series, vol.884: c.121).

This change of policy was nowhere more evident than in the speeches and amendments which came from the Conservative benches during the parliamentary debates on the Labour government's Trade Union and Labour Relations Bill, in the summer of 1974, which repealed the Industrial Relations Act. This meant that the closed shop once again became legal, although provision was made to exempt employees from the requirement to join a closed shop trade union if they could show that they had 'reasonable' grounds for refusing, such as religious conviction or conscientious objections. Rather than attack the closed shop *per se*, Conservatives focused their attention on specific areas of contention, namely the alleged narrowness of the criteria by which an individual employee could be exempted from the requirement to join a closed shop trade union, and the means of redress available to those employees who did lose their jobs due to the operation of a closed shop.

Thus, whilst most Conservatives objected to the closed shop in principle, most simultaneously acknowledged the impracticability of outlawing it outright. Instead, the official policy was to tolerate the closed shop, so long as adequate safeguards and reasonable grounds for exemption existed for employees who strongly objected to joining a trade union. In addition to the impracticability of outlawing the closed shop entirely, there was also the need to recognise the majority principle intrinsic to democracy. This meant acknowledging that very often the closed shop existed because a majority of workers – and sometimes employers themselves – in a particular company or industry supported it. Thus James Prior took the view that 'We shouldn't try to stop closed shops if that's what employers and unions wish to go for' (Cabinet Minister in Thatcher government to this author).

By adopting such a stance towards the closed shop the Conservative Party simultaneously highlighted the importance of its 'individual rights' strategy, its pragmatism in the context of what was deemed practicable *vis-à-vis* the closed shop, and its concern to avoid giving the electorate – and trade unionists – the impression that the return of a Conservative government would herald a new bout of conflict and confrontation. This 'human rights' stance, inextricably connected to the Conservative Party's renewed emphasis on the 'individualist' strand in its general philosophy or principles, also reflected an acknowledgement by those who had been involved in the introduction of the Industrial Relations Act that there were limits to what could be effected by legislation itself.

However, there remained many Conservatives who were highly critical both of the closed shop itself, and of their party's willingness to tolerate it. Their criticisms gained added resonance in the wake of the Labour government's Trade Union and Labour Relations (Amendment) Act, 1976, which revoked the right of an individual to object to membership of a closed shop union, on 'reasonable' grounds. For some in the Conservative party, the leadership's approach to the closed shop issue was far too acquiescent (see, for example, the editorial in *Crossbow*, autumn 1977). There were calls for the closed shop to be proscribed absolutely. Not only did it render trade unionism a 'tyranny', it was claimed, but the unions actually held down, rather than increased, the incomes and living standards of their members. Indeed, it was suggested that without a century of trade unionism, the majority of British workers would have been able to rise to 'middle-class affluence' (Shenfield 1975: 36).

The Trade Union and Labour Relations (Amendment) Act also aroused the concern among the Conservative rank-and-file over the closed shop and their party leadership's qualified acceptance of it. The extent to which constituency concern over the issue increased in the wake of the Act was indicated by the fact that, whereas only four of the fifty-nine motions on Employment and Industrial Relations submitted to the Conservative Party's 1975 Annual Conference were directly related to the closed shop, no less than forty-six of the 113 Employment and Industrial Relations motions sent to the 1976 Conference were critical of the closed shop, with a considerable number of them imploring the party leadership to pledge its intention of outlawing the practice when next elected.

For more prescient Conservatives, however, the closed shop was perceived as something from which the party could actually gain a positive advantage. It was envisaged that the reality of total trade union membership afforded an excellent opportunity for mobilising 'non-socialist' elements in the unions against the Left. On the assumption that those who usually sought to avoid joining trade unions were likely to be 'moderates' (as opposed to those most active in trade unions, who were deemed to be predominantly left-wing), it was thought that the closed shop could enable the Conservative Party to encourage these 'moderates' to become more involved in union affairs, precisely so that they could counter the Left. For some Conservatives, therefore, so long as adequate safeguards existed for individual objectors, the closed shop was not the 'necessary evil' which many others in the party considered it to be (see, for example, the editorial entitled 'Prior commitments' in *The Spectator*, 17 September 1976). Indeed, David Mitchell, backbench MP and former secretary of the Conservative parliamentary employment committee, made it clear that in his view it was preferable for a Conservative worker who objected to joining a trade union to became a member anyway, and subsequently play an active role in ensuring that the union had a 'moderate' leadership, pursuing 'moderate' policies, than for a Conservative employee to refuse trade union membership, thereby permitting the union to become dominated by political 'extremists' (*HC Debates*, Standing Committee E, 1974, vol. IV, c.863).

THE SIGNIFICANCE OF 'THE GRUNWICK DISPUTE'

It was the dispute at the Grunwick photographic film-processing plant in north London, during 1976–7, which really fuelled controversy in the Conservative Party over the closed shop, for although this was primarily a dispute concerning union recognition, and the right to join or form a trade union, Conservative neo-liberals and 'moral individualists' turned the dispute on its head by referring to it in the context of a right not to join a trade union. Consequently, during the course of the Grunwick dispute, many Conservative backbenchers became more vociferous in urging the party leadership to adopt a tougher stance against the closed shop. Indeed, according to a member of the backbench employment committee at the time, the Grunwick dispute 'drove parts of the party mad with rage at the trade unions' (former senior member of the Conservative backbench employment committee to this author).

According to George Gardiner, a backbench MP elected in February 1974, speaking from the platform at the Conservatives' 1977 Annual Conference, the party's *de facto* acceptance of the closed shop might have been a 'sensibly cautious line' to have adopted a year or so previously, but subsequent events had created a situation in which such a policy was no longer an adequate response to a 'scandalous' situation. Gardiner thus called upon the Conservative leadership to pledge that it would get rid of the closed shop, when next elected. Elsewhere, the leader of the Freedom Association – an organisation which included several Conservative MPs amongst its membership (and which was also charged with 'extremist infiltration' of the party, by a former Conservative Minister, William Van Straubenzee (*The Times*, 26 May 1978) – was convinced that James Prior constituted 'a positive liability' to the party, and suggested that while he remained shadow spokesperson on employment, it would be impossible to believe that the Conservative Party was ready to seize the historic opportunity of playing the role of liberator (*The Times*, 12 September 1977).

Tension in the Conservative Party was heightened when Norman Tebbit, a backbench MP elected in 1970, praised the Freedom Association for its role in upholding the rights of individuals who found themselves in conflict with 'big, greedy, arrogant, powerful mobsters' calling themselves trade unionists. According to Tebbit, there were people in the Conservative Party with the morality of Laval and Petain, people who were willing not merely to tolerate evil but to excuse it, and, by so doing, to profit from it. In complaining that the doctrine of appeasement was still to be heard from the 'faint-hearts' in the Conservative Party, Tebbit suggested that it was all the more necessary to deal with evil before it became any stronger (*The Times*, 10 and 13 September 1977).

Even so, Tebbit was not alone amongst Conservatives in abhorring the closed shop whilst simultaneously acknowledging that it was not really feasible to ban it outright. The Monday Club, for example, recognised that a future Conservative government would not outlaw the closed shop because it would be impractical to do so. The point was also made that 'a government which preaches "freedom of choice" and then legislates to prevent a group of employees from choosing, of their own free will, to form an all-union coterie, would be guilty of inconsistency' (Monday Club 1979: 4).

In the wake of the Grunwick dispute, therefore, the Conservative leadership sought to reiterate its 'individual rights' approach, laying strong emphasis on the protection of those who held strong objections to joining a trade union, whilst acknowledging the impracticability of actually banning the closed shop outright. Such an approach clearly accorded with James Prior's predominantly voluntarist inclinations, and his opinion that some limitations on freedom were acceptable if they helped to bring order and stability into the world of industrial relations. With regard to eradicating particular problems or trade union 'abuses', Prior sought to convince delegates at the Conservatives' 1977 Annual Conference that 'example' was much better than 'coercion', and that 'jaw-jaw' was better than 'war-war'.

Throughout the years in opposition, therefore, Conservative policy on the closed shop remained one of reluctant toleration, combined with a commitment to provide protection and, where necessary, compensation for those who were unwilling or unable to join a trade union which operated a system of compulsory membership.

THE COMMITMENT TO TRADE UNION BALLOTS

The Conservative Party's advocacy of individual rights for trade union members *vis-à-vis* their union organisation and leadership also entailed calls for ballots to be introduced, both for the election of union leaders, and to determine the degree of support for proposed strike action. Indeed, the Conservatives' new commitment to trade union ballots was also mooted as a major means of democratising Britain's labour movement, thereby making union leaders and their activities accountable to the mass membership. This particular approach indicated a fundamental change of thinking in the Conservative Party since the Industrial Relations Act; a fundamental premise upon which the 1971 Act had been predicated was that trade union leaders no longer enjoyed sufficient authority or control over their members. After the 1974 election defeats, however, the Conservative Party began arguing the opposite, namely that ordinary trade union members no longer had any control over their professed representatives.

One particular note of circumspection which was expressed with regard to trade union ballots concerned the assumption that the outcome would be the election of more 'moderate', and less 'militant', officials at senior level. According to Rhodes Boyson, a backbench MP elected in February 1974, so long as union leaders were conferred with 'exceptional' powers and privileges, it would be the 'militants', not the 'moderates', who would fight hardest and longest, by hook or by crook, to gain control (Boyson 1978: 48). Other Conservatives also wondered whether ordinary trade union members really were more 'moderate' than their leaders, but decided that they had to be trusted and given the opportunity of exercising their judgement (Cabinet Minister in Thatcher government to this author).

To a considerable extent, this approach was a response to the emergence of several left-wing trade union leaders during the 1970s, yet it also accorded perfectly with the Conservative Party's 'individual rights' strategy, entailing an appeal to 'ordinary' trade unionists. The Conservative Party thus suggested that it was the union leadership which needed to be 'disciplined' or 'controlled' by the rank-and-file, not vice versa, as had been the case prior to 1974.

This new perspective was endorsed by Conservatives from across the whole spectrum of the party. According to Ian Gilmour, trade union leaders were as unrepresentative of their rank-and-file as the medieval church had been of the laity (Gilmour 1978a: 237), while for Geoffrey Howe, some trade union leaders were akin to 'medieval barons and bishops, and even 18th century Dukes' (*The Times*, 7 January 1978). Opposition spokesperson on Treasury affairs, David Howell, meanwhile, was highly critical of 'the self-interested mafia' and 'well-heeled princes of trade union officialdom' who, he alleged, prowled the upper reaches of the trade union bureaucracy (*The*

Times, 13 November 1976), whilst a senior Monday Club official scathingly referred to the 'tinpot Marxist gauleiters' and 'Red fascists' in Britain's trade unions (Buckmaster 1977: 4–5). With Norman Tebbit alluding to the 'evil, destructive, and malignant Marxists who have seized control of the Labour Party and the TUC' (Tebbit 1975), and Margaret Thatcher, now party leader, referring to 'over-bearing and unrepresentative trade union leaders' (*The Times*, 10 January 1978), it was perhaps not surprising that these criticisms found expression in the Conservative Party's 1979 Election Manifesto, which noted that 'too often, trade unions are dominated by a handful of extremists, who do not reflect the common-sense view of most union members.'

The Conservative response to this 'problem' was to promise the introduction of secret ballots and the provision of public funds for postal ballots. These ballots were to be held both for the election of senior union officials, and to gauge support among union members for strike action. With regard to the former, the Conservative Party argued that the existing system served to encourage the election of 'extremists' to senior trade union posts, not least because 'the Left' was more organised and more prepared to 'pack' meetings which were otherwise poorly attended.

At the same time, a strong body of Conservative opinion maintained that votes in favour of strike action were often the result of fear or intimidation, for where voting was by show of hands, individuals opposed to strike action might be afraid to be seen opposing a strike call by the union leadership. Secret or postal ballots for union elections and strike calls were thus envisaged as a means of breaking the 'grip' of the Left under the guise of enhancing the 'rights' of individual trade unionists, and democratising the unions. In believing most 'ordinary' union members to be 'moderates', the Conservative Party clearly reckoned that the involvement of more rank-and-file members in union ballots would result in a more 'moderate/representative' leadership being elected, and less industrial action being pursued.

This individual rights strategy was undoubtedly intended to ensure that future battle lines were drawn between 'ordinary' trade unionists and their union leaders, rather than between trade unions *per se* and the government. If trade union leaders were to challenge a future Conservative government, it was envisaged that the party could appeal to the rank-and-file to call their senior officials to account, and refuse to endorse such action. The genius of such a strategy, the Conservative Party believed, was that it could hardly be denounced or portrayed as a partisan attack on the trade unions, when it promised a far greater role and degree of influence for 'ordinary' trade union members.

THE CONSERVATIVE TRADE UNIONISTS ORGANISATION

In order to assist the 'democratisation' and 'depoliticisation' of the trade unions, 1975 saw the Conservative Party reactivate its Conservative Trade Unionists organisation, whose primary objective was to encourage greater participation and representation by Conservatives and 'other moderates', both in the workplace and in the trade union movement itself. This was to include putting up 'Conservative' candidates in union elections, particularly once secret ballots had been introduced, on the grounds that trade unionists could then vote free from fear of intimidation from the Left.

The CTU was also intended to provide a conduit of communication between the Conservative Party, particularly at parliamentary level, and employees and trade unionists on the shopfloor. It was envisaged that the members of the CTU in the workplace could advise Conservatives in Parliament of the views of ordinary employees, particularly in terms of the sort of measures they would support or oppose, whilst simultaneously explaining to employees and trade union members the Conservative Party's objectives with regard to industrial relations.

A further role played by the CTU was that of explaining to trade unionists their right to opt out of paying the political levy, and, to a considerable degree, encouraging them to do so. This even entailed making available pre-printed forms enabling trade unionists to opt out of paying the political levy. On this issue in particular, the CTU has been credited with doing 'a very good job' (former senior member of Conservative backbench employment committee to this author).

The CTU also 'had considerable influence on public opinion, in that it showed the public that there were a lot of trade unionists who were prepared to come out in Conservative colours' (Cabinet Minister in Thatcher government to this author). This was clearly important in seeking to convince the electorate that Conservatism and trade unionism were not mutually exclusive phenomena, for ever destined to be in irreconcilable conflict. Indeed, a former senior official at Conservative Central Ofice, Andrew Rowe, recalls that during the latter half of the 1970s, the CTU occasionally played a valuable role in parliamentary by-elections, as in the Penistone constituency in July 1978. Although the Conservative Party failed to win this safe Labour seat, Rowe suggests that the 'increased Tory vote on a reduced poll in this highly trade unionised constituency (steel, coal, etc.) was in part due to the the very active campaign by CTU members in the by-election'. This, he suggests, 'showed how the use of trade unionists to canvass and work in areas which have been traditionally unsympathetic to the Conservative Party could achieve impressive results' (Rowe 1980: 229 n.12, 219).

Elsewhere, it was claimed that if the party was serious in its desire to tackle the problem of industrial conflict, it could start immediately by encouraging well-organised participation by Conservatives in trade unions (Mahony 1976: 15). Similarly, a representative of the party's Trade Union National Advisory Committee told delegates attending the Conservatives' 1975 Annual Conference that it was no use them moaning about the fact that so many union officials were left-wing, for much of the responsibility could be attributed to Conservatives themselves and the people on the shopfloor who either elected left-wing union leaders or failed to vote at all, letting them in by default. It was up to the delegates themselves, the CTU representative declared, to become involved in trade union affairs, via attendance at union meetings and participation in union elections.

Thus it was evident that whilst ballots for the election of trade union leaders could reasonably be advocated by invoking the discourse of 'democratisation', 'handing unions back to their members', and 'individual rights', there was also a clear expectation that 'moderates' in the trade union movement would more readily be mobilised against the Left when union elections were being held.

However, Rowe has spoken of the suspicion and snobbery which existed in the party, particularly at constituency level, towards trade union activity and organisation by Conservatives, for these were often regarded as something of a nuisance due to 'the type of person' who might be attracted. Indeed, according to Rowe, 'Conservative activists were not only ignorant about trade unions ... they came from the very groups most obviously threatened by their spread. People of independent means, small businessmen and professionals were ideologically unsympathetic to trade unions' (Rowe 1980: 217). Furthermore, Rowe points out:

> There are Conservatives who will argue passionately that the attempt to build an effective CTU on the basis of loyalty to trade unionism is to build a Trojan horse filled with corporatists who

will spill out one dark night finally to subdue the Conservative
liberal tradition of individual freedom.

(ibid.: 213)

Certainly, the CTU was strongly in favour of a cautious policy by
the Conservative Party with regard to trade unionism and industrial
relations. Whilst clearly critical of much trade union activity and
behaviour, the CTU was also critical of those in the Conservative
Party who constantly called for 'tough' action and legislation against
the trade unions. Certainly, the CTU's role in encouraging greater
activity within the trade unions by Conservatives themselves was
partially intended to effect a reduction in 'militancy' and 'extremism',
by undermining the alleged or perceived dominance and influence
of the Left. This, in turn, would partly solve 'the trade union
problem' without recourse to a panoply of prescriptive or punitive
legislation, the invoking of which would probably exacerbate the
very problems it was intended to solve, and possibly alienate
the 'moderates' who might otherwise have been amenable to
Conservatism. There was certainly a feeling within the CTU that the
Conservative Party 'often appears quite long on legal and constitutional knowledge, but disastrously short on personal experience of
union matters' (ibid.: 228). This both reflected and reinforced the
CTU's role of simultaneously persuading ordinary trade unionists of
the case for Conservatism, whilst also 'educating' fellow Conservatives generally, both at parliamentary and constituency level, of
the reality of trade unionism and life on the shopfloor, thereby
encouraging a more constructive attitude and strategy towards the
trade unions and their members.

One aspect of trade unionism which clearly illustrated the CTU's
essentially cautious approach to reform was that regarding the closed
shop. Whilst sharing the concern common to all Conservatives about
the denial of individual liberty engendered by compulsory union
membership, the CTU recognised that: 'The closed shop chiefly exists
because large numbers of people wish to enter and maintain one at
their place of work and because many employers find it convenient to
deal with one.' Whilst acknowledging that some legislation might be
needed from the next Conservative government to remedy those
'aspects of the closed shop ... which are unacceptable', it was also
acknowledged that 'CTU members would certainly prefer that abuses
were modified by action from members within unions rather than
by intervention by government ... it is essential that some forward-
looking compromise is reached', because 'no solution will work which

is imposed from above' (Rowe 1980: 214). Whilst the influence of the CTU should not be exaggerated, it is none the less worth noting that the general stance adopted by the parliamentary Conservative Party towards the trade unions during its period in opposition was broadly in line with that espoused by the CTU itself.

AMBIGUITY OVER INCOMES POLICY

For much of its period in opposition, the Conservative Party was characterised by a degree of ambivalence and ambiguity over the issue of whether or not it intended to adopt an incomes policy. With Margaret Thatcher expressing her intention of not having a statutory pay policy, and yet refusing to state categorically and unequivocally that she would never have one, the party generally oscillated between complete rejection of all formal incomes policies, and the possibility of pursuing an informal or voluntary one which might constitute part of an annual economic forum. For example, Sir Geoffrey Howe, the Shadow Treasury Minister, called for the Conservative Party to seek a middle way between those who rejected incomes policies outright, and those who saw them as a valuable weapon in the battle against inflation. 'If not an incomes policy', Sir Geoffrey argued, then at least 'a policy for incomes'. Elaborating on this issue, he suggested 'a more open approach to economic management . . . possibly in the form of an extended NEDC' (Howe 1976). The latter option certainly seemed to be favoured by Peter Walker, a former Minister in Heath's Cabinet, who claimed that 'such is the strength of union power at the present time that a policy of free collective bargaining cannot successfully be pursued' (Walker 1977a: 67). Yet such was the ambiguity of the Conservative leadership's stance that Peter Walker made a call, early in 1976, for the party generally, and the Shadow Cabinet in particular, to clarify its position on the issue of incomes policy (*The Times*, 19 January 1976).

Walker's call, however, went largely unheeded, save for references by the Conservative leadership to a return to 'responsible' collective bargaining. According to Prior, the Shadow Employment Minister, the debate on pay policy in Britain was too often seen in simple black and white terms, with the issue being polarised into a stark choice between rigid pay control or a complete free-for-all (*Conservative News*, October 1978).

The ambivalence had certainly not been resolved by the 1976 publication of the Conservative Party policy document, *The Right Approach*. Whilst pointing out that experience did not suggest that a fully-fledged prices and incomes policy was the best means of finding a long-term solution to the problem of inflation, *The Right Approach* blandly noted that the same experience demonstrated the 'unwisdom' of flatly and permanently rejecting the idea (Conservative Central Office 1976: 37). Needless to say, this did little to placate the impatience of those Conservatives such as Timothy Raison, who demanded far greater clarity and coherence in party pronouncements on the vexatious issue of incomes policy (Raison 1977: 12). Indeed, when such clarity and coherence were still lacking a couple of years later, an editorial in *The Spectator* on the issue was titled 'Fifty–seven varieties', a wry reference to the range of differing options and opinions being put forward by Conservatives with regard to incomes policy (*The Spectator*, 14 October 1978).

THE CASE FOR AN INCOMES POLICY

To those Conservatives who continued to favour an incomes policy, the question was not solely about reducing inflation by restraining pay increases; it was also about the pursuit of social justice and national unity. For Conservatives such as Peter Walker, Ian Gilmour, and – post-1972 – Edward Heath, incomes policies offered a means through which a sense of industrial partnership and co-operation could be developed, which, in turn, would do much to create One Nation.

Indeed, such was the support amongst some Conservatives for an incomes policy that they not infrequently found themselves endorsing the Labour government, which itself was pursuing a series of pay policies. According to Heath, it was 'essential' that the government should pursue an incomes policy, because this had become an 'inevitable and inescapable . . . part of economic management' (*HC Debates*, 5th series, Vol.891: c.1707–8). Similarly, Peter Walker argued that there was 'a basic necessity for an incomes policy', and that such a policy was 'of paramount importance'. Indeed, he even called on the Labour government to pursue 'a tougher incomes policy'. In so doing, Walker insisted that the difficulties of an incomes policy 'are nothing compared with the difficulties created by having no incomes policy', for these were 'unsurpassable' (*HC Debates*, 5th series, vol.904: c.732; vol.909: c.495–501).

Such sentiments were echoed by David Knox, whose only criticism of the Labour government's incomes policy was its 'absence of any real teeth'. Even so, he called upon his Conservative colleagues to give the Labour government their full support, because an incomes policy was 'essential' (*HC Debates*, 5th series, vol. 909: c.522–8), a point which was endorsed by Peter Tapsell when he declared that it would 'never again be possible anywhere in the Western World efficiently to run an industrialised parliamentary democracy without an incomes policy' (*HC Debates*, 5th series, vol. 914: c.1236–42).

Meanwhile, five years after his original attempt, Reginald Maudling succeeded in having his memorandum – in which he strongly advocated an incomes policy – circulated in the Shadow Cabinet. He continued to argue that as long as the trade unions held the power to destroy businesses and bring the economy to a halt, then 'any talk of a return to free collective bargaining or the operation of a "free market" is meaningless' (Maudling 1978: 266–7). Support for an incomes policy was also expressed by Robert Carr, when he declared that those Conservatives who believed that incomes policies could, or should, be abandoned were living in 'a fool's paradise' (Carr 1975).

IN DEFENCE OF TRIPARTISM
AND NEO-CORPORATISM

Many Conservative supporters of incomes policy were also advocates of neo-corporatism. Not only did they believe that 'tripartite' discussions between government, trade unions, and employers would contribute to the creation of One Nation and social harmony, but also that such a mode of consultation and decision-making would serve to channel trade union power into a more constructive direction. Peter Walker firmly believed that the nature of modern society necessitated genuine dialogue between government, management, and trade unions. The means by which this could best be achieved, he suggested, was the creation of an industrial assembly, the membership of which would be drawn from all areas of economic life. Such an assembly would meet on a regular basis to discuss matters pertaining to Britain's economic and industrial situation, and hopefully, as a consequence, would find some solutions. If this could be achieved, Walker claimed, then a new climate could be forged in British industry (Walker 1977a: 81). An industrial assembly was also favoured by Ian Gilmour, for whom it constituted the best means by which government could deal with the power of the trade unions 'and other producer groups', and work with them through consultative procedures (Gilmour 1978a: 243). Other leading Conservative advocates of some mode of neo-corporatism during the second half of the 1970s included Edward Heath (*HC Debates*, 5th series, vol.914: c.1427–8) and Maurice Macmillan, the latter urging the creation of a 'Council of Industry', based on a significantly strengthened NEDC, coupled with a greater parliamentary representation of the trade unions – 'a bench of union barons to match the bench of bishops' (*HC Debates*, 5th series, vol.891: c.1674).

For such Conservatives, therefore, incomes policies, tripartism, and neo-corporatism were to be supported on two grounds. First, they constituted a 'realistic' response to the power of the trade unions in a modern, complex, interdependent economy; a legislative attack on organised labour was considered neither feasible nor desirable. Any attempt at placing significant curbs on organised labour was deemed likely to prove both impracticable – as shown by the experience of the Industrial Relations Act – and dangerous for industrial stability and social cohesion. Conservatives subscribing to this perspective were certainly critical of many of the attitudes and activities of Britain's trade unions, but they believed that the very power of the trade unions which Conservatives – and a majority of the British public (according to a number of opinion polls published during this period) – objected to was itself an obstacle to any comprehensive legislative strategy. Instead, such Conservatives sought to harness trade union power more constructively, through incorporation into the machinery of government and economic decision-making. This was simultaneously intended to serve an 'educative' function, helping to illustrate to trade union leaders the economic and industrial facts of life, so that they would recognise for themselves the need for greater 'moderation' and 'responsibility'.

The second rationale for this approach was that it accorded perfectly with the One Nation tradition in the Conservative Party, which MPs such as Ian Gilmour strongly subscribed to. Incorporating the trade unions constituted an integral part of a strategy to eradicate 'them and us' attitudes in industry, and class conflict in society generally, by fostering a sense of partnership and common interest between management, trade unions, and the British state. National unity and the establishment of One Nation were thus to be secured through greater responsibility and reciprocity all round.

THE NEO-LIBERAL COUNTER-ATTACK

Such Conservatives, however, found themselves increasingly on the defensive from 1974 onwards, as the Conservative Party under Margaret Thatcher's leadership moved in the opposite direction, towards neo-liberalism. This meant renunciation of both neo-corporatism and incomes policy, in favour of a return to the free market in which economic decisions, including employment and wages, were to be determined by market forces and the laws of supply and demand. For many Conservative supporters of this approach, such as Margaret Thatcher herself, Norman Tebbit, Sir Keith Joseph, Rhodes Boyson, Nicholas Ridley, John Biffen, Nick Budgen, and Jock Bruce-Gardyne (to name but a few), it had been a cardinal error of the Heath government to have capitulated to the trade unions in 1972, thereby abandoning its Manifesto commitments to reduce trade union power and return to free collective bargaining. This capitulation to trade union power meant that the unions were granted a key position in economic decision-making at the very highest level. Not only did this undermine the operation of 'the market', it was also deemed to undermine the authority and sovereignty of Parliament itself. For neo-liberals such as Margaret Thatcher and Sir Keith Joseph, it was the Heath government's pursuit of a neo-corporatist strategy from 1972 which, to a considerable extent, 'converted' them to neo-liberalism.

The neo-liberals' objection to neo-corporatism and incomes policies was founded on three premises. First, as just intimated, it was held that market forces and, ultimately, the capitalist system itself would be destroyed. Decisions concerning a whole range of economic and industrial matters would be determined by governments and dominant producer groups (namely the TUC and the CBI) rather than by the natural laws of 'the market' itself. Not only was this held to be wrong in principle, it was also argued that decisions taken by governments, rather than determined by 'the market', were often less efficient, and as such either exacerbated the very problems they were intended to resolve or led to the emergence of new problems. Either way, the consequence was for further government intervention in the economy in a doomed attempt to 'put things right'. The logic of this process, neo-liberals warned, was that eventually the state, aided and abetted by the dominant producer groups with which it had formed a corporatist alliance, would seek to control or regulate every sphere of industrial and economic activity, thereby signalling the end of private enterprise, the free market, and capitalism itself (see, for example, Biffen 1977; Budgen, *HC Debates*, 5th series, vol.914: c. 1239–40; Raison 1979a: 13).

The second premise upon which the Conservative neo-liberal objection to neo-corporatism was based concerned the – allegedly concomitant – erosion of individual liberty and independence from the state. First, it was claimed that neo-corporatism would require that everyone in a particular industry or sector of the economy would need to become a member of their 'representative' institution, for there would otherwise be little point in either the government or the organisation concerned entering into any agreement. In the case of the trade unions, therefore, the obvious consequence would be an extension of the closed shop, whereby employees would be compelled to join the 'appropriate' trade union. Neo-corporatism was therefore attacked for its implications for individual liberty. Second, it was argued that having ascribed a major role in industrial and economic policy-making to the dominant producer groups in society, the state would subsequently require them to 'police' their members, so as to ensure that the agreements were adhered to. This would render the key 'representative' institutions mere agents or adjuncts of the state, charged with the responsibility for administering government policies. Conservative neo-liberals such as David Howell and Timothy Raison were fearful that the incorporation of key producer groups into the formulation and administration of economic policies was a means through which the state would further increase its power and control over the individual citizen (Howell 1972; Raison 1979b: 26).

The third objection which Conservative neo-liberals levelled against neo-corporatism concerned its allegedly detrimental effect on the sovereignty of Parliament and on the authority of the state itself. As Rhodes Boyson argued, every step towards the replacement of 'the market' by government direction took the country further down the road to political agitation and civil disorder. With ever more economic decisions being taken away from the influence of market forces, the outcome would be intense political lobbying almost amounting to blackmail, increasing resort to direct action by workers, and growing disenchantment among ordinary citizens who would becoming increasingly aware that economic rewards were being disbursed through the political system itself, rather than through 'the market'. Consequently, the more the government took decisions out of 'the market', and placed them in an arena of political favouritism, the more groups in society were set against each other, thereby undermining social cohesion, whilst simultaneously serving to diminish the authority of, and respect for, Parliament and the state (see, for example, Boyson 1978: 72; Shenfield 1975: 36).

Following on from this particular point, Conservative neo-liberals also pointed out that state intervention in the economy, coupled with successive or permanent incomes policies, resulted in a politicisation of economic affairs generally, and of trade union activities and objectives in particular. It was argued that an industrial dispute concerning a pay claim during a period of incomes policy invariably brought the trade union involved into conflict with the government itself. This then raised the question of whether such a dispute was genuinely industrial in nature, or whether it was politically motivated. Norman Tebbit (1974), for example, was firmly of the view that the strike activity which had 'brought down' the Heath government in 1974 had been 'politically motivated'.

With regard to incomes policies *per se*, Conservative neo-liberals were emphatic that this was the wrong strategy for reducing inflation. It was increases in the money supply, unmatched by corresponding increases in output, productivity, and economic growth, which constituted the root cause of inflation, Conservative neo-liberals insisted.

By the time of the 1979 general election, however, the party had clearly rejected an incomes policy for the private sector, believing that pay settlements 'should be left to the companies and workers concerned'. Furthermore, the Conservative Party declared, 'no one should or can protect them from the results of the agreements they make.' Pay bargaining in the public sector, however, was to 'take place within the limits of what the taxpayer and rate-payer can afford', thereby placing it 'on a sounder economic footing' (Conservative Central Office 1979: 12).

Clearly, therefore, the emphasis was very much on the concept of responsible collective bargaining, with employees having to suffer the consequences of pursuing 'excessive' pay claims (i.e. unemployment, bankruptcies, etc.). Some Conservatives envisaged that this would also serve to encourage the election of more 'moderate' trade union leaders, as employees learnt that 'large' wage claims pursued by 'militant' union officials were quite likely to result in job losses.

The debate over the question of incomes policy took place in the context of a move towards neo-liberalism in Conservative economic thinking. Not surprisingly this was also a cause of concern and controversy in the party, particularly because of the envisaged social consequences, most notably high(er) unemployment. Yet for neo-liberals, the enemy which faced the party in the 1970s was not the doctrinaire laissez-faire of the mid-nineteenth-century, but *étatisme* (Blake 1978: 8).

In the wake of the 1974 election defeats, there was increased advocacy in Conservative circles of economic liberalism, and the need for the party to seize the opportunity of pursuing a 'social market' strategy (see, for example, Ridley 1974; Beloff 1976; Centre for Policy Studies 1978). Indeed, it was for this purpose that Margaret Thatcher and Sir Keith Joseph founded the Centre for Policy Studies in 1974 – to 'survey the scope for replacing increasingly interventionist government by social market policies, and to seek to change the climate of opinion in order to gain acceptance for them' (Joseph 1975). In undertaking this task, the growing neo-liberal bloc in the Conservative Party was aided and abetted by a whole host of individuals and institutions, not least Samuel Brittan – 'no-one in this country has done more than Samuel Brittan, in his books and articles, to explain the social market concepts which animate our thinking' (ibid.: vii) – and the Institute of Economic Affairs (Cowling 1978). These were in addition to the influence already derived from the ideas of Milton Friedman and Friedrich Hayek whose ideas had originally been articulated in such texts as *Capitalism and Freedom* (Friedman 1962) and *The Constitution of Liberty* (Hayek 1960), for example.

What greatly added to the concern felt by some Conservatives over their party's move towards neo-liberalism was the significantly increased levels of unemployment which would ensue. To those who alleged that the abandonment of an incomes policy and the enhancement of market forces would lead to higher unemployment, neo-liberals pointed out that the number of people out of work had risen quite significantly since the mid-1960s, irrespective of whether or not an incomes policy had been pursued. The neo-liberal approach to the relationship between 'excessive' wage increases, higher unemployment, and 'the market' was clearly indicated by David Price, a former economist, when he suggested that free collective bargaining, in the context of Britain's depressed economic position, would act as a far more potent restraint upon excessive pay demand than any social contract formula agreed between the TUC and the government (Price 1977).

Instead, neo-liberals sought to ensure that wages would, in future, be determined by the market, approximating to the laws of supply and demand. If there was a significant rise in unemployment, in the wake of a reversion to free collective bargaining, then the blame would be laid at the door of the unions, for pursuing 'excessive' wage demands which ignored the 'economic facts of life'. As backbench MP Nicholas Ridley succinctly stated: 'people must be made to suffer the consequences of their actions, or inaction, once more' (Ridley 1974). It was suggested that willingness to allow a higher level of unemployment would have the 'incidental advantage' of greatly concentrating union leaders' minds on the task of preserving their members' jobs, thereby distracting them from more political ends (Mahony 1976; Martin 1976: 13). Furthermore, there was a claim that some unemployment was preferable to increasing inflation, the rationale being that the effects of unemployment were mostly limited and localised, only affecting individuals and their families, and often for a relatively short period of time. By contrast, inflation affected everyone, particularly those on low or fixed incomes, whilst also causing far more damage to the nation's economy generally (Hodgson 1975).

Conservative neo-liberals thus increasingly challenged the apparent taboo of post-war British politics, namely that unemployment *per se* was unacceptable, so that full employment had to be preserved at – literally – any cost. A Selsdon Group publication in the mid-1970s was highly critical of those politicians who had inherited, in their formative years, a deep fear and loathing of mass unemployment, to the extent that any unemployment was deemed unacceptable, and symptomatic of failure. Against this orthodoxy, it was argued that only mass involuntary unemployment needed to give cause for concern (Bourlet and Roots 1974: 3). At the same time, a leading neo-liberal in the Conservative Party was complaining that Britain had an 'unemployment complex', and was therefore afraid to implement the policies necessary to control inflation (Howell 1974). This fear, it was emphasised, had to be overcome. According to Jock Bruce-Gardyne, for example, it had become a 'manifest truth' to the electorate that a particular level of employment could not be permanently maintained by the actions of politicians, however well-intentioned. Yet the assumption by successive post-war governments that they had a responsibility for maintaining full employment had resulted in a fundamental shift in the balance of power towards the trade unions. Consequently, Bruce-Gardyne lamented, union leaders were no longer inhibited by the fear that wage demands might jeopardise the continued employment of their members (*The Times*, 9 October 1975).

Neo-liberals were confident, however, that this situation could be reversed. To this end, Nicholas Ridley urged the Conservative Party to recognise what it was that had controlled trade unions for a century: a proper balance of supply and demand in the labour market (Ridley 1974, 1976: 12). Sir Keith Joseph was rather more explicit, suggesting that trade unions ought to be 'free to price their people out of jobs, or bankrupt their employers, if their members really wished them to' (*The Times*, 1 April 1976).

It was precisely these kinds of perspectives and pronouncements which alarmed the One Nation Conservatives, and those in the party with managerial or industrial experience. They tended to emphasise the potential threat to social and political stability in Britain, coupled with increased bitterness and hostility on the shopfloor in industry, should such an approach be implemented by a future Conservative government. Edward Heath, for example, was convinced that the Conservative Party would never be able to win popular support for an economic system which tolerated, with genial indifference, a steady one or two million – or more – people out of work for any length of time. Neither would it deserve to, he added (*The Times*, 22 November 1975). This warning was echoed by Ian Gilmour, when he sought to remind his neo-liberal colleagues in the Conservative Party that high unemployment was unlikely to help the promulgation of free market doctrines, or cement loyalty to the nation's democratic institutions. To those Conservatives who might favour 'smashing' trade union power through high unemployment, Gilmour pointed out that Britain's 'free society' would probably be smashed at the same time (Gilmour 1978a: 242). Ironically, in advancing this line of argument, Gilmour actually drew attention to a warning issued by the doyen of neo-liberalism Friedrich Hayek, who had himself pointed out that a monetary policy which would break the coercive powers of the trade unions by producing protracted and extensive unemployment had to be avoided, because 'it would be politically and socially fatal' (Hayek 1960: 281–2). Not dissimilarly, Peter Walker expressed concern that high unemployment might lead to the re-emergence of 'class war' in Britain, and he therefore urged the Conservative Party not to abandon its longstanding commitment to full employment (*The Times*, 23 June 1975, 28 September 1975).

TOO LEGALISTIC OR TOO LITTLE?

In seeking to tread a cautious path with regard to proposals for trade union reform, the Conservative Party's parliamentary leadership found itself being criticised both by those who still feared it was going too far, and simultaneously by those who complained that it was not going far enough.

With regard to the former of these two criticisms, some Conservatives, particularly those with experience of industry or management, or who subscribed to the One Nation vision of Conservatism, felt that the party's approach remained too reliant on legislative remedies and punitive measures. Peter Walker was concerned that some of the proposals being contemplated by the Conservative Party, such as abolition of social security payments to strikers' families, new laws on picketing, the training of 'reserves' to break strikes, could prove 'disastrous' if actually implemented. He feared that the antagonism aroused by such policies might well divide the nation, and create a bitterness not experienced since the Jarrow Hunger Marches of the 1930s. Walker thus insisted that such measures could not be pursued by any Conservative government that was serious in its desire to establish a good relationship with the trade unions (Walker 1977a: 67–8).

James Prior, meanwhile, emphasised that the national interest demanded an even-handed approach to problems, and this could only be achieved through conciliation and co-operation. As such, Prior expressed his desire to achieve voluntary agreements with the TUC, so that change could be brought about by persuasion and codes of practice. His approach was to proceed, as far as was possible, on the basis of maximum agreement with the trade unions, and to deal pragmatically with each issue or problem as it arose (interview with John Torode in the *Guardian*, 15 September 1977; quoted by Paul Routledge in *The Times*, 21 March 1978). Prior sought 'a broad consensus across industrial boundaries', so as to secure the consent of ordinary working people (*The Times*, 9 August 1975), whilst Gilmour was adamant that 'a peaceful settlement' between the Conservative Party and the trade unions would only be achieved if the party's approach and policies were appealing and attractive to sufficient numbers of rank-and-file union members (Gilmour 1978b).

Not for the first time, Pressure for Economic and Social Toryism (PEST) were involved in the advocacy of a conciliatory approach, their chairman insisting that "Selsdon Man" must not be resurrected.' Instead, he urged the Conservative Party to continue on 'the uphill road' which it had so painfully discovered at the beginning of 1972. In other words, he argued, the party needed to stick to the road of co-operating with the trade unions, not confronting them. In proffering this advice, the chairman of PEST condemned the Industrial Relations Act for having been 'a far too legalistic document drafted without any consideration of human relations' by Conservative lawyers (Raffen 1974: 600).

Another proponent of a more conciliatory, voluntarist stance was Robert McCrindle, MP, a company chairman and director, who was deeply concerned at the 'tough' approach to trade unions which some of his Conservative colleagues were demanding. For many in the party, he lamented, the efforts which would have to be made to come to terms with the trade unions were unacceptable, so attractive and ingrained had the idea of confrontation become (*The Times*, 14 May 1974). Meanwhile, at the party's 1977 Annual Conference, a Conservative trade unionist warned: 'as the Party which stands for law and order ... do not bring in a law which you cannot enforce.' The same individual was also concerned that the Conservative leadership might 'turn the issue of trade unions at branch or constituency Party meetings into a Party war'.

By contrast, a number of Conservatives were of the opinion that the party's policy in opposition conceded far too much to voluntarism and the perceived necessity of not offending the trade unions or frightening the electorate. Many of them were MPs from more 'professional' backgrounds, such as law or journalism, and probably failed to comprehend fully the concerns of those of their fellow Conservatives who had closer contacts with, or experience of, industry or management. For example, one Conservative barrister, John Peyton, called for strikes to be outlawed in certain 'key' industries and services (*The Financial Times*, 30 March 1974), whilst Rhodes Boyson, a former headmaster, was of the opinion that the party had been wrong to enter the October 1974 election pledging not to introduce another Industrial Relations Bill. Far from soothing the concerns of voters over the prospect of further confrontation, Boyson alleged that the pledge had actually lost the Conservative Party votes, not least amongst the working class itself (*The Times*, 11 May 1974).

Certainly some Conservative critics of the party's policy in opposition feared that constant reiteration of the need to avoid conflict or confrontation with the trade unions might serve to persuade voters that the Conservatives had no solutions to the trade union 'problem' and were not, therefore, worth voting for. As Richard Barber of the Bow Group argued, the party's policy towards the trade unions in opposition appeared to consist of reassurances that they had nothing to fear, and that their privileges would remain intact. Such an approach, Barber warned, was giving the impression that the Conservative Party lacked resolve in facing up to the various aspects of trade union power, a misconception which was likely to persuade voters that there was little to be gained by a change of government, and that they might as well vote for the party which was 'unequivocally subservient to trade union interests' (Barber 1976).

Similar concerns were expressed by other Conservatives, such as Angus Maude, who also referred to a widening of the 'already alarming gap' between the Conservative leadership in Parliament and its supporters in the country. Speaking about the party's desire to avoid antagonising the trade unions, Maude asserted that to have a case which was both correct and electorally popular, and yet to renounce it, was symptomatic only of a death-wish (*The Times*, 7 May 1974).

The cautious, somewhat ambiguous, policies enunciated by the Conservative leadership, with regard both to trade union reform and incomes policy, during the years in opposition from 1974 to 1979, reflected not only the disagreements on the party's backbenches but also divisions within the Shadow Cabinet itself. Throughout this period, the Shadow Cabinet picked by Margaret Thatcher was notable for its ideological balance in spite of – or perhaps because of – the general perception that the Conservative Party was moving to the Right. Within the Shadow Cabinet, ascendent neo-liberals from the 'New Right' were countered by One Nation Conservatives valiantly seeking to uphold the tattered flag of Tory paternalism. This judicious ideological balance was obviously a major factor in determining the cautious stance which was adopted over the twin issues of trade union reform and incomes policy, although, as has already been noted, many of those on the Right of the Conservative Party – especially within the Shadow Cabinet – were mindful of the experience of the Industrial Relations Act, and this itself was instrumental in moulding a less legalistic or repressive trade union policy than might otherwise have been expected. As the Shadow Employment Secretary recalled:

> The zeal of the monetarists was tempered by the rest of us who were advising that we should remember that our experience in Government last time had been rather different from the approach which we had planned to adopt in Opposition: the realities of office had forced us to jettison a load of ideological baggage.
>
> (Prior 1986: 109)

Indeed, the fact that James Prior was the Shadow Employment Secretary was itself highly significant, for his appointment was clearly intended to dampen or disguise anti-trade union attitudes in the Conservative Party, and thereby allay fears among voters that the election of a Conservative government would once again result in a bout of intense industrial strife as a consequence of an attack on the trade unions (although by 1979, after the 'winter of discontent', the premise that only a Labour government could work with the trade unions, and thus guarantee industrial peace, was thoroughly discredited. In any case, by this time many voters would doubtless have welcomed a pledge to declare all-out war on the trade unions). Not surprisingly, therefore, Prior's occupancy of the post of Shadow Employment Secretary was not popular with those on the neo-liberal or Right tendency of the Conservative Party. Indeed, many such Conservatives suspected that Prior himself 'had no intention of carrying out any serious reforms of trade union law' (Ridley 1991: 14).

Yet in spite of her renowned hostility towards trade unionism, Margaret Thatcher not only tolerated Prior as Shadow Employment Secretary, but herself generally refrained from appearing too antagonistic towards the trade unions. As one of her staunchest allies later pointed out:

> she was content, while still in Opposition, not to stir up either the trade unions or Jim Prior. She could wait to attain office to work out the details. Also, it was not an issue which she judged had electoral appeal. She just let Jim Prior carry on being his emollient self and did not expose her true intentions until she had the power to implement them.
>
> (ibid. 1991: 15)

As another Minister recalls: 'It needed further hard experience culminating in the Winter of Discontent in 1978 . . . before the British people were ready to give continuous backing to a Government for trade union reform' (Whitelaw 1989: 75–6). The 'winter of discontent' also served to harden opinion in the Conservative Party against the idea of an incomes policy or some mode of economic forum. Whilst a few One Nation Conservatives still clung to the idea of wages being determined within a framework jointly agreed between government, employers, and trade union leaders, their ranks in the Conservative Party had dwindled significantly by early 1979. Certainly, by this time, Margaret Thatcher herself was 'highly sceptical about the role of pay policy in controlling inflation, and indeed by the prospect of any useful understanding with organised labour' (Halcrow 1989: 127).

7   The 'step-by-step' approach to trade union reform, 1979–1994

THE STYLE AND APPROACH OF THE THATCHER–MAJOR GOVERNMENTS

Although the Conservative Party won the May 1979 general election in the aftermath of the 'winter of discontent', and thus at a time when public hostility towards the trade unions was particularly pronounced, it came to power with relatively little by way of a detailed or predetermined programme for trade union reform. Whilst, as we have already noted, certain objectives and policy proposals had been agreed and formulated during the time in opposition, it would be wrong to assume that the new Conservative government possessed a detailed or long-term package of firm proposals beyond those already agreed. On the contrary, much of the trade union legislation implemented by the Thatcher and Major governments has been devised pragmatically and incrementally, guided undoubtedly by certain principles, but none the less developed in a rather *ad hoc* manner. It is only with hindsight that the reforms introduced since 1979 appear to represent a coherent strategy meticulously prepared and implemented. For example, whilst the closed shop was finally outlawed by the 1988 and 1990 Employment Acts, the Conservative Party had entered office in 1979 insisting that outright prohibition of the closed shop was not practicable. Thus were many of the Conservative government's policies towards the trade unions evolved and developed whilst in office, rather than having been predetermined. Indeed, the first Employment Secretary, James Prior, had envisaged, or at least hoped, that his 1980 Employment Act alone would be sufficient to bring about greater 'responsibility' and 'moderation' by the trade unions, to the extent that a return to dialogue and consultation over economic policy and wage determination between trade union leaders and the government would follow. Prior certainly did not expect, or desire, a whole series of trade union laws, and thus did not envisage or intend that his 1980 Act would merely be the first of many.

Prior was very much isolated, however, for most Conservatives were eager to see far more reforms – and far more far-reaching, radical reforms – being pursued by the party's parliamentary leadership. From 1979 onwards, therefore, the main disagreement within the Conservative Party over the issue of trade union legislation primarily concerned the pace, rather than the desirability, of reform. Few Conservatives any longer deviated from the view that trade union reform was both desirable and necessary. What did cause disagreement and debate in the Conservative Party was how quickly the parliamentary leadership ought to proceed.

In this respect, something of a generational difference manifested itself, with newer, younger backbenchers believing the parliamentary leadership to be too slow and cautious. For such critics, the Conservative Party had gone from one extreme to another: having tried too much too soon in the early 1970s, it was criticised for doing too little, too slowly, a decade later.

These newer backbench MPs, particularly those first elected to the House of Commons in 1979 or 1983, had not been party to the traumas experienced by the Heath government in its dealings with the trade unions, and thus failed to appreciate the reservations of those who had held ministerial office under Heath in the early 1970s. Many of those who had been in the Heath government certainly recognised the need to reform the trade unions, but were also equally aware of the need to proceed with caution, so as to avoid the mistakes of the early 1970s. Thus, what some newer, younger Conservative MPs perceived as lack of determination by the party leadership was, in fact, a sober recognition of what was feasible and practicable in the political minefield of industrial relations. However much senior Conservatives might have shared the emotional or ideological hostility to the trade unions articulated by their younger colleagues, political experience and parliamentary socialisation had inculcated in them a reluctant recognition that pragmatism and practicability were too important to ignore. Their refusal to embark upon another instant, all-out attack on the trade unions signified, not the absence of commitment, but the presence of wisdom.

Nor was underestimation of the Conservative leadership's determination to tackle the trade unions confined to backbench critics in the party. The TUC itself singularly failed to appreciate just how serious the Thatcher government was about reforming trade unions and industrial relations. In other words, many Conservative backbenchers and the TUC doubted the government's commitment, both 'groups' anticipating that the proposed reforms would not amount to much or be pursued for long. Conservative backbenchers feared, and the TUC hoped, that political 'reality' would temper the Thatcher government's commitment to trade union reform, and that after a short while the Conservative leadership would seek, as the Heath government had done, a closer, co-operative working relationship with the trade unions. The underestimation of the Thatcher government's commitment, and of the extent to which it was adopting a long-term strategy, was candidly acknowledged by the then TUC General Secretary, Len Murray: 'We didn't believe that they would do what they were threatening to do. We didn't believe that they meant it' (Lord Murray to this author).

What the Conservatives were 'threatening' to do – according to their 1979 Election Manifesto – was, initially at least, to introduce three main changes, namely: to review the law on trade union immunities with regard to picketing; to ensure 'ample compensation' for employees who lost their jobs as a consequence of their refusal to join a trade union; and to encourage secret ballots, financed by the government, 'for union elections and other important issues'. There was also a promise that a Conservative government would 'ensure that the unions bear their fair share of the cost of supporting their members who are on strike', a clear indication that social security payments to strikers would be curbed.

Disagreement in the Conservative Party over the issue of trade union (and industrial relations) reform manifested itself at the very highest levels of government within days of its election victory. In emphasising his desire to avoid confrontation with the trade unions, and pledging, instead, his intention of consulting, and co-operating with, the two sides of industry, James Prior immediately found himself at odds with Margaret Thatcher, the new Prime Minister. Upon being appointed Employment Secretary, Prior requested that Barney Hayhoe be permitted to continue serving as his deputy. This request was turned down by Thatcher, who offered Prior a barrister in the form of Leon Brittan as his Junior Minister at the Department of Employment. This time, it was Prior who responded in the negative, arguing that Brittan's 'manner as one of my Deputies in Opposition had already upset both the CBI and the TUC'. Furthermore, Prior felt that it would be a mistake to have as his deputy a Conservative barrister who had been so closely associated with industrial relations reform, claiming that it would look too much like 'a re-run of Geoffrey Howe's handling of industrial relations in the early 1970s' (Prior 1986: 113–14). A number of other candidates for the post suggested by Prior proved unacceptable to Margaret Thatcher, or were otherwise unavailable. Eventually, Prior had to accept the appointment of Patrick Mayhew, another barrister, as his Junior Minister, with Thatcher declaring her determination to have '*someone* with backbone' in the department (ibid.: 114).

Thatcher further declared that trade union reforms would be on the Statute Book by Christmas (1979), thereby sending a clear signal to Prior that there was to be no prevarication or procrastination. Under pressure to act swiftly (from many backbenchers as well as from the Prime Minister), Prior immediately set about drafting what was to become the Employment Act, 1980. Yet at the same time, he sought to maintain a dialogue with trade union leaders in the hope that changes could be effected predominantly through persuasion, and therefore with a minimum of conflict or confrontation. Indeed, whilst acknowledging the need for at least some trade union reform, Prior still inclined significantly towards voluntarism, believing that legislative measures should be kept to the absolute minimum.

Consequently, he made it clear that once his 'limited but vital proposals' had been enacted, he expected the main responsibility for improving industrial relations to lie with the two sides of industry (ibid.: 113–14). Elsewhere, Prior insisted that 'the key to good industrial relations was to be found in the way in which people conducted their affairs at the place of work'. In consequence, he claimed that beyond the imminent 1980 Employment Act, the government had no plans for major legislative changes in the sphere of industrial relations (*Daily Telegraph*, 21 July 1979).

Such utterances were endorsed by a former senior official of the CTU, who warned the government against pursuing massive programmes of restrictive legislation against the trade unions. What was needed, he claimed, was for the Conservative government and the trade unions to develop a working relationship with each other, irrespective of what individuals on either side said about the other (Bowis 1979a: 5–7).

The Employment Bill was introduced to Parliament at the end of 1979, and enshrined four main objectives. First, government funds were to be made available to finance ballots for union elections and strike calls. Second, picketing was to be limited to an employee's own place of work; secondary picketing (picketing of another employer or place of work) was thereby outlawed. Third, the Bill sought to amend the closed shop, by stipulating that all new closed shop agreements would have to secure the support of at least 80 per cent of the workforce, as registered in a secret ballot. 'Substantial compensation' was also to be made available to employees who lost their jobs as a consequence of not joining – on grounds of conscience or deeply held conviction – a trade union which operated a closed shop. The fourth objective of the Bill, following on from the third to some extent, was to deal with 'coercive union recruitment tactics', such as the 'blacking' of those employees who declined to join a trade union.

These proposals, however, caused dismay in some quarters of the Conservative Party, where it was felt that they did not go far enough. Instead, they were deemed 'to represent no more (at the most) than the bare minimum of what is necessary' (editorial in the *Daily Telegraph*, 10 July 1979). As such, the Employment Bill had the effect of exacerbating impatience in the Conservative Party over the issue of industrial relations and trade union reform, as Prior's 'step-by-step' approach irked those backbenchers, and a few of his Cabinet colleagues, who desired a bolder, more robust approach from the Employment Secretary.

Not for the first time, Prior found himself having to remind his colleagues of the dangers of rushing through punitive legislation which might well be seen by the unions and the British public as vindictive or excessive, and thus less likely to be successful, due to lack of popular support and legitimacy (BBC Radio 4, *The World This Weekend*, 3 February 1980). Prior sought constantly to convince his Conservative critics that to pursue the hard-line approach to trade union reform which they demanded would be to antagonise and provoke the unions, thereby resulting in the same kind of confrontation and conflict that had been engendered by the Industrial Relations Act. He was adamant that the Conservative Party could not afford to tread the same path again, emphasising that 'it behoved us to go fairly carefully in what we said and what we did.' He feared that 'if one tried to do too much again too quickly, one could get outright rejection again of anything you tried to do' (former Cabinet Minister to this author). Prior therefore sought 'to bring about a lasting change in attitude by changing the law gradually, with as little resistance, and therefore as much by stealth, as was possible' (Prior 1986: 158).

Prior's caution was also born of recognition of the importance of practicability; trade union legislation which might have satisfied Conservative backbenchers and constituency activists was not necessarily legislation which could effectively be implemented. Prior was emphatic that: 'It would be wrong to pass legislation which the courts could not enforce, as had been the case with the 1971 Act.' In any case, he argued:

> It would have been too easy for the Government to go too far in changing the law and to do so too fast: we would then find that not only the unions but also business and most of the country would unite in saying that we had produced a scheme of law which was unworkable. . . . If Labour's legislation had been unbalanced in one direction, favouring the unions, we had to be wary of not tilting the balance too far back in the other.
>
> (Prior 1986: 158, 169)

This cautious stance was particularly evident over the question of ballots for union elections and strike calls. Whilst many of his colleagues – including the Prime Minister herself – were in favour of compulsory ballots, Prior was emphatic that it was not practicable for every decision to be taken only after a secret ballot of the mass membership of a trade union. Instead, he argued, the decision as to whether a ballot should be conducted ought to rest with the trade unions themselves, particularly if such ballots could be demanded by ordinary union members.

A similar view was enunciated by a former senior official of the CTU, who argued on more than one occasion that whilst it was right for union members to be able to demand a secret ballot, it would be impracticable to insist on one for every decision, not least because some problems arose, and were then resolved, in less time than it would take to organise a ballot. Other problems, meanwhile, by their very nature, necessitated immediate action, health and safety matters for example. Thus, whilst not disagreeing with the principle of secret ballots, the former CTU official argued that there were 'insoluble problems about making it compulsory for all issues', as in the case of a genuine walk-out for health and safety reasons, which by its very nature could not wait for the outcome of a secret ballot (Bowis 1979b: 19–20).

However, Prior's defence of his cautious approach was not helped by the major strike at British Steel which began in January 1980. There was general concern not only at the implications of a strike in a key industry, but also over the secondary picketing of private steel firms which accompanied the strike. Having been 'walking a political tightrope in my effort to stick to a gradual approach to trade union reform', Prior suddenly found that 'there was a gale almost blowing me off the rope as the action of steelworkers and their supporters led to renewed demands for much tougher measures to curb trade union power' (Prior 1986: 161).

Indeed, such was the unease on the backbenches with Prior's 'softly-softly' approach to the trade unions, that the Conservative Party Chairman, Peter (Lord) Thorneycroft, visited the Employment Secretary to warn him that pressure in the party for tougher action on union immunities might become irresistible. Certainly, George Gardiner, MP, was prominent in demanding a more hard-line approach by Prior (*Sunday Express*, 3 February 1980), whilst similar calls for tougher measures were heard at a crowded meeting of the Conservative 1922 Committee at the beginning of February 1980.

At the same time, Prior was busy fending off criticism from some of his Cabinet colleagues over his cautious approach. For example, John Nott wrote to Prior urging a radical clampdown on trade union immunities, whilst another former lawyer, Geoffrey Howe, made it clear that he favoured a return to the wholesale reform of industrial relations that had been attempted with the 1971 Industrial Relations Act. Meanwhile, the Cabinet committee on economic strategy held a number of meetings at which Prior had to fend off demands for tougher action against the trade unions.

The Cabinet's economic strategy committee held a crucial meeting on 12 February 1980 at which Prior's approach to trade union reform was the main item on the agenda. Prior had the task of persuading his ministerial colleagues to accept his policy. Indeed, so important was this meeting that Prior decided that he would resign as Employment Secretary if he was defeated. In order to prevent such an eventuality, Prior spent the day before the meeting holding a series of private audiences with some of his Cabinet colleagues, in order to convince them of the wisdom of his approach, and thus to elicit their support in the Cabinet committee meeting.

In the event, the meeting was characterised by a deep division amongst Prior's ministerial colleagues; Margaret Thatcher's desire for a rather tougher approach towards the trade unions was shared in the Cabinet committee by Humphrey Atkins, John Biffen, Sir Geoffrey Howe, David Howell, Patrick Jenkin, Sir Keith Joseph, and Angus Maude. By contrast, Prior received support for his moderate approach from Nicholas Edwards, Sir Ian Gilmour, Lord Hailsham, Francis Pym, Peter Walker, and George Younger. The remaining members of the Cabinet committee – Mark Carlisle, Michael Heseltine, Norman St John-Stevas, and Lord (William) Whitelaw – were all somewhat equivocal on the issue. The resultant compromise was that Prior's approach was to be supported on condition that a major review of trade union immunities would be conducted in the not-too-distant future, with a view to further legislation in the next parliamentary session.

Yet this compromise was insufficient to assuage some of the neo-liberal critics on the government's backbenches. Appearing before the House of Commons Select Committee on Employment in February 1980, Prior was rhetorically asked by John Gorst, MP, whether he was 'afraid' of going further in his reform of industrial relations and the trade unions in case he provoked a general strike. Gorst then insinuated that Prior was guilty of 'cowardice', 'abdication of responsibility', and of 'giving in to threats of blackmail'. Further-more, Gorst made it clear that his wish was to see trade union immunities not reviewed, but revoked. Prior faced further hostility from another Conservative on the committee when John Townend pointedly asked him whether he was concerned with seeking the consent of 'minority power blocks', rather than of the majority of the population.

Prior's response was to emphasise his desire to win the consent of both the public and the trade unions. He reiterated yet again his belief in both the desirability and the necessity of a cautious, consensual approach to trade union reform, and in so doing, expressed his regret that some politicians still favoured 'fierce action' which would probably lead to greater industrial unrest and civil disorder. Predictably, perhaps, Prior's allusion to a consensual approach was characterised as a euphemism for appeasement of the trade unions (*The Spectator*, 16 February 1980, 3).

Nowhere was Prior's emollient approach more evident than in the parliamentary debates over the 1980 Employment Bill, in particular its highly cautious provisions concerning the closed shop. In explicitly acknowledging that many of his Conservative colleagues would have liked him to have been much tougher, to the extent of outlawing the closed shop altogether, Prior emphasised that this had been tried back in 1971 and simply had not worked (*HC Debates*, 5th series, vol.976: c.59, c.62).

More generally, in response to criticisms of other aspects of the Employment Bill, Prior found himself repeatedly warning his parliamentary colleagues that their suggestions and proposals for tougher action were 'fraught with danger and risks', and that if adopted, the government might well create more problems than it actually solved. He did not want Parliament to put itself in the position of passing legislation which could not subsequently be enforced. This was a deliberately cautious policy, taking careful account of practicability and circumstances, Prior proclaimed, and thus one which perfectly accorded with the traditional 'pragmatic Tory approach' (*HC Debates*, 5th series, vol.983: c.627–35). He also suggested that those most critical of the moderate character of his legislation were those who were furthest away from the day-to-day problems of British industry, and who thus had a simplistic belief that industrial relations problems could be solved merely by invoking the law. Prior rejected this perspective, insisting that whilst the law had an important part to play in establishing the overall framework within which employers and employees conducted their affairs, 'the main responsibility for improving industrial relations rests with those in industry' (*HC Debates*, 6th series, vol.17: c.766–7).

It was no secret that Prior's voluntarist inclinations were sharply at odds with the rather more radical approach favoured by Margaret Thatcher, several Cabinet colleagues, and many Conservative back-benchers; few were surprised when Prior was replaced in Thatcher's first Cabinet reshuffle in the autumn of 1981. Indeed, there was a sense of delight among many Conservatives at all levels of the party that Norman Tebbit was appointed Employment Secretary in place of Prior. Tebbit had acquired a reputation among friends and foes alike of being a 'union-basher', and as such, his appointment raised hopes – and in some quarters of the parliamentary party, fears (former Cabinet Minister to this author) – that the Conservative government was about to embark on a fundamental and full-scale legislative attack on the trade unions.

Yet to the consternation of many Conservatives on the Right of the party, Tebbit immediately made it clear that he too intended pursuing a 'step-by-step' approach to trade union reform, albeit with a slightly quicker, longer gait. He was 'determined first to form public opinion, and then to be always just a little behind, rather than ahead of it' (Tebbit 1988: 185). Tebbit, like Prior before him, was cognisant of the dangers in proceeding too quickly, or of introducing legislation which proved unworkable or unenforceable. His instinctive or ideological hostility towards trade unionism was thus considerably tempered by a hard-headed realism about what was feasible.

There was, however, a further reason for the maintenance of a 'step-by-step' approach, namely electoral calculations. It was recognised that such an approach offered the advantage of keeping trade union reform high on the political agenda, thereby enabling further legislative proposals to be unveiled in the run-up to a general election. This neatly fitted in with Tebbit's notion of always leaving the public wanting a little bit more. The 'step-by-step' approach sustained by Tebbit thus ensured that the issue of trade union reform would be kept 'on the boil'. (It is thus no coincidence that each Conservative election victory since 1979 has been followed within a year or so by the introduction of new trade union legislation.)

Yet Tebbit's pragmatic approach disappointed those Conservatives who had eagerly expected his 'trade union basher' image to be matched by legislative deeds. When this proved not to be the case – particularly with regard to his refusal to outlaw the closed shop in his 1982 Employment Act – some on the Right of the Conservative Party began fearing that Tebbit too was backtracking and succumbing to the traditional arguments about 'realism' and 'practicability' which many viewed as mere euphemisms for prevarication and procrastination. Tebbit was certainly wary of going too far on certain issues, hence his refusal to replace 'contracting out' of political levy payments with 'contracting in'. Tebbit was acutely aware that whilst such a measure would have been warmly welcomed on the Conservative backbenches, an outright attack on the Labour Party's main source of funding 'would not have been equitable ... it would not have been in the interests of a democratic system to leave one of the two main parties bereft of its prime funding'. It was also recognised that if the political levy was attacked, a future Labour government might well 'retaliate' by legislating against business donations to the Conservative Party (former Cabinet Minister to this author; see also Kirwan 1983).

None the less, some of the most radical and far-reaching trade union reforms – those enshrined in the 1984 Trade Union Act – such as the measures on trade union ballots for leadership elections, strike action, and political funds, were originally drafted by Tebbit, although by the time the Bill was introduced to Parliament, Tebbit had been replaced as Employment Secretary by Tom King. It was this piece of legislation which, more than any other, represented the centre-piece of the Thatcherite desire to 'democratise' Britain's trade unions, and 'hand them back to their members'.

With the 1984 Trade Union Act on the Statute Book, however, there followed something of an interregnum in the programme of trade union legislation, with no further reforms introduced until 1988 – the year following the next election victory. There were a number of reasons for this hiatus in Conservative trade union legislation. First, the scope and substance of the 1984 Act provided for the sort of measures which many Conservatives had long been demanding. Indeed, there were some in the Conservative Party who wondered whether it was necessary – or desirable – to introduce any further legislation. From a few quarters, a Baldwinian call was heard urging the parliamentary leadership to start pursuing a more conciliatory, constructive approach towards the trade unions, re-establishing dialogue and rebuilding bridges. Such calls, however, were totally unheeded. Not only did there remain an ideological antipathy towards trade unionism throughout much of the Conservative Party, there was also the fact that from the parliamentary leadership's point of view, there was no need to seek a rapprochement with the trade unions. A combination of legislation, high unemployment, and ministerial willingness to stand firm in the face of industrial action had all combined to weaken the power of the trade unions. The Thatcher governments of the early 1980s had disproved the generally held assumption of post-war British politics, namely that no government could govern without seeking the co-operation of trade union leaders. In this context, there was absolutely no need for Ministers in the mid-1980s to start proffering olive branches to the trade unions.

The second reason for the hiatus in trade union legislation between 1984 and 1988 was the 1984–5 miners' strike, which was obviously a major preoccupation for the Thatcher government during this time. In any case, the eventual defeat of the miners itself served to weaken and demoralise Britain's trade unions: if the traditionally powerful NUM could now be defeated by the Thatcher government, then what chance did any other trade union have of securing victory through industrial action? Admittedly, the government might have chosen to use the defeat of the miners as the occasion to introduce further legislation, but refrained from doing so. It was also the defeat of the miners' strike which prompted some of the calls for a more conciliatory approach towards the trade unions to be adopted, although it is inconceivable that these were actually instrumental in persuading Ministers to exercise restraint.

The third reason for the hiatus in trade union legislation between 1984 and 1988 was that the Employment Secretary who succeeded Tom King in September 1985, Lord Young, had little interest in introducing further union reforms *per se*, claiming that the three Acts already passed had 'restored a better balance between employers and employees'. Instead, he was more concerned to 'find a way to make the Department concentrate on employment and enterprise' (Young 1990: 162).

It was not until 1988, the year following another Conservative election victory, that a further bout of trade union legislation was introduced (although the measures had been promised in the Conservatives' 1987 Election Manifesto), by which time Lord Young had been replaced at the Department of Employment by Norman Fowler. The 1988 Employment Act addressed issues dealt with in the previous three Acts, but radically reformed and extended them, so that, for example, pre-entry closed shops (hitherto permissible if 80 per cent of employees voted in favour) were now prohibited. Yet the 1988 Employment Act received no mention in Fowler's autobiography, and the subsequent piece of legislation, the 1990 Employment Act, which built upon its predecessor – although it did include abolition of all closed shops – only warranted brief mention over a couple of pages (Fowler 1991: 324–5). Both pieces of legislation, however, were publicly presented as logical extensions of the government's programme of trade union 'democratisation' and enhancement of the rights of individual trade union members *vis-à-vis* their unions and union leaders.

The 'step-by-step' policy of trade union reform, with a further piece of legislation always being introduced in the year following a Conservative general election victory, was maintained with the 1993 Trade Union Reform and Employment Rights Act, which not only declared further aspects of trade unionism in need of reform, but also confirmed that John Major was not prepared merely to consolidate the trade union reforms introduced under his predecessor's premiership, or to adopt a more conciliatory approach to the unions. Indeed, it is significant that shortly after the 1992 general election victory, the NEDC was finally abolished, thereby dashing any expectations that the style of leadership associated with John Major – gentler, and more inclined to listen and discuss collegially – might herald a return to a more regular and constructive rapport between the Conservative government and the trade unions.

Indeed, although David Hunt (Employment Secretary since May 1993) spoke on the platform of a TUC conference in July 1994, and apparently invited the trade unions to work more closely with the government in devising measures to pursue full employment, the overall attitude of 1990s Conservatism remains antipathetical towards trade unionism. Indeed, contemporary Conservative orthodoxy is that job creation and reductions in unemployment can only be achieved by not restoring trade union power or influence, but by pursuing further measures to increase labour market deregulation and flexibility.

Furthermore, many Conservatives are still in favour of further trade union reforms, particularly legislation to prohibit or curb strikes in 'essential services'. This issue was revitalised in the summer of 1994 when signal workers virtually halted train services by undertaking industrial action in support of a pay claim significantly in excess of the government's own public sector pay limit. Although previous Employment Secretaries, most notably Norman Tebbit, had shied away from legislating against strikes in 'essential' or public services, the series of 24- and 48-hour strikes organised by the Rail, Maritime and Transport Union pushed the issue of outlawing such action back up the political agenda. Those Conservatives in favour of legislation would doubtless see it as a fitting finale to the trade union reforms of the previous fourteen years.

TRADE UNION LEGISLATION UNDER THATCHER AND MAJOR

Rather than adopt a merely chronological approach to the trade union legislation introduced since 1979, the Thatcher–Major governments' trade union and industrial relations reforms will be delineated in a more thematic manner. This will entail noting the reforms introduced concerning particular aspects of trade unionism and industrial relations, and, where appropriate, the rationale proffered by the Thatcher–Major governments to justify or explain these measures. Given that it is strike action which has been so widely viewed as the key industrial relations problem – 'the British disease' – by politicians since the late 1950s and early 1960s, it is to the legislation introduced since 1979 concerning strikes that we first turn our attention; this is followed by an overview of reforms introduced concerning trade union leadership elections, the closed shop, and the maintenance of political funds.

Trade union ballots prior to strike action

Conservatives obviously portrayed ballots as the means of 'democratising' Britain's trade unions, and thus making union leaders accountable to the views of their members. This was considered particularly crucial in the sphere of strike action. Conservatives frequently claimed that because trade union leaders were more militant, and thus 'unrepresentative' of their rank-and-file membership, many strikes were not supported by ordinary workers. Instead, it was alleged that trade unionists often obeyed strike calls by their union leaders reluctantly, or through fear of disciplinary action by their union, such as termination of their membership, which in the case of a closed shop trade union might well result in loss of employment. On the premise that ordinary trade unionists were usually more moderate than their leaders, many Conservatives envisaged that strike ballots would result in far fewer strikes actually taking place, because trade union members would, it was believed, often reject strike calls by their leaders. For the Thatcher governments, therefore, strike ballots were envisaged to have the dual advantage of both 'democratising' the trade unions and reducing the incidence of strikes.

Provision for strike ballots was initially included in the 1980 Employment Act, which made state funds available to trade unions to enable them to conduct postal ballots prior to strike action (although some on the Right of the party viewed with consternation the offer to the trade unions of state finance to pay for postal ballots by a government supposedly committed to reducing public expenditure and reliance on the state). Such funding was intended to pre-empt trade union claims that they could not afford to conduct postal ballots. However, at this stage, whether trade union leaders wished to conduct such ballots was entirely up to them; there was no legal obligation to do so.

It was the 1984 Trade Union Act, however, which actually made secret ballots obligatory prior to strike action. A trade union which called its members out on strike without previously having obtained their (majority) support in a secret postal ballot would not enjoy legal immunity, and would therefore be liable to civil action from affected employers who could subsequently seek a High Court injunction or sue the union concerned for damages.

The issue of strike ballots was further addressed by the 1988 Employment Act, which endowed trade union members with a legal right to a postal ballot, the implication clearly being that this would enhance secrecy, and eradicate the scope for intimidation of ordinary trade union members which might otherwise occur in the workplace.

Finally, the 1993 Trade Union Reform and Employment Rights Act stipulated that all strike ballots had to be postal and subject to independent scrutiny. The Act also required trade unions to give employers at least seven days' notice from the result of the ballot before commencing strike action.

Strike action

Apart from the introduction of pre-strike ballots, the Thatcher–Major governments introduced a number of measures intended to limit the capacity of trade unions to engage in strike activity. First, through the 1982 Employment Act, the definition of a 'trade dispute' was narrowed, thereby ensuring that certain kinds of industrial action no longer carried legal immunity. In particular, a trade dispute was redefined to mean 'a dispute between workers and their employers which relates wholly or mainly to' terms and conditions of employment and other closely related matters. The deliberate, intended effect of such a definition was to render unlawful industrial action in connection with such matters as demaracation disputes between trade unions or attempts to compel workers or employers in another firm or industry to operate a closed shop. Very importantly also, the 1982 Employment Act's redefining of 'a trade dispute' rendered unlawful 'politically motivated' strikes. As one sympathetic commentator observes: 'This direct removal of legal immunity from the trade unions in particular cases was distinctly the most radical element in the whole programme of Conservative trade union reform' (Hanson 1991: 17). The 1988 Employment Act, meanwhile, made it unlawful to pursue any form of strike activity in support of a closed shop, even in the immediate workplace.

The 1988 Employment Act also introduced a second significant change concerning strikes, namely that trade unions could no longer discipline members who refused to participate in industrial action. As the 1987 Green Paper *Trade Unions and their Members* had emphasised: 'No union member should be penalized by his trade union for exercising his right to cross a picket line and go to work.' This clearly accorded with the Thatcherite emphasis on the 'individual rights' of trade union members *vis-à-vis* their unions and officials, whilst also serving to undermine solidarity amongst trade unionists during times of industrial action. Indeed, this measure was also portrayed as upholding the individual's 'right to work', a phrase whose incantation by Ministers during industrial action assumed the aura of tragic irony, given that those same Ministers were happy to oversee the contraction of whole industries, entailing tens of thousands of redundancies, and to preside over unemployment of between two and three million. Such was the context in which the strike-breaker's inviolate 'right to work' was proudly proclaimed by Conservative Ministers.

A third aspect worth noting with regard to strike action is the provision enshrined in the 1990 Employment Act permitting employers to sack workers engaged in unofficial strikes. At the same time, if and when such workers were dismissed, industrial action in their support would itself be exempt from legal immunity. Unofficial strikers would themselves have to accept 'individual responsibility' for their actions.

Trade union ballots for leadership elections

As with strike ballots, the Thatcher government's introduction of ballots for the election of trade union leaders was proudly portrayed as an innovation intended to 'democratise' Britain's trade unions, and 'hand them back to their members'. At the same time, this policy was largely premised on the widely held assumption that the vast majority of 'ordinary' trade union members were more moderate (i.e. less left-wing) than their allegedly 'extremist' or 'militant' leaders. It was therefore assumed that the introduction of leadership ballots would result in the election of more 'moderate' trade union leaders, ones who would be far more reflective and representative of the 'commonsense' views of their members. This, in turn, Conservatives envisaged, would mean fewer strike calls and lower wage claims.

As with strike ballots, the first steps towards imposing leadership elections were modest indeed, the 1980 Employment Act merely making available public funds for those trade unions which wished to conduct a ballot of their members in order to elect (or re-elect) their leader. It was the 1984 Trade Union Act which laid down a requirement that members of trade union executive committees who held voting rights at executive meetings were to be subject to election by their rank-and-file membership in ballots to be conducted at least once every five years. Ballot papers were to be sent to the home address of each union member, and members were also entitled to return them completed by post. However, at this stage, postal ballots were not made obligatory; secret ballots could be conducted at the workplace if certain conditions were met. It was the 1988 Employment Act which extended to trade union members the right to vote for their leaders in a postal ballot. At the same time, General Secretaries or presidents of trade unions were themselves to be subject to five-yearly elections, a move which perfectly accorded with the avowed objective of 'democratising' the trade unions, and of making union leaders accountable to their members.

Eliminating the closed shop

As has been noted in previous chapters, the closed shop had always been subject to fierce Conservative criticism, largely on the grounds that it constituted a denial of individual liberty, but also because it represented an infringement upon management's right to manage.

With the Thatcher government which came to power in 1979 committed to restoring this right to management, and simultaneously espousing a vigorous 'individualist' philosophy, it was inevitable that the closed shop would come under increased attack. Yet many Conservatives were surprised – and dismayed – by the caution displayed by the parliamentary leadership in tackling the closed shop. As noted earlier in this chapter (pp. 160–5), many back-benchers wanted Prior or Tebbit to outlaw the closed shop entirely, and were thus extremely disappointed by the apparent timidity displayed in the trade union legislation of the early 1980s.

The 1980 Employment Act, for example, stipulated that all new closed shop agreements were to be subject to ballot by the employees concerned. Furthermore, the support of at least 80 per cent of these employees (voting in a secret ballot) would be required before a new closed shop could actually be established. At the same time, employees whose employment was terminated as a consequence of their refusal, on grounds of conscience or other deeply held conviction, to join a trade union, would be entitled to sue for unfair dismissal and to claim 'substantial compensation' if their case was upheld. Similar compensation could also be paid to employees who lost their job because the trade union itself refused to allow them membership.

To many Conservatives, such provisions were deemed wholly inadequate, and consequently the parliamentary debates concerning the 1980 Employment Act witnessed a number of backbenchers castigating Prior for the modesty of his proposals. Indeed, during the committee stage of the Bill, John Gorst teamed up with the Liberal MP Cyril Smith to table an amendment which would establish an employee's legal right not to have to join a trade union 'on any grounds whatsoever'. In moving this amendment, Gorst listed four particular objections to the closed shop. First, it served to concentrate excessive and coercive power in the hands of trade union officials. Second, it entailed compulsory membership of a hitherto voluntary association. Third, it denied employees the right to choose which trade union – if any – they wished to join. Fourth, it created a monopoly in the supply of labour in particular occupations or industries. In situations where the closed shop operated, Gorst complained, the employer had responsibility without power, whilst the trade union had power without responsibility (*HC Debates*, Standing Committee A. 1979–80, vol.1: c.700–9).

Whilst some of Gorst's colleagues on the standing committee shared his sentiments, they declined to support the amendment in the lobbies, largely on grounds of pragmatism. Not only were some of them concerned that Gorst's amendment would undermine the Bill's chances of success (by antagonising or alienating moderate trade unionists, for example), there was also a reluctant recognition of how deeply embedded in British industrial life the closed shop had become. Indeed, Jocelyn Cadbury referred to his own managerial experience in arguing that 'whether I like it or not, the closed shop is rooted in our industrial life', and so 'to abolish the closed shop outright would create too much divisiveness in the country'. In any case, he added, 'I do not think it is practicable' (ibid.: c.755).

The same concern over practicability also informed Norman Tebbit's provisions on the closed shop in the 1982 Employment Act – 'I rejected the pressures to "ban" the closed shop, it simply would not have worked' (Tebbit 1988: 185) – which extended the requirement for a ballot to existing closed shops, and also stipulated that either 80 per cent of the relevant workforce, or 85 per cent of those actually participating in the ballot, would have to vote in favour in order for the closed shop to remain immune from legal action by any employees who lost their job for refusal to join the trade union in question. For those employees who were deemed to have lost their job unfairly by virtue of refusing to join a trade union, particularly when that union had failed to conduct a ballot and obtain the requisite majority in favour of operating a closed shop, the amount of compensation was also increased (and has been increasing ever since to take account of inflation).

Yet in spite of the repeated claims that outright abolition or prohibition of the closed shop was not feasible or practicable, the 1988 Employment Act did remove all legal immunity for trade unions which operated a post-entry closed shop, irrespective of whether it commanded the support of the overwhelming majority of employees or union members. Trade union democracy was no longer the issue, but the rights of individual employees *vis-à-vis* the union itself. The 1988 Employment Act thus termed it 'unfair' for any employee to be dismissed from employment for refusing to join a trade union. The Act also removed all immunities from any trade union which took industrial action in order to enforce a closed shop.

In the wake of these provisions, it was little surprise when the next main bout of trade union legislation – the 1990 Employment Act – took the inevitable, logical step of removing legal immunity for pre-entry closed shops. In other words, all closed shop agreements, and attempts to enforce them, were now deemed illegal, and liable to civil action by aggrieved employees whose employment suffered as a consequence of trade unions seeking to maintain a closed shop of any kind. Ironically, one of the reasons cited by the Conservative government for its prohibition of all closed shops was that it was abiding by the European Community's Social Charter, which contained the stipulation that individuals ought to be endowed with the right to belong or not to belong to a trade union. This is the only provision enshrined in the Social Charter which the Conservatives have been happy to incorporate into domestic law: no 'opt-out' here.

Trade Union 'Political Funds'

Trade union links with, and financial donations to, the Labour Party have always been a target for considerable Conservative condemnation. Conservatives have routinely insisted that the trade unions should 'keep out of politics', and not align themselves financially and organisationally with a particular political party. Furthermore, the point has frequently been made by Conservatives that many trade union members whose union subscriptions included a small donation to the Labour Party via the political fund or levy were not themselves Labour Party supporters. For such reasons, the Conservative Party has always viewed trade union political funds and levy payments with the utmost distaste and displeasure, yet throughout the post-war period up until the 1980s it refrained from legislating against them, not least because it was felt that the antagonism and aggravation which would probably be provoked were not worth while. Such caution and restraint had reflected the Conservative Party's desire to foster a sense of trust between itself and the trade unions from 1945 onwards. By the 1980s, this was no longer a consideration, hence no longer such a constraint.

The Conservative government's main objections to the existing political funds or levy system were enunciated in the Green Paper, *Democracy in Trade Unions*, published at the beginning of 1983. Among other things, it was alleged that the existing system whereby a ballot in favour was treated as once-and-for-all, so that no subsequent ballots were required, was undemocratic, for it failed to give union members a regular opportunity to express their views (which may have changed since the ballot), whilst also preventing subsequent union members from expressing their wishes concerning the maintenance of a political fund by their union.

The main legislative attack on trade union political funds and levy payments was enshrined in the 1984 Trade Union Act, which stipulated that trade unions would have to conduct a secret ballot of their members at least once every ten years, in order to obtain their consent for the maintenance of a political fund financed from a proportion of their membership fees. To the dismay of many Conservatives, the Act did not specifically address the question of trade union donations or affiliations to the Labour Party, and so was viewed by some as a missed opportunity. Ironically, Norman Tebbit, the Employment Secretary who drafted the Trade Union Bill (before being reshuffled, so that the Bill was actually introduced by his successor, Tom King), had himself been in favour of replacing 'contracting out' of the political levy with 'contracting in'. However, he was persuaded from incorporating such a provision, partly on the advice of the Party Whips, who warned that it might be too provocative, and subsequently leave the Conservative Party vulnerable to retaliation by a future Labour government seeking revenge by legislating against business donations to the Conservatives (Tebbit 1988: 197–8).

Tebbit's decision not to replace 'contracting out' of the political levy by a system of 'contracting in' proved a grave disappointment to many Conservative backbenchers, ninety of whom supported an amendment, tabled by John Townend, MP, during the third reading of the Trade Union Bill, which would free trade unionists from any obligation to contribute towards their union's political fund unless they had expressly declared, in writing, a desire to do so. Townend acknowledged that the government was unlikely to accept his amendment at that point in time – it did not – but declared his hope that it would serve as a warning to Ministers about the breadth and depth of opposition on the backbenches to the 'contracting out' system, and thus 'put down a marker for the future' (*HC Debates*, 6th series, vol. 57: c.722–5).

In fact, for whatever reasons, no further legislative action has been invoked to curb the political funds operated by many trade unions, in spite of the widespread support that this would doubtless command among many Conservatives. It would seem that subsequent Employment Secretaries have either had other priorities, or have shared Tebbit's concern that tougher action against trade union political funds might appear too partisan, and leave the Conservative Party vulnerable to retaliatory action against business donations should a Labour government ever be elected.

Other aspects of the Thatcher–Major governments' programme of trade union reform which warrant passing mention are:

1 the creation, via the 1988 Employment Act, of a Commission for the Rights of Trade Unionists, to which trade union members could turn for legal advice and possibly financial assistance if they felt that they had suffered as a consequence of 'unlawful' trade union activity or behaviour;
2 the right of employers to offer financial 'incentives' to employees to give up their trade union membership; this provision was included in the 1993 Trade Union Reform and Employment Rights Act;
3 the declaration in the same Act that employers could only continue lawfully to deduct employees' trade union membership fees – the 'check off' arrangement – from their wages or salaries if those employees provided written permission every three years confirming their wish for such deductions to be made.

Vital though such legislation has been in seriously weakening the trade unions, other factors are also of signal importance when considering the Conservative onslaught against trade unionism since 1979; the law has only been one weapon in the Thatcher–Major governments' armoury.

THE MINERS' STRIKE 1984–5

No overview of the Thatcher governments' attitude and approach towards the trade unions would be complete without some reference to the year-long miners' strike which occurred during 1984–5. The strike came to symbolise the Conservatives' determination to destroy the power of Britain's trade unions once and for all, and in many respects the stance adopted by the Thatcher government against the NUM was just as significant as the content or volume of any legislation against the trade unions. Not only did the Thatcher government's unyielding stance ensure the eventual collapse of the strike, it also sent a signal – precisely as intended – to other trade unions that attempts to 'take on' the Conservative government were futile.

Although the miners' strike officially began in March 1984, its origins can be traced back to 1978, with the leaked publication of the so-called 'Ridley Report', outlined in the previous chapter (p. 130). Having implemented Ridley's proposals during the preceding five years, the Conservative government had carefully placed itself in an extremely strong position to stand firm against the miners when they were finally provoked into strike action in protest against the government's pit closures programme. At the time, as part of its propaganda war against the miners, the Conservative government repeatedly denied the claims of the NUM leader, Arthur Scargill, that there was a plan to run down the coal industry, entailing the closure of dozens of pits and the redundancies of tens of thousands of miners, as a prelude to privatisation, although history has subsequently vindicated Scargill's allegations.

Margaret Thatcher had actually favoured an attack on the miners in 1981, but had been persuaded that the time was not then ripe for a confrontation with the NUM. The proposals enshrined in the 'Ridley Report' had not then been fully implemented. It was to be another three years before the Conservative government was ready to take on the NUM in a trial of strength.

Many Conservatives claimed that the election of Arthur Scargill as president of the NUM in April 1982 made a confrontation between the government and the miners inevitable, the view being that Scargill himself, as a Marxist, would seek to instigate a miners' strike in order to bring down a Conservative government. Sooner or later, the irresistible force would meet the immovable object. Scargill and Thatcher were in fact quite similar in certain respects. Both were ideologues and populists who believed that any compromise was tantamount to betrayal. Both saw themselves as fighting for 'their' class; Scargill for the working class of northern England and the industrial regions, Thatcher for the *petite bourgeoisie* of Middle England and the City. Both were prepared to condone (or at least refused to condemn) picket-line violence on 'defensive' grounds; Scargill condoned (or at least refused to condemn) violence by striking miners 'in defence' of their jobs and their pit communities, whilst Thatcher condoned (or refused to condemn) violence by police officers 'in defence' of miners defying the strike and exercising their 'right to work'. (It was most odd that a government should talk of the 'right to work' of men whom it has subsequently, as intended throughout, made redundant.)

Margaret Thatcher herself apparently

> always knew, even as far back as 1978, that she would face a pitched battle mounted by Arthur Scargill. She knew it would be ostensibly an industrial dispute, but in reality it would be a political assault designed to overthrow her Government.
>
> (Ridley 1991: 67)

After Scargill's appointment as NUM president, the imminence and inevitability of a miners' strike was compounded by the government's selection, in September 1983, of Ian MacGregor as the new chair-person of British Coal. MacGregor had already presided over a major rationalisation (i.e. contraction and redundancy) programme at British Steel during the early 1980s, so it was abundantly clear what the government was expecting of him at British Coal. As one leading commentary on the miners' strike noted, 'MacGregor's record of taking on the trade unions in the USA's mining industry commended him to Margaret Thatcher as an ideal figure to take on Arthur Scargill.' MacGregor 'had no commitment to public-sector enterprise. He was an out-and-out private enterprise zealot, American style with a record in the USA for anti-unionism' (Goodman 1985: 27–8).

The miners' strike, which formally began in March 1984, following the announcement that the Cortonwood colliery in South Yorkshire was to be closed down, was soon to involve or highlight a number of features germane to the Thatcher government's 'programme' of trade union reform, and thus add to the pressure on the party leadership for further, tougher legislation. Of particular significance was the issue of ballots prior to strike action. Conservative Ministers constantly challenged the legitimacy of the miners' strike because of the NUM's refusal to conduct a ballot of its members to see if they actually supported strike action. (But strangely enough, neither the government nor the media ever called for a ballot of coal miners to ask them if they wished to have their pits closed down, their industry decimated, and their communities destroyed.) In view of the Thatcher government's avowed intention to 'democratise' Britain's trade unions, the NUM's refusal to conduct a ballot was clearly controversial, with Scargill being characterised and condemned as precisely the sort of 'bully-boy' trade union leader from whom the Conservative Party claimed it wanted to 'liberate' ordinary union members through the introduction of strike ballots.

Also raised by the strike was the issue of ballots for the election of trade union leaders themselves. Conservatives portrayed Scargill not only as a 'bully-boy' and a 'tyrant', but also as the archetypal 'extremist' leader who was not only totally unrepresentative of the views of most of his ordinary mass members, but also unaccountable.

The 1984–5 miners' strike also served to place renewed emphasis on the issue of picketing, as picket-line violence repeatedly attracted media attention. This in turn rendered the conduct of the miners' strike as much a law-and-order issue as an industrial relations one. Numerous reports about attacks on those miners continuing to work in defiance of the strike, coupled with injuries sustained by police officers as a consequence of violence on the picket line, were frequently cited by Ministers as evidence that many of those engaged in picketing were simply 'thugs', 'bully-boys' and 'rent-a-mob extremists'. The question was once again raised as to what curbs ought to be placed on picketing, and how they should – or could – be enforced. Certainly, from the government's perspective, the large police presence at picket lines was an example of the need for order and the rule of law to be maintained so as to uphold freedom, in this case the freedom of those miners wishing to continue working in defiance of the strike and the pickets: 'there would be no surrender to the mob and the right to go to work would be upheld' (Thatcher 1993: 346).

At a more general level, the miners' strike afforded the Thatcher government with an excellent opportunity to display its mettle in standing firm when faced with a challenge from a traditionally powerful, and militant, trade union. This obviously fitted in well with the image of a 'conviction government' determined to maintain order, and uphold the national interest and authority of the state when faced with a concerted or determined challenge from a 'vested sectional interest', one which was also deemed to be politically motivated. Hence Margaret Thatcher's notorious allusion to the striking miners as 'the enemy within', who had to be defeated with the same determination and courage as the Argentinians had been two years previously in the Falklands War. Indeed, in drawing an analogy between the Falklands War and the miners' strike, the Thatcher government portrayed both as instances where democracy was blatantly threatened by dictators and politically motivated tyrants.

As had been the case in the General Strike in 1926, therefore, many Conservatives considered that, ultimately, the most important issue at stake during the 1984–5 miners' strike was the continued existence of British parliamentary democracy itself. One Cabinet Minister involved declared that the defeat of the NUM meant that 'Parliament had regained its sovereignty', and suggested that 'had the Thatcher Government been broken and the craven Mr Kinnock installed in office by Scargill's thugs Britain would have been a grim place indeed' (Tebbit 1988: 238–9).

One other significant aspect of the miners' strike in terms of the Conservative government's approach to trade union and industrial relations reform was the reticence shown in instigating legal action during the dispute. The Thatcher governments were committed to reforms which exposed 'illegal' industrial action to civil action from affected parties such as employers, and certainly during the miners' strike 'Norman Tebbit and others on the right of the party ... were anxious to use immediately the legislation we had passed to stop secondary picketing at premises which are not the pickets' own' (Walker 1991: 172). However, Peter Walker, Energy Secretary at the time of the miners' strike, persuaded his Cabinet colleagues, and in particular Margaret Thatcher herself, 'that when you are fighting Mr Scargill, the legislation was unlikely to work', in which case: 'The government would be made to look a fool and people would say the legislation was unworkable' (ibid.: 173).

Walker also insisted that legal action against the miners might have prompted active solidarity from other trade unions whose support for the NUM had remained largely rhetorical, rather than practical. It was deemed essential to avoid legal action which might precipitate a closing of trade union ranks. 'If I had turned it into a battle involving Tory trade union legislation, it could well have provoked other trade unions ... to join in the dispute' (ibid.: 173). Whilst not all of his Cabinet colleagues were entirely persuaded by these arguments, Walker's cautious approach none the less enjoyed the support of Margaret Thatcher (Thatcher 1993: 353).

REJECTION OF INCOMES POLICIES

The Thatcher government's rejection of formal incomes policies constituted a distinct departure from the trend of the previous two decades. As was noted in previous chapters, successive governments throughout the 1960s and 1970s had pursued incomes policies in an attempt at controlling inflation. Proceeding on the assumption that inflation was largely caused by 'excessive' wage increases (i.e. wage increases not based on increased productivity, which therefore led firms to raise prices in order to cover their increased wage bill; this in turn, of course, led to further wage demands in order to cover price rises and the increased cost of living), governments sought to secure agreements with the trade unions as to the level of pay increases each year. If the unions could be persuaded to restrain their pay demands, it was believed, then inflation itself could be reduced.

The Thatcher government rejected this approach. Insisting that inflation was caused by governments excessively increasing the money supply, and seeking to solve socio-economic problems merely by printing more money and pumping it into the economy, the Thatcher government argued that incomes policies were a waste of time. Not only were incomes policies predicated upon an incorrect understanding of the cause of inflation, they would not work anyway, it was claimed, because trade unions were unable – or unwilling – to keep their side of any agreements with government concerning pay. Agreements entered into by trade union leaders concerning pay restraint were often not adhered to by their members on the shopfloor. Consequently, the Thatcher government's perspective was that if trade union leaders were unable to deliver their side of the bargain, then there was little point in government entering into negotiations with them in the first place.

The Thatcher government's rejection of incomes policies was also due to the fact that they served to politicise the whole issue of wages and salaries. Disputes over pay brought government and trade unions into conflict and confrontation. It became difficult to ascertain whether industrial action, in support of a pay claim in excess of government recommendations, was simply an industrial dispute concerning terms of employment, or whether it constituted a politically motivated strike against the government itself. (Many Conservatives, for example, believed that the miners' strike which allegedly led to the downfall of the Heath government early in 1974 was politically motivated, and that the pay claim was very much a means of disguising and legitimising the NUM's real objective at the time, namely to bring down the Heath government.) Such experiences reinforced the Thatcher government's rejection of incomes policies.

Following on from this perspective was the Thatcher government's firm belief that wages ought to be determined by 'the market'. Levels of pay, it was maintained, had to be determined by criteria such as what a firm or employer could afford, the relationship between the supply of, and demand for, a particular occupational skill, etc. Market forces, not agreements between government and unions, were to determine levels of pay.

The corollary of this approach was that increases in pay would have to emanate from increased profitability, increased productivity, or increased unemployment. Thus the Thatcher government's abandonment of incomes policies was linked to its abandonment of any commitment to the maintenance of full employment, a commitment which previous post-war Conservative governments had largely subscribed to. By contrast, Thatcherism made it clear that increases in unemployment were, to a significant extent, to be blamed on the trade unions, on the grounds that they were pressing for levels of pay which their employers could not afford, and which therefore led either to bankruptcy or to a shedding of staff in order to finance the wages of those who remained. Either way, the Thatcher government sought – with considerable success, in the early 1980s at least – to lay the blame for rising unemployment on 'greedy' trade unions who were allegedly pricing their members out of work. This had the double advantage for the government of deflecting the blame for high unemployment onto the trade unions rather than its own monetarist policies, and also of reducing public sympathy for the unemployed; the government could claim that many of those who were out of work had only themselves or their unions to blame, because they had demanded excessive pay rises. As such, the Thatcher governments anticipated that high(er) levels of unemployment would eventually prove far more effective in encouraging lower pay claims by the trade unions than any formal incomes policy agreed between government and union leaders.

One other important reason for the rejection of formal incomes policies by Thatcherism was the fact that they were clearly unpopular with many workers and trade unionists themselves, particularly amongst the skilled working class. The most obvious manifestation of this unpopularity was the propensity of rank-and-file union members to pursue wage claims in excess of those agreed between their union leaders and the government. However, there was also a recognition by Thatcherite Conservatives that resentment against incomes policies was particularly strong amongst skilled workers. This was because Labour's incomes policies had provided the lowest-paid with wage increases additional to, or in excess of, the stipulated pay norm or guideline, as part of an attempt at reducing poverty, and ensuring that incomes policies enshrined notions of social justice and fairness. The consequence, however, was that sections of the skilled working class witnessed the differentials between themselves and unskilled workers being eroded, a trend which they bitterly resented. To sections of the skilled working class, therefore, the Conservative Party's pledge to reject incomes policies, and return instead to free collective bargaining, was particularly appealing, especially as it was accompanied by talk of the need to restore incentives and differentials, and an insistence 'that effort and skill earn larger rewards' (*Conservative Manifesto* 1979: 12). This was music to the ears of those workers who possessed special skills or qualifications, for they clearly believed that they could secure higher remuneration in the context of 'the market' than under a government-imposed incomes policy.

Yet it is perhaps worth noting that not all Conservatives were, or are, opposed to incomes policies. Throughout Margaret Thatcher's premiership, some Conservatives hankered after a formal policy on pay, derived from consultation with the trade unions. The Thatcher government's first Employment Secretary, Jim (now Lord) Prior, 'became increasingly worried ... by the complete rejection of any form of incomes policy', for he 'believed that we had to have a policy to encourage voluntary restraint' (Prior 1986: 109). However, such a belief was clearly out of sync with the Thatcherite insistence that matters such as wages should be determined solely by managers and 'the market'. As another Conservative proponent of an incomes policy lamented, 'Dogma prevented any arrangement for wage bargaining other than ministerial exhortation, ill-treatment of the public sector, and unemployment' (Gilmour 1992: 82).

THE REJECTION OF CORPORATISM

Intimately and inextricably related to the Thatcher government's rejection of incomes policies was the rejection of corporatism. To a considerable extent, the development of corporatism in Britain had proceeded *pari passu* with the establishment of incomes policies. In order to secure any agreement on pay levels and wage increases, successive governments had negotiated with trade union leaders on a range of economic and industrial issues. Union leaders were only willing to accept wage restraint if they were offered 'benefits' in return. These 'benefits' invariably concerned the provision of the social wage, whereby government accepted responsibility for welfare benefits, old age pensions, public services, etc. Incomes policies and a drift towards corporatism thus developed in tandem.

Thatcherism rejected corporatism on a number of grounds. First, it was considered that such a mode of policy-making was totally incompatible with the neo-liberal belief that economic matters should be determined by market forces, and the laws of supply and demand. Decisions concerning issues such as investment, productivity, (re)location, and labour recruitment were deemed to be the concern and responsibility of firms and employers themselves, operating in the context of phenomena such as market forces, consumer demand, and profitability. Such decisions were not deemed to be the responsibility of government, according to the Thatcher–Major governments, and they were certainly not matters which the trade unions should seek to determine. In reviving the role of the market, therefore, Thatcherism made it clear that there was no place for the trade unions in determining economic policy. Therefore, by 1988, Lord Young (one of Margaret Thatcher's

Employment Ministers) was able proudly to proclaim that: 'We have rejected the TUC; we have rejected the CBI. We do not see them coming back again. We gave up the corporate state' (*The Financial Times*, 9 November 1988). Indeed, in the same year, the government published a White Paper (Command 278) on its plans for encouraging greater private enterprise and competition in which it declared that:

> The ability of the economy to change and adapt was hampered by the combination of corporatism and powerful unions.... Corporatism limited competition and the birth of new firms whilst, at the same time, encouraging protectionism and restrictions designed to help existing firms.
>
> (Department of Trade and Industry 1988: 1)

Second, and following directly on from this last point, Thatcherite critics of corporatism argued that such a system served to politicise decisions which had hitherto been taken on purely economic grounds. It was claimed that policies would increasingly be adopted on the grounds of social desirability or political expediency, rather than market criteria such as economic efficiency or commercial viability.

Third, and, again, following on from the above point, it was held that under a corporatist system, the state itself increasingly became the focus of demands and group lobbying. Before long, the state would find itself overwhelmed by the plethora of organised interests demanding that it pursue particular policies. The consequence was held to be twofold. Initially, there would be an 'overload of government' (King 1975), whereby the state would no longer be able to cope with, or respond satisfactorily to, the number and nature of the demands made upon it. Then, once this stage was reached, the government and the state would become the target of increasing resentment from those groups and citizens whose demands it was no longer able to satisfy. The danger of this situation was deemed to be that the authority and legitimacy of the state itself would be undermined. It was thus felt by Conservative critics of corporatism that the state had, for its own sake, to withdraw from many of the socio-economic activities and responsibilities it had hitherto taken on board, whilst also disengaging from the partnership established with organised interests such as the trade unions. Those who had previously looked to the state to protect or advance their interests would in future be expected to look to 'the market', and their own efforts.

Fourth, it is argued that the role and sovereignty of Parliament itself is undermined if and when vital decisions are determined by Ministers, civil servants, and the leaders of key interest groups. Indeed, it is argued that 'the drift of power from Parliament to industrial interests will serve only to weaken the authority of Parliament in general. As Parliament weakens, so the strength and legitimacy of bodies like the unions will grow' (Raison 1979a: 33). Clearly, therefore, the fear is that the advance of corporatism proceeds *pari passu* with the decline of parliamentary democracy. Conservative critics of corporatism thus suggest that if the trade unions wish to participate in politics and policy-making, then they ought to put up their own candidates in general elections.

Fifth, and finally, Conservative critics of corporatism suggest that it effectively disenfranchises those who are not members of the key interest groups in society, these invariably being 'producer' groups (i.e. those engaged in industrial and economic production, such as trade unions and employers' associations). Either individuals will be compelled to join an 'appropriate' group, which would constitute a denial of individual liberty and freedom of association, or they would be unrepresented in the making of a range of important policies. According to Raison, 'corporatism is never concerned with the individual, but only with the collectivity, never with the consumer, but only the producer' (Raison 1979a: 37). This particular objection was especially pertinent in the context of Thatcherism's strong emphasis on individualism.

Apart from its rejection of a formal incomes policy, the other manifestation of the Thatcher–Major governments' rejection of corporatism was the downgrading – and eventual abolition – of the National Economic Development Council, which met less and less frequently during the Thatcher years and was finally abolished in the spring of 1992. As far as most members of the Thatcher governments were concerned, the NEDC was a waste of time. The reduction of state intervention in the economy (trade union reforms notwithstanding) and the rejection of incomes policies were deemed to render the NEDC redundant. It was seen by Conservatives as the institutional relic of a bygone corporatist era, and to this extent it is perhaps surprising that it was not abolished sooner. Certainly Nigel Lawson, the Chancellor of the Exchequer from 1983 to 1989, was of the opinion that 'no useful purpose was being served by the National Economic Development Council, and . . . it should therefore be abolished' (Lawson 1992: 713). He articulated the view of many senior Conservatives when he declared that 'the deliberations of the

Council itself were a complete waste of valuable Ministerial time' (ibid.: 714). However, in keeping with the government's step-by-step approach, the NEDC was wound down gradually, meetings becoming less frequent. Shortly after the 1987 election victory, meetings of the NEDC were reduced from one a month to one a quarter. The writing was clearly on the wall, but it was not until a couple of months after the general election victory in April 1992 that the NEDC was finally abolished.

THE SIGNIFICANCE OF HIGH UNEMPLOYMENT

It would be a mistake to see the Conservative government's attack on trade unions as consisting solely of legislative reforms and restrictions, vitally important though these are. It is also necessary to consider, however briefly, the significance and impact of high unemployment on British trade unionism in the 1980s and 1990s. Surely no one can still be in any doubt that the Thatcher–Major governments have viewed high unemployment as a weapon which can be wielded against the trade unions, so as to destroy their powers and effectiveness? Even if one wishes to dispute this, and argue (as the government itself does) that unemployment is due to extraneous factors, such as world recession, which are beyond the control of any single government, the fact remains that high unemployment impacts upon trade unions in a number of ways.

First, high unemployment – arguably – serves to damp down wage demands, as fear of losing their jobs encourages workers to accept more modest pay increases. When unemployment is high, or rising, many employees will gratefully accept whatever pay increase they are offered, on the grounds that 'at least I've still got a job'. On similar grounds, workers are often reluctant or unwilling to engage in strike activity during times of high unemployment. However, the reason for qualifying the statement that high unemployment damps down wage demands and pay increases is that during the 1980s, many of those in work experienced significant increases in their living standards, casting some doubt on the assumption that there is a correlation between high unemployment and low pay rises. None the less, it does seem plausible to maintain that high unemployment will, in many instances, serve to exert a downward pressure on pay increases. (The increased living standards which many enjoyed in the 1980s may well have been attributable to lower inflation, tax cuts, and the relative ease with which some people obtained 'credit' or loans). When and where this is the case, the trade unions will clearly be in a weaker bargaining position, because they – and management – will be aware of the lower expectations of the workforce, and the unwillingness of workers to risk their jobs by participating in strike action.

The second way in which high unemployment impacts upon trade unions so as to reduce their powers is by depleting their membership. Clearly, as unemployment rises, so union membership will fall, unless those losing their jobs were not members of a trade union in the first place. Certainly in Britain during the 1980s, there was a marked decline in trade union membership. In 1979, for example, out of a national employment total of 23,173,000, the trade unions had 13,289,000 members (57.3 per cent of those in work). By 1987, however, the national employment total had fallen to 21,584,000, whilst trade union membership had declined to 10,475,000 (48.5 per cent of those in work).

Yet it does not follow that if unemployment itself falls, then trade union membership will increase. Indeed, towards the end of the 1980s, unemployment did fall slightly, yet trade union membership continued to decline. There is no real mystery involved. Many of the industries and firms which did expand and recruit workers during the 1980s do not allow or acknowledge trade unions, whilst in others, the terms and conditions of employment are deemed sufficiently favourable by the employees to preclude any desire to join a trade union. It ought to be noted that of the three million jobs which the government claims have been created since about 1985, most have been in the service sector, often part-time or temporary, and often recruiting women. Such employment also tends to be characterised by low levels of union membership.

It is also reasonable to assume that the outlawing of the closed shop effected by the 1988 and 1990 Employment Acts has served to reduce trade union membership. One other factor which might account for the decline in trade union membership is simply that in the context of high unemployment, some employees consider the trade unions to be ineffective and impotent, and thus not worth joining. This clearly puts trade unions in a no-win situation. If they are seen as being weak and ineffective, employees will consider them a waste of time. Yet if they are seen to be strong or active, they will be condemned for being too powerful or influential, thereby attracting further legislative curbs from the government.

AMBIVALENCE OF THE TORY PATERNALISTS

Many of those Ministers or MPs on the 'Left' or One Nation wing of the Conservative Party were uneasy and ambivalent about their government's reform of the trade unions during the 1980s, and its concomitant rejection of incomes policies and neo-corporatist bargaining with organised labour. These Conservatives generally accepted that after the events of the 1970s in the sphere of industrial relations, some trade union reform was both desirable and necessary – 'trade union reform was Margaret Thatcher's most important achievement' according to one of her most trenchant critics in the party (Gilmour 1992: 79) – particularly measures to democratise the unions, and make their leaders accountable to the mass membership. This type of reform was one which all Conservatives could wholeheartedly endorse.

However, paternalist Conservatives often remained anxious about many other reforms, and the government's commitment to trade union reform generally, fearing either that the party leadership was in danger of going too far, or that a more constructive element ought to be introduced in its approach to trade unionism, a 'carrot-and-stick' approach, rather than repeated waving of the stick and nothing else. By the middle of the 1980s in particular, there were some Conservatives who were suggesting that in the wake of three pieces of legislation, and the humiliating defeat inflicted on the miners, it was time for the party to adopt a more constructive and conciliatory approach towards the trade unions. Whilst one backbencher was suggesting that the time was ripe for the government to take the initiative in establishing a new working political relationship with the trade unions, based on discussion and dialogue (Baldry 1985: 10–11), a former Minister was similarly declaring that instead of viewing the defeat of the miners' strike as the signal for a new legislative onslaught against the trade unions, it ought to be viewed as the opportunity to 'introduce a more positive element to its strategy'. What was envisaged was the 'creation of a partnership between Government, industrial management and unions' (Pym 1985: 160–2, 182).

Indeed, even during the early 1980s, before the miners' strike, there were calls for the establishment of a partnership between the government and the trade unions to accompany the legislative reforms. It was envisaged that as the trade unions were rendered more responsible and moderate as a consequence of legislation, so they would be better placed to participate meaningfully in discussions and dialogue with Ministers and managers over industrial and economic affairs. In any case, it was believed that if reform and rehabilitation could be pursued in tandem, then the trade unions would have less justification for claiming that they were being subjected to a vindictive, vengeful attack by the Thatcher governments. For Conservatives subscribing to this perspective, what was being mooted (as it had been during the debates in opposition in the latter half of the 1970s) was the establishment of some kind of economic forum, in which Ministers, the TUC, and the CBI could meet on a regular basis in order to discuss economic problems and policies (Patten 1983: 128–9). Meanwhile, Conservatives such as Gilmour were reiterating the call for an industrial parliament, in which a significant number of 'seats' would be held by appointees from the trade unions and industry (Gilmour 1983: 206).

Yet these calls, and the paternalistic One Nation sentiments which underpinned them, went unheeded. Under the hegemony of Thatcherism, the Conservative governments of the 1980s were not ideologically inclined to pursue a neo-corporatist, conciliatory approach towards the trade unions. On the contrary, as noted earlier, the Thatcher–Major governments were expressly concerned to downgrade and dismantle corporatist mechanisms and institutions, and remove trade unions from the domain of economic policy-making. In any case, if the trade unions could be weakened through legislation and unemployment, then what need was there for the government to consult or negotiate with them? Neo-corporatism had partly been a strategy to channel or contain trade union power, rather than attack it. Yet if that power had subsequently been eradicated, then the whole rationale for incorporating the trade unions into economic decision-making dissipated. Whereas the 'Left' of the Conservative Party tended to the view that trade union reforms would render the unions more amenable to 'responsible' behaviour and participation in economic affairs, the 'Thatcherite' wing of the party was emphatic that if the power of the trade unions could be legislated away, then there was no need subsequently to ascribe them any role in economic discussions or policy-making at all. They could, for all practical purposes, be ignored.

Those Conservatives on the One Nation wing of the party were also deeply concerned at the high levels of unemployment which the Thatcher governments were willing to tolerate, fearing the potentially damaging consequences for social stability and political legitimacy in Britain. Writing in the early 1980s, Gilmour refuted the claims of many neo-liberal Conservatives and monetarists that unemployment was often beneficial to the economy (in terms of reducing inefficiency, overmanning, etc.), and that many of the unemployed were voluntarily out of work and thus needed cuts in their benefits in order to compel them to take whatever jobs were available. Instead, One Nation Conservatives such as Gilmour pointed out that 'far from the unemployed being volunteers, they have been press-ganged ... unwillingly conscripted into a growing army of the unemployed' (Gilmour 1983: 5). Quite apart from the economic costs of high unemployment – social security payments, lost income tax revenues and national insurance receipts – Gilmour warned that far from helping the economy to adjust, so that it would be revitalised and invigorated, high or long-term unemployment results in a loss of skills and resources which may never be replaced or regained, even after economic recovery: 'not only does human "capital" deteriorate; factories close and there is a sharp decline in investment. Future prospects are therefore diminished. So unemployment damages the economy along with everything else' (ibid.: 7).

Furthermore, Gilmour ominously warned that whilst the unemployed did not endure the hardship suffered by those out of work in the 1930s, 'we should be wise to remember Burke's remark about there coming a time when men would not suffer bad things merely because their ancestors had suffered worse' (ibid.: 7).

On a number of grounds (economic efficiency, social justice, and political legitimacy), therefore, One Nation Conservatives disputed the Thatcherite assumption or assertion that 'there is no alternative', and that governments should, or could, do little more than create the right conditions for the smooth, effective functioning of 'the market', by controlling the money supply, reducing state ownership and interference, and curbing the power of the trade unions. Whilst One Nation Conservatives could readily support such measures, they emphasised that they were not enough, and that a more positive, constructive approach was required to accompany this strategy. Hence Francis Pym was amongst those suggesting that the Thatcher governments 'should ease the overwhelming priority given to economic policy and acknowledge the importance of social policy ... a balance between economic needs and social needs'. This, he argued, ought to include 'more generous benefits ... to the poor and to the unemployed'. To this extent, like most of his colleagues on the One Nation wing of the Conservative Party, Pym declared: 'I oppose laissez-faire if it is based on the assumption that is a virtue for a Government to do as little as possible and if its effect is to perpetuate unfairness and hardship' (Pym 1985: 143).

Again, however, their calls went unheeded. The Thatcher Government's view was that on economic grounds it could not, and on ideological grounds it should not, implement measures which sought significantly to reduce unemployment. The prevailing perspective was that ultimately the creation of new jobs was dependent upon the revival of 'the market' and encouraging wealth creation, both of which required less, not more, intervention by government and the state. The type of policies mooted by the One Nation Conservatives were dismissed by Thatcherites as precisely the sort of measures which had been pursued throughout the post-war period, and which had got Britain into such an economic and political mess in the first place. In any case, the Cabinet reshuffle in the autumn of 1981 witnessed the removal of a number of One Nation Conservatives – 'the weaker willed, the craven-hearted and the embittered failures amongst the Conservative Party' – so that 'the balance in the Cabinet was decisively changed' (Tebbit 1988: 181). In any case, the re-election of the Thatcher government in June 1983, at a time when unemployment stood at around three million, destroyed once and for all the hitherto prevailing orthodoxy that no government presiding over mass unemployment could win an election. That the Thatcher government did win the 1983 general election against the backdrop of high unemployment served to weaken the position and the credibility of the One Nation Conservatives even further. They were never to recover. Their decline was terminal.

ANY TRADE UNION STONES LEFT UNTURNED?

The Conservative onslaught since 1979 against the trade unions has been so thorough and so relentless that it is tempting to assume that nothing more could be done. Yet there remain a number of Conservatives who believe that more could – and should – be done by way of reforming the trade unions, and reducing further what little power or effectiveness they still possess.

Certainly there exists a widespread desire amongst Conservatives to see pay determined through individual contracts and negotiations, rather than through collective bargaining conducted between employers and trade unions. As well as further marginalising trade unions, individual bargaining is viewed by Conservatives as a means of applying, to each employee, criteria such as improved performance, productivity, merit, etc., rather than awarding 'across the board' pay increases irrespective of individual effort or contribution. The displacement of collective bargaining is deemed particularly desirable for the public sector (Hanson 1991: 89). The governments of Margaret Thatcher and John Major have been keen to move to a system whereby the terms and conditions of employment pertaining to each employee 'reflect their own skills, efforts, capacities and circumstances' rather than being 'solely the outcome of some distant negotiation between employers and trade unions' (Department of Employment 1988: 18). To this end, it has been suggested that:

> many existing approaches to pay bargaining, beloved of trade unions and employers alike, will need to change if we are to secure the flexibility essential to employment growth. In particular, 'the going rate', 'comparability' and 'cost of living increases', are all outmoded concepts – they take no account of differences in performance, ability to pay or difficulties of recruitment, retention or motivation ... National agreements ... all too often give scant regard to differences in individual circumstances or performance.
>
> (ibid.: 1988: 23–4)

It is clearly the hope of many Conservatives that a move towards individual – instead of collective – bargaining will render the trade unions virtually redundant. Indeed, this objective was reiterated in the White Paper *People, Jobs and Opportunity* (Department of Employment 1992), which suggested that:

> There is every reason to be confident that by the end of the 1990s we will have moved decisively away from the collectivist pay arrangements which restricted individual choice and damaged employment growth to a situation where the pay of the great majority of employed people will reflect their contributions at work.

If this form of individual pay bargaining does become the norm, then the role of the trade unions will be further – and significantly – undermined. This, of course, is precisely the intention.

Another area in which many Conservatives desire to see further action against the trade unions is that of strikes in the 'essential services' (a point noted in the first section of this chapter). Up until 1994, the post-1979 Conservative administrations had balked at implementing legislation against such strikes, although it had been mooted in the 1987 Green Paper entitled *Trade Unions and their Members*, which was the precursor to the 1988 Employment Act. A major reason for Conservative reticence on this issue has been the determination to avoid entering a legal minefield involving complex disputes over the precise meaning of 'an essential service' (Tebbit 1988: 198; Thatcher 1993: 275). This once again indicates the constant concern to avoid unenforceable legislation or measures which would bring the law itself into disrepute, even though such measures might command a great deal of instinctive or ideological support amongst Conservatives. None the less, the strike action conducted by the Rail, Maritime and Transport Workers Union during the summer of 1994, in connection with a pay claim by signal workers, has served to place the issue of outlawing strikes in 'essential' or public services back on the Conservatives' policy agenda.

Certainly, a number of Conservatives have always been highly sceptical of the arguments put forward against such legislation, perceiving them to be manifestations of cowardice and a woeful lack of political will-power on the part of their ministerial colleagues. There have been suggestions that the Conservative government should legislate to impose a 'statutory duty to maintain the supply of a specified short-list of essential services, including health, gas, water, electricity, telephone and fire services', thereby ensuring 'the removal of all trade union immunities in the relevant industries' (Hanson 1991: 92; see also Roberts 1987: 17). In return for giving up their right to strike, it has been suggested, employees in 'essential services' might be offered a lump-sum cash payment by way of compensation.

Conservative concern over the operation of the political levy has also remained, in spite of – or probably because of – the 1984 Trade Union Act, which was evidently too half-hearted a measure for many in the party. The Act's requirement that trade unions ballot their members once every ten years to see if they wished to continue maintaining a political fund fell a long way short of the demand for 'contracting out' of political levy payments to be replaced by 'contracting in'. The argument advanced by Conservative critics was – as it had always been – that 'contracting out' placed the emphasis on those who objected to making payments towards the political levy, rather than on those trade unionists who actually wanted to pay it. In other words, the existing provisions actually assisted trade union political funds by virtue of the apathy of those trade union unionists who could not be bothered to 'contract out', or as a consequence of the ignorance of those union members who were unaware of their right to do so.

In the meantime, in the wake of the 1993 Trade Union Reform and Employment Rights Act, and pending any further reforms, the Major government's approach seems to be one of virtually ignoring and bypassing the trade unions altogether. With union membership having fallen to about nine million (one-third of the workforce), as a consequence of high unemployment and the changing patterns of employment during the 1980s and 1990s (the decline of manufacturing and heavy industry, and the rise instead of a predominantly non-unionised service and tertiary sector, often employing female and part-time workers), an apparent trend away from collective bargaining and national-level agreements, and the unions ensnared in an intricate web of legislation, the Major government evidently views trade unions largely as an irrelevance. Indeed, it is apparent that many Conservatives are hoping, if not expecting, that 'unions will continue to decay and will eventually cease to be important as social institutions' (Roberts 1987: 27).

8 Conservatism and trade unionism in Britain

Trade unions have always been problematic for the Conservative Party. For a political organisation committed to such principles and precepts as the market economy, individualism, the paramount importance of profit-making, maintaining the confidence of the City and the wider business community, 'sound' money, management's right to manage, and capitalism generally, trade unions have constituted a major problem.

The institutions of organised labour have long been accused by Conservatives of subverting or sabotaging all of the above. To this list of charges have been added other indictments, such as their political activities and objectives (inextricably related to their financial and organisational link with the Labour Party), their 'irresponsible' use of the strike weapon, and the unrepresentative and unaccountable character of trade union leaders *vis-à-vis* their mass membership.

Yet the Conservative Party has had repeatedly to profess support for trade unionism in Britain, partly because of the need – prior to 1979 – to obtain the grudging consent and co-operation of organised labour when the party has been in office, and partly, when in opposition, to dissuade voters from believing that it would deliberately seek confrontation with the unions, thereby causing further industrial conflict and social unrest. The Conservative Party has sought to temper its anti-trade union image in a number of ways.

First, it has actually attempted to portray itself as a friend of trade unionism. Such an image has been assiduously cultivated by citing various laws passed by Conservative administrations since 1824, which, the party has variously claimed, granted trade unions immunities and privileges previously denied to them. Balfour, for example, claimed that he looked back 'not only without regret, but with pride, on the part which the Conservative Party had played, in putting the trade unions upon a sound basis' (*The Times*, 6 October 1910). Meanwhile, in the year that Baldwin's government introduced the Trade Disputes Act, a Conservative MP was proclaiming that 'the Conservative Party has done more for trade unionism than any other party, and we intend to do more in the future' (*HC Debates*, 5th series, vol.202: c.647–8). Similar proclamations have been expressed periodically ever since.

Conservative leaders have also, on occasions, sought to praise British trade unionism by portraying it as a vital component of British industry. Once again, Balfour gave clear expression to such a view, announcing that 'it conduces to the general peace of society, in connection with the controversies between Capital and Labour, that Labour should be organised, and . . . able to meet on equal terms with employers.' He insisted that only through the 'wise working' of trade unions could industrial peace be attained (*The Times*, 6 October 1910). Forty years later, the Conservative Party's 1950 Election Manifesto proclaimed that 'we have held the view, from the days of Disraeli, that the trade union movement is essential to the proper working of our economy, and of our industrial life.'

A further means invoked by the Conservative Party to play down its instinctive and ideological antipathy towards the trade unions has been to posit a distinction between 'responsible' and 'irresponsible' trade unionism. The former is deemed to apply to those trade unions which pursue 'modest' pay claims, do not resist managerial authority, co-operate in initiatives to enhance productivity, rarely – if ever – engage in strike activity, and recognise the supremacy of the national interest over the sectional interests of the union itself. Needless to say, 'irresponsible' trade unions are held to be those who press for 'excessive' wage increases, impede managerial authority, obstruct attempts to increase productivity, have little compunction about invoking strike action, and place their sectional interests above those of the nation.

This dichotomy is coupled with a demarcation between the industrial objectives and activities of trade unions, which are largely considered legitimate, and their political aspirations, which are roundly condemned. This demarcation initially arose as a conse-quence of the trade unions' financial and organisational links with the Labour Party, with Bonar Law declaring that:

> from the time the trade unions became captured by a particular political party, and became a political organisation, I was opposed to them. But from the point of view of the purposes for which

trade unions were created – the purpose of using combinations of men to obtain better terms for themselves, and a larger share of the profits in the business in which they work – I am entirely in favour of trade unionism.

(*HC Debates*, 5th series, vol.31: c.1647–8)

The insistence that trade unions ought to steer clear of politics was subsequently reinforced by the 1926 General Strike, although it was mainly after the Second World War that the involvement of the trade unions in politics became more problematic for the Conservative Party. With the establishment of a mixed economy, and the drift, via incomes policies, towards a mode of corporatism, governments increasingly found themselves in direct contact with trade union leaders on a regular and routine basis, and reliant upon the co-operation of the unions for the success or otherwise of economic policy. Consequently, the apparent distinction between the 'industrial' and the 'political' objectives of the trade unions became ever more blurred, and Conservatives increasingly attributed 'political' motives to industrial action taken by organised labour, particularly when such action was taken by workers in the public sector, or in defiance of an incomes policy.

A final polarity alluded to by the Conservative Party on innumerable occasions has been that between the trade union leadership on the one hand, and the mass membership on the other. According to this characterisation, the former have invariably been deemed 'extremists', unrepresentative of, and unaccountable to, the union membership, and often 'politically motivated'. By contrast, the mass membership is portrayed as being comprised of 'ordinary', 'decent', 'moderate', 'sensible', 'patriotic', working people, who are often misled and manipulated by their union leaders. This dichotomy has frequently underpinned populist appeals by the Conservative Party to 'ordinary' trade union members, no more so than under the Thatcher governments.

The history of the Conservative Party's attitude towards, and relationship with, the trade unions from the early nineteenth century to the middle of the twentieth century was largely one of grudging toleration, punctuated by the General Strike and the subsequent 1927 Trade Disputes Act (the latter serving to fuel trade union suspicions that the Conservative Party was innately anti-trade union and anti-working class). The repeal of the Combination Acts in 1824 had been secured partly out of recognition that the mere passage of legislation through Parliament did not always achieve the desired results; in this case, combinations of workers continued 'underground' in surreptitious secrecy. Conservative leaders subsequently – until the 1971 Industrial Relations Act – were mindful of the risk of introducing unenforceable legislation, and this was to be a significant factor in accounting for the reluctance of successive Conservative premiers to accede to ritual backbench demands for punitive legislation against the trade unions. The refrain was frequently heard that the type of legislation demanded was not practicable. To pass unenforceable legislation, Conservative leaders repeatedly warned, would be to bring the law into disrepute, and possibly undermine the authority of the state itself.

The Industrial Relations Act had represented the culmination of a change of policy orientation whose antecedents could be discerned a decade earlier. By the early 1960s, concern over Britain's deteriorating economic situation, poor industrial performance, and increasing industrial relations problems had significantly eroded the Conservative government's faith in the voluntarist policy towards the trade unions which it had endorsed throughout the 1950s. Throughout that decade, the party's parliamentary leadership emphatically rejected calls for legislation on trade unions to be introduced. Two main reasons were cited to justify this refusal, in addition to the issue of whether such legislation was actually enforceable or practicable.

First, senior Conservatives repeatedly claimed that the activities and affairs of the unions were matters best left to the unions themselves to deal with. Intervention by government, especially a Conservative one, it was reckoned, ran the risk of undermining the strenuous efforts which had been made, by successive Ministers of Labour, to win the trust of the trade union movement. Given that memories of the 1926 General Strike, the 1927 Trade Disputes Act, and the 1930s Depression were still relatively fresh in the minds of both trade union leaders and politicians during the 1950s, senior conservatives were anxious to avoid any course of action which might open up old wounds between their party and the trade unions (Brittan 1976: 169).

A second reason why the Conservative Party's parliamentary leadership steadfastly adhered to a voluntarist industrial relations policy throughout the 1950s, was the prevalence of a 'human relations' approach to problems on the shopfloor. This perspective held that much of the conflict which occurred in British industry was explicable in terms of the socio-pyschological situation of those employed on the shopfloor. It was claimed that many workers experienced feelings of alienation and boredom, coupled with a suspicion and distrust of management, born of a lack of communication between the two sides of industry.

According to this analysis, employees often found it difficult to comprehend the role and significance of the particular tasks which they performed, particularly in a large enterprise where they might not see the finished product. In an age of mass production and large-scale enterprises, many Conservatives believed that this problem was one which underpinned much of the industrial unrest which Britain continued to suffer from during the 'boom years' of the 1950s. Greater prosperity, it seemed, did not reduce feelings of frustration at the place of work itself.

For Conservatives subscribing to this 'human relations' approach, the solution was not to be found in legislation; on the contrary, this would probably exacerbate the problem. Instead, the response of the Conservative parliamentary leadership throughout the 1950s was to call repeatedly for closer communication and co-operation between the two sides of industry. It was held that the way to eradicate feelings of distrust and discontent on the part of employees was to instil in them a sense of 'belonging' to the firm in which they worked, and a sense of 'worth' in the functions which they performed. The means to securing such objectives were to be found through encouraging greater consultation and dialogue, between employers and employees. By virtue of closer communication, it was envisaged that workers would become more appreciative of the responsibilities of management, whilst management was expected to develop greater cognisance of the anxieties harboured by its workforce. The outcome, it was hoped, would be a greater spirit of partnership and sense of shared purpose between the two sides of industry, and ultimately a marked decline in industrial conflict.

Yet by the 1960s, industrial conflict was increasing, as were inflation and unemployment. Also increasing, in consequence, was concern in the Conservative Party over a whole host of industrial and economic indicators, particularly the incidence of unofficial strikes, not so much because of any increase *per se*, but because figures for this particular mode of industrial action were only published from 1961 onwards. Hitherto, the scale of this problem had not been fully recognised. By the early 1960s, therefore, Britain's increasing industrial and economic difficulties served to undermine the hegemony of voluntarism in the parliamentary Conservative Party, thereby polarising opinion within the party over how best to 'answer' the 'trade union question'.

For the Conservative Party's neo-corporatists and One Nation paternalists, it was imperative that organised labour, through its leadership, be incorporated into national-level discussions and decision-making in the realm of economic affairs. Not only was this considered to be a means of furthering the ideal of eradicating class divisions and thus fostering One Nation, but, more importantly perhaps, was intended to have the effect of educating trade union leaders with regard to the economic facts of life, particularly in the context of Britain's growing industrial and economic problems. It was hoped that this would encourage greater 'moderation' and 'responsibility' by the trade unions. Ultimately, such a strategy was intended to reverse Britain's worsening economic situation, and obviate any need for trade union legislation. In this sense, neo-corporatism was to supplement voluntarism, rather than replace it outright. The incorporation of the trade union leadership into the policy machinery of the state was intended, amongst other things, to pre-empt any need for the government to intervene directly in the internal affairs of the trade unions.

In sharp contrast, a growing body of opinion on the Conservative backbenches was inclined towards the view that the party leadership was appeasing the unions instead of having the courage and commitment to tackle their powers and privileges directly. For them, the incorporation of the trade unions was utterly reprehensible. It signified a continued drift towards collectivism and corporatism, both of which were considered the antithesis of Conservatism. For those Conservatives subscribing to this perspective, what was required was an approach which sought to reduce the power and influence of the trade unions, rather than seeking to accommodate or come to terms with them. This would entail both legislation and a return to the free market, so that a combination of politico-legal and economic constraints could be imposed on organised labour. It was this strategy which acquired increasing support within the Conservative Party during the course of the 1960s and beyond.

Yet whilst it can be clearly demonstrated that the Conservative Party's conversion to a legalistic trade union policy corresponded closely with the developing crisis of the British economy during the 1960s and 1970s, reference to economic variables provides only a partial explanation of the change in policy. An economic reductionist account does not, in itself, provide an adequate explanation of either the changing character of Conservative attitudes and approaches towards trade unionism or of the debates which occurred within the party over the direction in which it ought to move. It is not enough to declare that the adoption of 'legalism' *vis-à-vis* the trade unions was simply the logical policy in view of Britain's deteriorating economic situation. The party might just as well have redoubled its efforts to pursue a neo-corporatist policy, and tried even harder to convince trade union leaders of the need for a change in attitudes and behaviour.

To understand more fully why it was a legalistic, rather than neo-corporatist, policy which acquired hegemony in the Conservative Party from the 1960s onwards, another factor needs to be considered, namely the changing character and composition of the Conservative Party itself. We would suggest that the type of approach towards the trade unions adopted by the Conservative Party from the 1960s onwards, and the type of debates within the party which reflected and reinforced this change of approach, owed much to the socio-economic background of many Conservative MPs, particularly the newer, younger recruits to Parliament. Without this 'new breed' of Conservative MPs, it is quite possible that neo-corporatism, rather than legalism, would have become more fully established as the predominant Conservative policy towards the trade unions.

Many of the Conservatives who dominated the higher echelons of the parliamentary Conservative Party from 1945 to the early 1960s were old enough to have lived through the bitterness engendered by the General Strike in 1926, and the deprivation and despair caused by the mass unemployment of the 1930s. Throughout the early post-war years, therefore, many such Conservatives were extremely anxious to pursue a much more constructive, conciliatory approach towards the trade unions, and to convince trade unionists that the Conservative Party bore them no ill-will. As Lord (Rab) Butler acknowledged 'a quite deliberate policy of appeasement was adopted. Winston Churchill still had unpleasant memories of the General Strike to live down' (Butler 1971: 164). Consequently, according to Lord Woolton, 'he was determined that there should be no industrial strikes during his period as Prime Minister' (Woolton 1959: 380). Much more recently, John Biffen alleged that, in the wake of the 1945 election defeat, the Conservative Party 'wouldn't touch trade union reform. As a consequence, it had relatively good trade union relations, but at a price.' In Biffen's view, 'one needed rather more aggression to lance that particular boil. However, the important thing in the 1950s was to live down the bad, black days of Britain' (Biffen 1968).

The likely influence of the 1920s and 1930s on the outlook of senior Conservatives from 1945 to the early 1960s can be deduced from the fact that over half of the Conservative MPs elected were over 50 years of age, and therefore clearly old enough to remember the bitterness of the General Strike and the deprivation of the Great Depression. This age factor was complemented by the fact that well over one-third of Conservative MPs in the 1955–9 Parliament had first been elected before or at the 1945 election. The significance of this generational factor was clearly recognised by Harold Macmillan himself, when he declared that 'the older ones have not forgotten. I was a Member of Parliament in those years [the 1930s] on Tee-side. As long as I live, I can never forget the impoverishment and demoralisation.' He was therefore 'determined, as far as it lies within human power, never to allow this shadow to fall again upon our country' (quoted in Ramsden 1977: 448–9).

From the early 1960s onwards, however, the natural decline in the number of Conservative MPs old enough to remember the pre-war era was matched by a tendency for the parliamentary Conservative Party to become younger. For example, whereas in the 1955 election, 51.7 per cent of Conservative MPs were under 50 years of age, by the 1979 election, the proportion had increased to 62 per cent. Obviously, there was a corresponding increase in the number of Conservative MPs under the age of 40, the proportion rising from 16.6 per cent in 1955 to 24.7 per cent in 1979. The experiences and outlook of most of these younger Conservatives tended to be markedly different to those of their more senior colleagues. Nowhere were these differences more in evidence than in the sphere of trade union reform and industrial relations policy.

The trend towards a younger Conservative Party owed much to a conscious, concerted effort by Central Office during the mid-1960s to modernise the party's public image, and make itself appear rather more representative of the society it sought to govern – a move prompted in no small part by the election of the relatively young, more meritocratic, Harold Wilson as Labour Party leader and Prime Minister. The exit from Parliament, in the 1964 and 1966 elections, of much of 'the Macmillan generation' was accompanied by a Central Office request that older Conservative MPs and prospective parliamentary candidates consider standing down, in order that new blood could be injected into the party at subsequent elections. However much pride there might have been at the party's achievements during thirteen years in office, there was also a widespread feeling, more particularly (but not exclusively) amongst younger Conservatives, that the party had lost sight of Conservative principles and had lost touch with the electorate.

The 1964 election defeat, followed by another, barely two years later, served to signal both the need, and the opportunity, to rejuvenate the Conservative Party's parliamentary membership, re-evaluate its principles and policies, and update its image in the eyes of the electorate. Many Conservatives themselves were concerned that the party was widely perceived to be too patrician and paternalist, dominated by aristocrats, old Etonians, and 'grandees'. Such an image was deemed an electoral liability, in the allegedly meritocratic, technocratic Britain of the 1960s.

From the 1960s onwards, not only did the Conservative Party experience a generational change in its parliamentary composition, there was also a corresponding change in the socio-economic background of many of its MPs. Some of the changes in the educational background of Conservative MPs were particularly noteworthy, not the least of these being the decline in the proportion of Etonians. Whereas over 22 per cent of Conservative MPs elected in 1964 had attended Eton, less than 12.5 per cent of the 1983 parliamentary intake had done so. Amongst new Conservatives, the decline was even more marked, for whilst just under 22 per cent of new Conservatives elected in 1964 were Etonians, only 6 per cent of new Conservative MPs in the 1983 election had been to Eton.

The same period also witnessed a marked decline in the proportion of Conservative MPs who had attended public school and/or Oxbridge. For example, whereas just under 83 per cent of the 1964 parliamentary Conservative Party had received a public school education, only 47 per cent of the 1983 intake had. During the same period, the proportion of Conservative MPs who were Oxbridge-educated declined from 56.3 per cent to 35 per cent. Meanwhile, the number of Conservative MPs who had attended both public school and Oxbridge fell from exactly one-half, in 1964, to precisely one-quarter, in 1983. Amongst new Conservative MPs, the corresponding period saw the public school element decline from almost 78 per cent to barely 64 per cent, whilst the proportion who had been to Oxbridge decreased from 54.3 per cent to 45.7 per cent. The number of new Conservative MPs who had attended both public school and Oxbridge declined from 49.3 per cent in 1964, to just over 37 per cent in 1983.

One other striking change in the educational background of Conservative MPs since the 1960s concerns the increasing number who had attended a state secondary school, followed by a non-Oxbridge university. In 1964, the proportion who had followed such a route stood at 7.8 per cent; by 1983, it had risen to 17.9 per cent.

Amongst new Conservative MPs, the figure rose from 9.3 per cent to 30 per cent.

The period since the 1960s has also witnessed significant changes in the occupational background of Conservative MPs, more and more of whom have come from careers which can be described as 'professional' rather than industrial or managerial. For example, between 1955 and 1979, the number of journalists and writers in the parliamentary Conservative Party almost trebled. Meanwhile, the proportion of Conservative MPs from the world of finance (banking, accountancy, insurance, etc.) increased from barely 6 per cent in 1955 to 17 per cent by 1983. On the other hand, the proportion of Conservative MPs whose primary occupation was that of company director declined from over one-third in 1959 to less than one-quarter in 1979.

Once again, these occupational changes were most marked amongst new Conservative MPs. In the 1970 election victory, for example, just over 10 per cent of new Conservatives were lawyers, whilst in the 1983 election, this figure had increased to over 25 per cent. By contrast, the proportion of new Conservative MPs who were company directors fell from nearly one-third in 1970, to less than 11 per cent in 1983.

These developments, we contend, are vital to a fuller understanding of the changing character of Conservative attitudes and approaches towards the trade unions since the mid-1960s. The increasingly evident decline of the British economy coincided with the recruitment of a new generation of Conservative MPs for whom the country's economic problems constituted both a reason and an opportunity for a marked change of policy direction, not least with regard to the trade unions. Without memories of the General Strike and the Great Depression to inhibit them and constantly prick their consciences, the new generation of Conservative MPs had less compunction about invoking the law against the trade unions, and permitting unemployment to increase, in order to reduce inflation. Indeed, many of them shared the view enunciated by Lord Coleraine, that the inability of Macmillan to 'clear his mind of these tragic memories must certainly have clouded his judgement, for the problems which he was called upon to face, twenty and twenty-five years later, were very different' (Coleraine 1970: 110). Equally importantly, these MPs lacked industrial or managerial experience, and so had far fewer doubts about the wisdom of industrial relations legislation than the company directors and industrialists in the Conservative Party. In short, these more meritocratic Conservative

MPs have not suffered from what Margaret Thatcher once termed 'bourgeois guilt'. On the contrary, it has been suggested that for these 'more aggressively minded' Conservatives, 'capitalism doesn't have an unacceptable face' (Roth 1984: 36). Not surprisingly, the rapidly dwindling band of Conservative paternalists have viewed these changes with no little despair and dismay. According to one senior backbencher, 'in recent years, the Conservative Party has become less patrician, less grand'. No longer were 'extensive business interests' a key characteristic of most Conservative MPs. Furthermore, the backbencher remarked, it was no longer enough to aspire to be a 'knight of the shire' – traditionally the ballast of the parliamentary party. Instead, it has undergone a 'process of petit-embourgeoisement' which 'has served to narrow the horizons of the Party' (Critchley 1978: 467; see also Thomas 1984: 161).

The role and influence of the meritocratic, professional element within the Conservative Party, particularly its lawyers, became evident with the pursuit of the Industrial Relations Act, a measure whose antecedents could be traced back to *A Giant's Strength* (Inns of Court Conservative and Unionist Society 1958). The Industrial Relations Act's emphasis on legislative solutions to Britain's growing trade union problem caused considerable consternation amongst the party's paternalists and industrialists alike. The former were concerned that the measure would irrevocably damage their efforts at gaining the confidence and co-operation of the trade unions, whilst the latter feared that the upshot would be even greater distrust and disruption in British industry.

There existed a strong feeling amongst many Conservative industrialists, company directors, etc., that the Industrial Relations Act typified the attitude and approach of those who totally lacked any industrial or managerial experience, and who therefore had a naive faith in the ability of the law to effect changes in such a complex and delicate sphere of policy. As Beer has pointed out: 'Unlike the Tory paternalists who had very much fancied tri-partism ... the lawyers and others who designed the Act ... refrained from consulting seriously with the CBI and TUC, while the measure was being deliberated' (Beer 1982: 87–8). Needless to say, criticism of the Industrial Relations Bill, during both its formulation and its passage through Parliament, tended to emanate from those in the Conservative Party who had industrial or managerial experience.

Yet by the time the first Thatcher government was elected in May 1979, support in the Conservative Party for a conciliatory, neo-corporatist approach *vis-à-vis* the trade unions had diminished markedly, partly because such a policy had become so discredited, but also because the type of Conservatives favouring this approach had themselves diminished in number. Indeed, the decline of the One Nation Conservatives was so marked that the main source of debate and disagreement in the Conservative Party under Margaret Thatcher's leadership, concerning trade union legislation, was primarily about the pace of reform.

Yet even here, one can discern a link between MPs' policy attitudes and their personal backgrounds, for the 'step-by-step' approach adopted by the parliamentary leadership was subject to constant criticism from many of the most recent Conservative 'recruits' in Parliament on the grounds that it was too little and too slow. Indeed, the 1980 and 1982 Employment Acts and the 1984 Trade Union Act were subject to considerable 'cross-voting' by Conservative MPs unhappy at the alleged modesty of the provisions enshrined in the legislation. A disproportionate number of these MPs were new entrants to the House of Commons having first entered Parliament in the 1979 or 1983 elections. In the former of these elections, seventy-four new Conservative MPs were elected, constituting nearly a fifth of the parliamentary party, whilst in the 1983 election, ninety-four Conservative MPs entered the Commons for the first time, this time constituting almost a quarter of the Conservatives' parliamentary representation. Put another way, approximately 45 per cent of the MPs sitting on the Conservative benches after the 1983 election had not been there prior to May 1979.

Consequently, these new Conservatives, who had not witnessed or experienced the problems encountered by their more senior colleagues concerning the introduction of the Industrial Relations Act in the early 1970s, tended to prove most critical of the circumspection exhibited by the party leadership during the first half of the 1980s in particular. This in turn suggests that 'parliamentary socialisation' is itself an important, yet often overlooked, phenomenon.

Of course, one other factor warrants passing mention, namely that of public opinion. It would be too simplistic to claim that the Conservative Party's increasingly 'legalistic' approach towards the trade unions was merely a response to the increasing unpopularity of the unions amongst the British electorate, as evidenced by countless opinion polls and attitude surveys from the 1960s onwards. Instead, the role of public opinion in this context is best understood in relation to the sociological changes which were taking place in the Conservative Party, as outlined above. In particular, whereas the patrician Conservatism of the One Nation Tories had placed considerable emphasis on 'educating' the people, elevating their condition not just materially but intellectually as well, the newer breed of Conservative was much more populist in nature, and thus inclined to follow public opinion much more readily and explicitly. Thus, whereas the Tory patricians often sought to tone down or defuse anti-trade union sentiments, either within the party or amongst sections of the British public, the populists of the 1970s and 1980s were more than happy to echo, and maybe exacerbate, the public hostility towards the trade unions which was subsequently to legitimise the anti-union legislation introduced during the 1980s. To this extent, the populists could claim to be far more in touch with the views of ordinary people than their patrician predecessors. Maybe, a century on from the leadership of Benjamin Disraeli, Conservative trade union policy in the 1980s and 1990s has reflected a new form of Tory democracy.

Bibliography

Abbott, Stephen (1966) *Industrial Relations* London, Conservative Political Centre.

Abbott, Stephen (1976) *How to Bring Democracy and Participation to the Trade Unions* London, Aims for Freedom and Enterprise.

Bagwell, Philip (1971) 'The Triple Industrial Alliance 1913–22' in Asa Briggs and John Saville (eds) *Essays in Labour History* London, Macmillan.

Baldry, Tony (1985) 'Time to talk', *Reformer* summer.

Baldwin, Stanley (1926) *On England* London, Philip Allan & Co.

Barber, Richard (1976) *The Trade Unions and the Tories* London, Bow Group.

Barber, Richard (1977) 'Direct action and the unions', *Crossbow* autumn.

Beer, Samuel (1965) *Modern British Politics* London, Faber.

Beer, Samuel (1982) *Britain Against Itself* London, Faber & Faber.

Behrens, Robert (1978) 'Blinkers for the carthorse; the Conservative Party and the trade unions 1974–78', *Political Quarterly* October–December.

Behrens, Robert (1980) *The Conservative Party from Heath to Thatcher* London, Saxon House.

Beloff, Max (1976) 'Pragmatism not enough', *Crossbow* summer.

Bevins, Reginald (1965) *The Greasy Pole* London, Hodder & Stoughton.

Bevins, Reginald (1973) 'Where have all the good men gone?', *The Spectator* 3 February.

Biffen, John (1965) 'School for Tories', *The Guardian* 27 August.

Biffen, John (1968) 'Intellectuals and Conservatism; a symposium', *The Swinton Journal* summer.

Biffen, John (1977) 'The elephant trap', *Conservative Monthly News* April.

Biggs-Davison, John (1969) *The Centre Cannot Hold: Or Mao and All That Marx* London, The Monday Club.

Birkenhead, Lord (1969) *Walter Monckton* London, Weidenfeld & Nicolson.

Blake, Lord (1976) *Conservatism in an Age of Revolution* London, Churchill Press.

Blake, Lord (1978) 'A changed climate' in Lord Blake and John Patten (eds) *The Conservative Opportunity* Basingstoke, Macmillan.

Body, Richard (1972) 'The road to freedom', *The Spectator* 1 July.

Bourlet, James and Roots, Michael (1974) *Step by Step Against Inflation* London, The Selsdon Group.

Bow Group (1965) *The Confidence Trick* London, Conservative Political Centre.

Bow Group (1972) 'Paying the price of reform', *Crossbow* July–September.

Bowis, John (1979a) 'Persuasion and progress: the realistic road for industrial relations', *Tory Review* August.

Bowis, John (1979b) 'Democracy in Britain's corporate state', *Tory Review* September–October.

Boyle, Edward (1966) *Conservatives and Economic Planning* London, Conservative Political Centre.

Boyson, Rhodes (1978) *Centre Forward* London, Temple Smith.

Brittan, Leon (1976) 'Where law can help', *Crossbow* summer.

Bruce-Gardyne, Jock (1969) 'The pursuit of the unobtainable', *The Spectator* 23 May.

Bruce-Gardyne, Jock (1974) *Whatever Happened to the Quiet Revolution?* London, Charles Knight.

Bruce-Gardyne, Jock (1984) *Mrs Thatcher's First Administration* Basingstoke, Macmillan.

Buckmaster, Clive (1977) 'Industrial progress or political anarchy?', *Tory Challenge* September.

Butler, Lord (1971) *The Art of the Possible* London, Hamish Hamilton.

Butler, David and Kavanagh, Dennis (1975) *The British General Election of October 1974* London, Macmillan.

Butt, Ronald (1973) 'Marching for Mr Heath with Mr Powell in mind', *The Times* 1 March.

Carr, Robert (1975) 'Incomes policy', *The Political Quarterly*, vol. 46, no. 4.

Centre for Policy Studies (1978) *Why Britain Needs a Social Market Economy* Chichester, Barry Rose.

Centre for Policy Studies (1983) *The Right to Strike in a Free Society* Chichester, Barry Rose.

Centre for Policy Studies; Trade Union Reform Committee (1980) *Liberties and Liabilities: The Case for Trade Union Reform* Chichester, Barry Rose.

Churchill, Winston (1906) *Randolph Churchill: Volume Two* London, Macmillan.

Clarke, David (1947) *The Conservative Faith in the Modern Age* London, Conservative Political Centre.

Clarke, Peter (1974) 'Too many rules; too little law', *Crossbow* December.

Cole, G. D. H. and Wilson, A. W. (eds) *British Working Class Movments: Selected Documents 1789–1875* London, Macmillan.

Coleman, Bruce (1988) *Conservatism and the Conservative Party in Nineteenth Century Britain*, London, Edward Arnold.

Coleraine, Lord (1970) *For Conservatives Only* London, Tom Stacey.

Conservative Central Office (1947) *The Industrial Charter: A Statement of Conservative Industrial Policy* London.

Conservative Central Office (1949) *The Right Road for Britain* London.

Conservative Central Office (1965) *Industrial Outlook* London.

Conservative Central Office (1968) *Fair Deal at Work* London.

Conservative Central Office (1970) *Fair Deal at Work* (revised edition) London.

Conservative Central Office (1971) *It's a Fair Deal* London.

Conservative Central Office (1976) *The Right Approach* London.

210 *Bibliography*

Conservative Central Office (1979) *The Conservative Manifesto 1979* London.
Conservative Industrial Department (1963) *Trade Unions and the Government* London, Conservative Political Centre.
Conservative Party (committeee on industrial relations) (1963) *Industrial Change: The Human Aspect* London, Conservative Political Centre.
Conservative Political Centre (1946) *Trade Unions and Employers* London.
Conservative Political Centre (1964) *Trade Unions and Industrial Peace* London.
Conservative Political Centre (1966) *Masterbrief 1: Economic Recovery, Productivity, Wages and the Trade Unions* London.
Conservative Political Centre (undated, but circa 1966) *Masterbrief 32: Strikes* London.
Conservative Political Centre (Notes on Current Politics, No. 2) (1967) *Briefing Notes* London.
Conservative Political Centre (1971) *Monthly Notes* No. 68, February.
Conservative Political Centre (1973–4) *Contact Brief, 60: Participation in Industry* London.
Conservative Research Department (1969) *Industrial Relations Reform* London.
Conservative Trade Unionists National Advisory Committee (1966) *Industrial Advance* London.
Cosgrave, Patrick (1978) *Margaret Thatcher: A Tory and Her Party* London, Hutchinson.
Cowling, Maurice (1978) 'The present position' in Maurice Cowling (ed.) *Conservative Essays* London, Cassell.
Critchley, Julian (1969) 'Conservative critics of the old Macmillanism', *The Times* 19 August.
Critchley, Julian (1973) 'Strains and stresses in the Conservative Party', *The Political Quarterly* October–December.
Critchley, Julian (1978) 'How to get on in the Conservative Party', *The Political Quarterly* October–December.
Critchley, Julian (1989) *Palace of Varieties* London, John Murray.
Daly, Ken/Conservative Trade Unionists (1981) *Participation – The Next Revolution* London.
Department of Employment (1988) *Employment for the 1990s* London, HMSO.
Department of Employment (1992) *People, Jobs and Opportunity* London, HMSO.
Department of Trade and Industry (1988) *DTI – Department for Enterprise* London, HMSO.
Dorfman, Gerald (1979) *Government Versus Trade Unions in British Politics Since 1968* Basingstoke, Macmillan.
Driscoll, James (1965) 'National wages policy', *Crossbow*.
Dykes, Hugh (1968) 'Trade unions: have we really got the answer?', *Crossbow*.
Eccleshall, Robert (1977) 'English Conservatism as ideology', *Political Studies*, vol. 25.
Eccleshall, Robert (1988) *Conservatism and the Conservative Party in the Nineteenth Century* London, Edward Arnold.

Eden, Anthony (1947) *Freedom and Order* London, Faber.
Eden, Anthony (1960) *Memoirs: Full Circle* London, Cassell.
Evans, Harold (1981) *Downing Street Diaries* London, Hodder & Stoughton.
Fowler, Norman (1991) *Ministers Decide* London, Chapman.
Friedman, Milton (1962) *Capitalism and Freedom* Chicago, University of Chicago Press.
Gilmour, Ian (1964) 'Enoch Powell's pipe dream', *The Spectator* 10 April.
Gilmour, Ian (1969) *The Body Politic* London, Hutchinson.
Gilmour, Ian (1974a) 'The Tory dilemma that followed the election', *The Times* 2 May.
Gilmour, Ian (1974b) 'How Mr Heath could establish industrial harmony', *The Times* 3 May.
Gilmour, Ian (1978a) *Inside Right: A Study of Conservatism* London, Quartet.
Gilmour, Ian (1978b) 'Restoring the state by making it work for the people', *The Times* 7 October.
Gilmour, Ian (1983) *Britain Can Work* Oxford, Martin Robertson.
Gilmour, Ian (1992) *Dancing with Dogma* London, Simon & Schuster.
Goldsmith, Walter (1980) 'Trade unions: the case for further legislation', *Free Nation* December.
Goodman, Geoffrey (1985) *The Miners' Strike* London, Pluto Press.
Griffiths, Eldon (1966) *The New Competitors* London, Conservative Political Centre.
Griffiths, Eldon (1977) *Fighting for the Life of Freedom* London, Conservative Political Centre.
Grigg, John (1976) 'The Tories and the TUC', *The Spectator* 9 October.
Guinness, Jonathan (1981) 'The danger of laissez-faire', *Monday World*.
Hailsham, Lord (1978) *The Dilemma of Democracy* London, Collins.
Hailsham, Lord (1990) *A Sparrow's Flight* London, Collins.
Halcrow, Morrison (1989) *Keith Joseph: A Single Mind* London, Macmillan.
Hanson, Charles (1991) *Taming the Trade Unions* Basingstoke, Macmillan.
Harris, Kenneth (1988) *Thatcher* London, Weidenfeld & Nicolson.
Harris, Nigel (1972) *Competition and the Corporate Society* London, Methuen.
Hayek, Friedrich (1960) *The Constitution of Liberty* London, Routledge & Kegan Paul.
Hayhoe, Barney (1977) 'Conscience and the closed shop', *Conservative Monthly News* July.
Heseltine, Michael (1986) *Where There's a Will* London, Hutchinson.
Hodgson, Patricia (1975) 'The moral appeal', *The Spectator* 19 May.
Hoffman, J. D. (1964) *The Conservative Party in Opposition* London, Macgibbon.
Holmes, Martin (1985) *The First Thatcher Government 1979–1983* Brighton, Wheatsheaf.
Hoskyns, John (1982) 'What are the unions for?', *The Times* 1 September.
Hoskyns, John (1982) 'The corrupting power of immunity', *The Times* 2 September.
House of Commons Debates London, HMSO.
Howe, Geoffrey (1976) *Policy for Incomes* London, Conservative Research Department.

Howell, David (date unknown) 'Managing the British economy' in Bow Group *The Conservative Opportunity*, London.

Howell, David (1972) 'Putting the boot into liberal society', *The Times* 25 April.

Howell, David (1975) 'Class war referee', *Crossbow* April.

Howell, Ralph (1974) 'Up to date sense about unemployment', *The Spectator* 24 August.

Hurd, Douglas (1979) *An End to Promises* London, Collins.

Inns of Court Conservative and Unionist Society (1958) *A Giant's Strength* London.

Institute of Directors (1983) *Democracy and Competitiveness* London.

James, Robert Rhodes (1972) *Ambitions and Realities* London, Weidenfeld & Nicolson.

Johnson, Nevil (1980) *In Search of the Constitution* London, Methuen.

Johnson, Paul (1980) *The Recovery of Freedom* Oxford, Basil Blackwell.

Joseph, Keith (1975) 'Foreword' in Samuel Brittan, *Second Thoughts on Full Employment* London, Centre for Policy Studies.

Joseph, Keith (1976) *Stranded on the Middle Ground* London, Centre for Policy Studies.

Joseph, Keith (1979) *Solving the Union Problem Is the Key to Britain's Recovery* London, Centre for Policy Studies.

Keegan, William (1984) *Mrs Thatcher's Economic Experiment* Harmondsworth, Penguin.

King, Anthony (1965) 'New stirrings on the Right', *New Society* 14 October.

King, Anthony (1975) 'The problem of overload', *Political Studies*, vol. 23.

Kirwan, Joseph (1983) 'Trade unions and party politics: the political levy is irrelevant', *Tory Review* October.

Lawrence, Ivan (1973) 'State-subsidised strikers – is there a remedy?', *Monday News* November–December.

Lawson, Nigel (1992) *The View From No. 11* London, Bantam Press.

Macdonald, D. F. (1960) *The State and the Trade Unions* London, Macmillan.

Macleod, Iain (1965) 'The pursuit of excellence', *The Spectator* 15 October.

Macmillan, Harold (1966) *Winds of Change* Basingstoke, Macmillan.

Macmillan, Harold (1972) *Pointing the Way* Basingstoke, Macmillan.

Macmillan, Harold (1973) *At the End of the Day* Basingstoke, Macmillan.

Macmillan, Maurice (1973) 'Employee involvement', *Industrial Outlook* October.

Mahony, David (1976) 'Union strategy wanted', *Crossbow* summer.

Martin, Peter (1976) *No Foundation – The Truth About Trade Union Power* London, Bow Group.

Maude, Angus (1964) 'And by opposing, end them?', *The Spectator* 30 October.

Maude, Angus (1966) 'Winter of discontent', *The Spectator* 14 January.

Maudling, Reginald (1978) *Memoirs* London, Sidgwick & Jackson.

Meyer, Anthony (1990) *Stand Up and Be Counted* London, Heinemann.

Middlemas, Keith and Barnes, John (1969) *Baldwin: A Biography* Basingstoke, Macmillan.

Ministry of Labour and National Service (1942) *Post-War Wages Policy* London.

Ministry of Labour and National Service (1943) *Draft Proposals for Legislation on Wage Agreements* London.

Monday Club, The (1979) *Tory Challenge – Election Supplement* April.

Monday Club, The (1980) *Towards Industrial Sanity* London.

Monypenny, William and Buckle, George (1929) *Life of Disraeli: Volume Two* London, John Murray.

Moran, Michael (1977) *The Politics of Industrial Relations* Basingstoke, Macmillan.

Moran, Michael (1979) 'The Conservative Party and the trade unions since 1974', *Political Studies*, vol. 27.

Mount, Ferdinand (1978) 'Mr Prior's green cross code', *The Spectator* 18 March.

Mount, Ferdinand (1980a) 'Mr Prior lays up short', *The Spectator* 9 February.

Mount, Ferdinand (1980b) 'It takes two to pussyfoot', *The Spectator* 26 April.

National Union of Conservative and Constitutional Associations (1873) *The Political Future of the Working Classes* London.

National Union of Conservative and Unionist Associations (1926) *The Test of Trade Unionism: The General Strike and After* London.

National Unionist Association (1924) *Unionist Worker Handbook: Co-partnership* London.

Nelson-Jones, John/The Bow Group (circa 1972) *The Wages of Fear: A Bow Group Memorandum on Pay, Inflation and Incomes Policy* London.

Nicholson, David (1973) 'Which freedom for Conservatives?', *Monday News* July–August.

Norton, Philip (1976) 'Dissent in committee: dissent in Commons Standing Committees 1959–74', *The Parliamentarian* January.

One Nation Group of MPs (1976) *One Nation at Work* London, Conservative Political Centre.

Oppenheim, Sally (1973) 'Freedom for workers – where it counts', *Conservative Monthly News* August.

Patten, Chris (1983) *The Tory Case* Harlow, Longman.

Pelling, Henry (1963) *A History of British Trade Unionism* Basingstoke, Macmillan.

Pimlott, Ben and Cook, Chris (1982) 'Introduction' in Ben Pimlott and Chris Cook (eds) *Trade Unions in British Politics* London, Longman.

Powell, Enoch (1968) *Conference on Economic Policy for the 1970s* London, The Monday Club.

Powell, Enoch (1969) *Freedom and Reality* Kingswood, Elliot Right Way Books.

Powell, Enoch (1972) *Still to Decide* London, Batsford.

Pressure for Economic and Social Toryism (PEST) (undated, circa 1967) *Stop Knocking the Unions* London.

Price, David (1977) 'Whither Labour's social contract?', *Tory Challenge* June.

Prior, James (1977a) *News for Trade Unionists* July.

Prior, James (1977b) Interview with John Torode, *The Guardian* 15 September.

Prior, James (1977c) 'Getting to know the unions', *The Times* 11 October.

Prior, James (1986) *A Balance of Power* London, Hamish Hamilton.

Pym, Francis (1985) *The Politics of Consent* London, Sphere.

Raffen, Keith (1974) 'Seconds out – the next round', *The Spectator* 18 May.

Raison, Timothy (1965) *Conflict and Conservatism* London, Conservative Political Centre.

Raison, Timothy (1977) 'Where do the Tories go from here?', *The Spectator* 25 April.

Raison, Timothy (1979a) *Power and Parliament* Oxford, Basil Blackwell.

Raison, Timothy (1979b) 'Can the Tories learn from the concordat?', *The Spectator* 17 March.

Ramsden, John (1977) 'From Churchill to Heath' in Lord Butler (ed.) *The Conservatives* London, George Allen & Unwin.

Ramsden, John (1980) *The Making of Conservative Party Policy* London, Longman.

Ridley, Nicholas (1969) 'The workers: participation, control or consultation', *The Swinton Journal* spring.

Ridley, Nicholas (1974) 'Why the Tories must break out of a make-believe world', *The Times* 30 December.

Ridley, Nicholas (1976) 'Against incomes policy', *The Spectator* 27 March.

Ridley, Nicholas (1991) *My Style of Government* London, Hutchinson.

Roberts, Ben (1987) *Mr Hammond's Cherry Tree: The Morphology of Union Survival* London, Institute of Economic Affairs.

Roth, Andrew (1972) *Heath and the Heathmen* London, Routledge & Kegan Paul.

Roth, Andrew (1984) *Parliamentary Profiles* London, Parliamentary Profiles Services.

Rowe, Andrew (1980) 'Conservatives and trade unionists' in Zig Layton-Henry (ed.) *Conservative Party Politics* Basingstoke, Macmillan.

Russel, Trevor (1978) *The Tory Party* Harmondsworth, Penguin.

St John-Stevas, Norman (1966) 'The Tory opportunity', *The Spectator* 2 September.

St John-Stevas, Norman (1984) *The Two Cities* London, Faber & Faber.

Salisbury, Lord (1860) 'The Budget and the Reform Bill', *Quarterly Review* April.

Salisbury, Lord (1866) 'The Reform Bill', *Quarterly Review* April.

Seldon, Anthony (1981) *Churchill's Indian Summer: The Conservative Government 1951–55* London, Hodder & Stoughton.

Shenfield, Arthur (1975) 'What about the trade unions?' in Rhodes Boyson (ed.). *An Escape from Orwell's 1984* London, Churchill Press.

Silvester, Fred (1973) 'Where the Tory Left has failed', *Crossbow* August.

Smith, Paul (1967) *Disraelian Conservatism and Social Reform* London, Routledge & Kegan Paul.

Stewart, Michael (1977) *The Jekyll & Hyde Years* London, J. M. Dent.

Taylor, Robert (1993) *The Trade Union Question in British Politics* Oxford, Blackwell.

Taylor, Teddy (1972) 'The struggle against inflation', *Monday News* July.

Tebbit, Norman (1974) 'Unions must abide by the law', *Industrial Outlook* June.

Tebbit, Norman (1975) 'Don't let's be duped by Labour', *Industrial Outlook* January.

Tebbit, Norman (1988) *Upwardly Mobile* London, Weidenfeld & Nicolson.
Tebbit, Norman (1991) *Unfinished Business* London, Weidenfeld & Nicolson.
Thatcher, Margaret (1993) *The Downing Street Years* London, Harper Collins.
Thomas, David (1984) 'The new Tories', *New Society* 2 February.
Waldegrave, William (1978) *The Binding of Leviathan* London, Hamish Hamilton.
Walker, Peter (1977a) *The Ascent of Britain* London, Sidgwick & Jackson.
Walker, Peter (1977b) 'Bringing reason back to the shopfloor', *Conservative Monthly News* December.
Walker, Peter (1987) *Trust the People* London, Collins.
Walker, Peter (1991) *Staying Power* London, Bloomsbury.
Whitelaw, William (1989) *The Whitelaw Memoirs* London, Aurum.
Wigham, Eric (1982) *Strikes and the Government 1893–1981* (second edition) Basingstoke, Macmillan.
Wood, David (1974) 'Mr Heath changes style and role', *The Times* 23 September.
Woolton, Earl of (1959) *Memoirs* London, Cassell.
Young, Hugo (1989) *One of Us* London, Macmillan.
Young, Lord (1990) *The Enterprise Years* London, Headline.

Index

218 *Index*